CONFIDENT LEADERS BY DESIGN

Do you feel confident at work? Are there times when you lack confidence but can't show it? The role of confidence in successful leadership is both significant and undisputed and yet organisations are full of leaders and teams who don't have as much as they want and, even worse, are not doing anything about it.

Attempts to develop confidence are usually confined to empty affirmations and vanilla-flavoured self-help books. In contrast, this book provides an evidence-based code that outlines the steps we can all take to positively shift our confidence and that of our teams. *Confident Leaders by Design* is for leaders at all levels looking for a rigorous yet accessible approach to confidence development. Through research and fascinating anecdotes it reveals the surprising secrets to supercharging leadership potential through confidence creation.

Alongside the theory, readers will practically locate their confidence sweet spot and explore activities like sludge audits, confidence curves and self-efficacy circles which will help them to immediately start growing confidence in themselves and their teams.

Chris Baker is a former teacher who now designs, delivers and assesses leadership development programmes at various scales across various domains. He has a doctorate in leadership self-efficacy, and fuelled by his own personal battles with low confidence is fascinated by its complex role in the way we think, feel and act.

"For those interested in applied psychology, particularly in leadership contexts, this book offers a valuable blend of theory, personal narrative, and actionable strategies."

Dr Paul Redford, *Associate Professor, University of the West of England*

"This book is an honest and informed exploration of the significant role that confidence, and specifically self-efficacy, plays in flourishing as a successful leader."

Alison Fletcher, *FCCT, Director of Professional Development, Cabot Learning Federation*

"Rooted in a truly impressive synthesis of available research, this is a timely reminder of the importance of self-efficacy and confidence for leaders at all levels. Highly recommend."

Andy Buck, *Founder of Leadership Matters*

"This is the book I wish I had read twenty years ago and is a must for anyone wishing to develop their own confidence and that of their team members."

Neil Thomas, *Director of Strata Leadership Development*

"Confidence is an essential part of successful leadership no matter what sector you work in, and this book provides a clear, evidence-based roadmap to get you there."

A. Jones, *Sargent (SGT), Australian Special Forces*

CONFIDENT LEADERS BY DESIGN

An Essential Guide to Confidence Creation

Chris Baker

Routledge
Taylor & Francis Group
LONDON AND NEW YORK

Designed cover image: Getty Images: amtitus

First published 2026
by Routledge
4 Park Square, Milton Park, Abingdon, Oxon OX14 4RN

and by Routledge
605 Third Avenue, New York, NY 10158

Routledge is an imprint of the Taylor & Francis Group, an informa business

British Library Cataloguing-in-Publication Data
A catalogue record for this book is available from the British Library

ISBN: 978-1-032-90621-8 (hbk)
ISBN: 978-1-032-89717-2 (pbk)
ISBN: 978-1-003-55893-4 (ebk)

DOI: 10.4324/9781003558934

Typeset in Joanna
by codeMantra

Access the Support Material: https://drchriswb.substack.com/s/clbd

To my teacher, Mr. Money, who believed in me when I didn't.

CONTENTS

INTRODUCTION

Before we jump into the book, I just wanted to take a moment to highlight some of the key aspects of it and how you can get the most out of it.

Deeply Personal

The content of the book is deeply personal to me, and the process of researching and writing it has been one of the most developmental processes I have ever engaged with. The book has emerged from a personal frustration about the huge amount of unmet potential that I felt during my early life because of a lack of confidence and an unawareness of how to make it better. As you will see in chapter 1, my confidence curve was fairly flat for a long time with the occasional spike due to some key people and experiences. The second half of my life has been the exact opposite because of the transformational impact of the secrets I am going to share with you as we move through the book. My greatest hope for you is that you open your mind, lean in to the challenging concepts and use the book's confidence code to start your proactive confidence growth a lot sooner that I did.

DOI: 10.4324/9781003558934-1

Everything on Purpose

The book has 'by design' in its title and lives and breathes that mantra itself throughout its structure and the practical strategies that it shares. Everything in the book is there on purpose and aimed to systematically develop your knowledge, understanding and confidence creation skills. The eagle eyed of you may have already noticed the book's thirteen chapters and winced at the associated bad luck, but this is also a purposeful decision and an explicit dismissal of the need for luck when you are doing what we are going to do and create confidence by design, not chance. The intellectual challenge level and vocabulary of the book is also a deliberate choice and is supposed to mirror the role that challenges just above our current ability can have on our confidence creation, so again, lean in, embrace the challenge and get your dictionary out.

All Pushing Towards Praxis

This is a practically focused book and a push against the vanilla-flavoured self-help books that promise much and deliver very little. Any use of theory is quickly linked to what Socrates called Praxis or 'practical application of theory' and put into modern, real-life scenarios. The aim is that each chapter drives both personal reflection and the application of newly acquired knowledge and understanding. At the end of each chapter there is a practical activity that you and members of your teams can use to explore your current levels of confidence and proactively develop them.

And one final word of caution: if at any point during the book you find yourself thinking "well this is just common sense," then I challenge you to question whether it is also 'common practice' as here lies our biggest problem. For lots of us, we think a good game, but our actions don't live up to our aspirations and we definitely don't do things by design.

1

YOU CAN'T CHEAT THE HARVEST

So, I want you to start this journey by thinking about how confident you are right now as you read this book. Not how confident you would say you are to others, but really how confident you feel on a day-to-day basis. Now think about how you got there. I would imagine you are like the vast majority of people in the world in that you can't really put a finger on how you became confident or unconfident, as it just seemed to happen little by little over the course of your life. You may be able to recount specific situations that had a big impact, and you may be wincing or smiling as you recount these experiences, but I bet that you have not systematically gone about your confidence building, and that is what we are here to change.

I hope you don't mind indulging me in a personal anecdote, but I feel it's important to unpack the rationale for this book and how some key events took me out of an apathetic state of low confidence and limited effectiveness into a supercharged upward spiral of confidence creation leading to personal and professional achievements that I would have never thought possible.

DOI: 10.4324/9781003558934-2

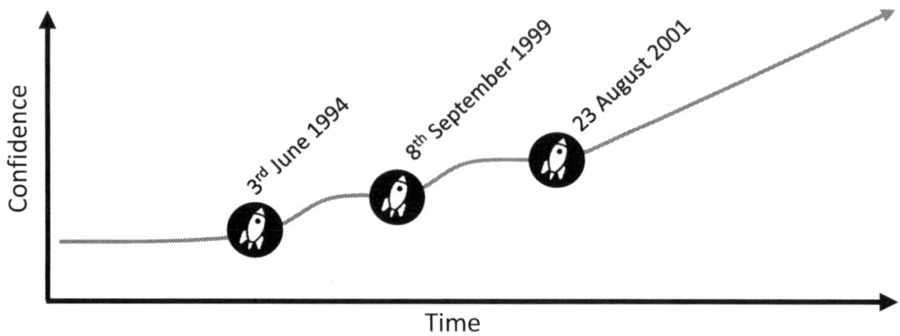

Figure 1.1 My own personal confidence curve

My story starts in a small town in the Southwest of England in a super supportive family and a seemingly perfect childhood. I was captain of school and community sports teams and had a large social network within which I felt accepted and of high status. All of this should have led to high levels of confidence, but what I didn't realise was that I had absorbed the thinking, feeling and behavioural norms of my family and my social groups. These norms included things like it wasn't cool to be good at learning, making people laugh was more revered than paying attention, travel outside of the town was for other people and careers were a continuation of what your father did. This sort of thinking left me bumbling along through my teenage years developing confidence tied to the wrong proxies and easily meeting the low expectations of my teachers and family.

In the summer of 1994, I was called into the headteacher's office to discuss my plans for the future and my choices for post-compulsory education, and that's where the story takes its first significant twist. My lacklustre response to the "What do you want to do with your life?" question was met with a swift set of affirmations about my inherent goodness, work ethic and hidden intelligence, which not only caught me off guard but was the first piece of positive feedback that I remember ever getting. The outcome of that meeting was much different from what my social and family groups would have expected, and I found myself continuing my studies for two more years. Sadly, my social groups did not change significantly enough to shift my levels of confidence, ability or agency, and I continued with the bumbling. Two years later I found myself back in the same office with the same headteacher having a very similar conversation about hidden intelligence and untapped potential. This time the result was attendance at the University of Portsmouth and the accolade of being the first person in my family's history to go that far in education.

My next big shift in confidence arrived almost as soon as I started University in the autumn of 1999 and was forced into different social groups with different perspectives on life and higher aspirations for themselves. Exposure to these new norms and a recognition that I was not too different from them in terms of ability and in some areas even in the ascendancy, meant that my confidence got a well-needed boost. Sadly again, the underlying, engrained beliefs about 'what a boy like me could do in life' prolonged the bumbling even further and a reluctance to allow myself out of first gear meant that my confidence remained lower than desired and required.

Fast-forward to 2001 and my second year of University when I had the opportunity to make my first solo trip abroad to work on a summer camp in Pennsylvania, USA. Little did I know that this would be the single greatest stimulus in my confidence curve and would set the tone for the rest of my life. The camp was eight weeks long and at the end the counsellors were all jumping in cars and planes back to their respective homes and I had the same plan. This was until a small group of people I had grown to call friends asked if I wanted to come to Florida for a couple of weeks before flying home. My membership to previous groups had left me with lower-than-average levels of confidence for the unknown and a contentment with the status quo, but I leaned in and listened anyway. To my surprise the almost nonchalant attitude of this new group to risk and the confidence that they brought from their upbringing uncovered a hidden confidence in me, and so before I knew it, I was sipping cocktails (well, dollar beers actually) on the beautiful Miami beach. The realisation that not everyone was unconfident like my social groups back home and the positive experience of stepping out of my comfort zone led to another six years of solo travelling and a transformational change in my confidence levels.

This is the point where the stimulus for this book was born, but little did I know that it would take me another twenty years to recognise the impact that my low confidence had on my early life and how passive I was about its development. That next section of my life and everything up to this very point has been dominated by an increasingly strategic approach to confidence creation with ever-increasing spirals fuelled by a thirst for challenge and a belief that with confidence and action I could achieve anything. This enhanced confidence has taken me through two Ironman triathlons, when previously I couldn't even swim; Master's and Doctoral degrees when I barely scraped through university; and keynotes at national and international conferences when I was too scared to even be in the school play.

If when you were reading my story, you found yourself nodding along and reflecting on how much your early life and maybe even current life has been dogged by low confidence and a lack of understanding about how to fix it, then strap in and let me share the secrets. It's not going to happen by osmosis though. Like the farmer who can't cheat the harvest and just turn up to their fields in the autumn and expect there to miraculously be crops to sow, you are not going to be able to blindly expect to build confidence. Confidence building, like growing crops, requires proactive, sustained effort and purposeful preparation. We need to prepare the land, sow the seeds and nurture the seedlings if we want to be the confident person that we know is somewhere deep inside.

The first step in that process is to understand how we got into this mess in the first place, and so the rest of the chapter is devoted to exploring why most of us have arrived at adulthood without the confidence we need to be effective or the knowledge of how to develop it.

Cultural Passivity

We are firstly going to look back into the past and think about the culture of the groups and family units that we grew up in as these may hold the first clues about how we did or did not accrue confidence. Consciously or often unconsciously we absorb the thoughts, feelings and behaviours of those we are surrounded by. John Locke, the famous 17th century English philosopher popularised the term 'Tabula Rosa' which translates to 'clean slate' from Latin and describes his belief that we are products of our environment. This concept was further strengthened over time by the work of psychologists Jean Piaget in cognitive development and B. F. Skinner in behavioural conditioning. A factor that I feel is rife in lots of groups and was certainly the case for me as a child growing up is this feeling of cultural passivity or the sense of apathy, determinism and conformity towards things. My suggestion is that this normalisation of passivity is one of the key reasons why people are void of the confidence they crave and have also done nothing about it.

Apathy

The first challenge for confidence creation and a possible characteristic of some social groups and their culture is apathy. Apathy in general terms can be described as a lack of feeling, emotion or concern, and typically shows itself as indifference towards things or a lack of care. People that suffer from general apathy or indifference have less motivation to take part in activities or achieve goals and experience reduced emotional reactions. An example for us would be someone indifferent about the benefits of increased confidence and the lack of motivation to change their current level. Briefly feeling this way about specific things or after a disappointment is completely normal but a wider, more chronic apathy can significantly affect confidence creation and may be a sign of a deeper issue. Chronic apathy can be a symptom of various mental health conditions such as schizophrenia, depression and post-traumatic stress disorder (PTSD) and have a much larger and sustained impact. People suffering this type of apathy experience a continuing lack of motivation and goal directed behaviour, difficulty planning or solving problems, isolation from society and a loss of interest in personal care. Attachment to groups or family settings where apathy is a strong characteristic can rob individuals of the need or want to improve their confidence levels and leave its development to chance.

Determinism

Group and individuals who believe that all events, including human choices and behaviours, are controlled by external causes are said to be deterministic. The philosophy of determinism dates as far back as Aristotle, who thought that everything strives towards a preordained purpose, through to Friedrich Nietzsche, who struggled with the concept because of its denial of free will, and more modern thinkers like Sam Harris, who see a place for both free-will and determinism. An example for us would be the person or group who finds no reason to try to build their confidence because "what will be, will be" and whatever level of confidence they arrive at is the one they were supposed to have. Interestingly, unlike apathy where the symptoms are typically negative, determinism does have some benefits. Believers typically accept things more easily and have greater levels of resilience due to the belief that the outcome was predetermined and so they just need to dust themselves off and try again. Determinism can also help reduce anxiety levels about future events or outcomes because of their fixed nature and thus lead to greater levels of calm and focus on the process. Negatively this belief can lead to something called learned helplessness where people give up on getting better because of a perceived lack of influence and an associated loss of agency which weakens self-belief and undermines motivation and confidence.

Conformity

Conformity is another factor that may influence an individual's passiveness to confidence creation, and flows from the influence of group cultures. Wanting to or being forced to be like others is something that feels like a normal part of the human experience, but researchers have found some complexity in it which has resulted in a deeper understanding. In 1958 American social psychologist Herbert Kelman suggested that changes to a person's thoughts, feelings and/or behaviours can happen at three increasingly stable levels due to an external influence. The weakest and most superficial level is 'Compliance' and is where we publicly conform to avoid negative consequences but privately think and feel differently. Compliant behaviour is often temporary because it typically only occurs in the presence of the influencing group or individual and only as long as it is seen as beneficial. An example for us would be thinking back to school where often in peer groups it was not cool to be clever or show confidence in subjects that clash with the group's norms, and so individuals hide those feelings internally. The group may verbally communicate a lack of confidence or demonstrate it through low expectations, and so the conforming individual aligns themselves so as not to stand out and possibly lose membership from the group or relationship.

Kelman's next level of conformity was 'Identification' which he suggested is even more closely linked to the desire to belong to a group, and is where a person identifies or agrees with the thoughts, feelings and behaviours of a group and therefore conforms in order to be a member. The big difference here is that there is a strong alignment between personal and group beliefs, and so the private and public personas are more aligned.

There is still some fragility in this level of conformity, though as disassociation from the group can result in a return to previously held or newly found beliefs. In our example, the difference at this level would be that the individual truly does believe what the group believes and that they are not very confident in specific school subjects or in learning more generally. There is no conflict between what they think and how they act as the two are aligned, but as peer groups change so might the level of conformity. Moving to a peer group where confidence and expectations are high may uncover unknown thoughts and feelings and create new behaviours. This was certainly true for me; I can remember a pivotal moment in my own confidence curve where a change in social group changed the whole trajectory of my confidence curve and effectively my whole life.

The final level suggested by Kelman was 'Internalisation' and is the deepest and most stable type of conformity, resulting in a profound and long-lasting acceptance of norms and values. At this level, individuals often get an intrinsic reward from the alignment which further strengthens the beliefs, and over time can become intertwined with their perceptions of themselves. In our example, continued membership to the low confidence group and acceptance of their beliefs may create a contentment and stability that feels nice and over time may internalise into a rigid personal perception of low confidence. It is important to highlight, however, that although identification can create fertile ground for internalisation, it is not a guaranteed outcome. Individuals who are open to new ideas and comfortable thinking critically are less likely to reach a permanent level of internalisation as are groups that promote reflection and inclusivity. Access to different perspectives can limit the chances of internalisation or reverse it as we saw in my experiences.

Unconscious Functioning

The next big element affecting confidence development and a contributing factor to its passive development is the very nature of confidence creation itself and how it is often an unconscious process. The notion that as humans we have lots of processes that are managed without conscious control dates back to the 17th century with researchers like Rene Descartes, who proposed mind-body dualism, and of course Friedrich Nietzsche, who emphasised the unconscious as a driving force of human behaviour and motivation. More recently the concept has been expanded by people like

Carl Jung, who believed in a collective unconscious shared by all humanity, and Daniel Kahneman, who highlighted its role in decision-making. Why we need to function unconsciously is a fascinating conundrum and continues to be the subject of a wide body of both physiological and psychological research. The body is an extremely efficient machine and so automating functions like breathing, digestion and blinking free up valuable cognitive resources for other things. Similarly, we can learn to automate behaviours like walking, riding a bike and even driving a car through habits in order to make them unconscious and leverage the same release of cognitive capacity. Research linking habitual functioning to the control of emotions and motivation may support our suggestion that confidence creation is largely unconscious and the concepts of implicit learning, classical and operant conditioning can help shine some additional light.

Implicit learning

Since the 1960s there has been a growing body of research into the concept of implicit learning which describes the learning of complex information in an unintentional manner, without any awareness of what has been learned. Much like unconscious functioning, there are some researchers that believe implicit learning has an evolutionary perspective and developed to allow rapid adaptation and survival without conscious effort or analysis. Some believe that repeated exposure to a stimulus strengthens connections between neurons because of the repeated activation which then leads to increase efficiency and performance. Another theory behind how we might implicitly learn is through what we pay attention to. We quickly learn how to ignore familiar aspects of environments and experiences and focus instead on the new and novel ones in order to understand them. Ignoring them does not mean that they are not encoded, and so this may be happening without use even knowing it. The growing consensus that we can learn things implicitly may also add weight to the idea that confidence creation is by default an unconscious process.

Classic conditioning

An unconscious way of learning that strongly affects us in the early years of our lives is called classic conditioning and describes how we learn things through association. Most people associate this way of learning to Ivan Pavlov's famous experiments with dogs in which he was able to create a learned association between a bell and the creation of saliva by always ringing a bell before providing food. American psychologist John Watson took Pavlov's work further by applying it to human behaviour and suggesting that all aspects of human functioning were simply patterns of stimulus and response. Watson's work suggested that people's responses are often learned through previous associations that they have made. An example from business might be how an individual typically feels fear when they hear shouting, and because they associate shouting with a particular member of staff, they feel fear when they interact with that member of staff even if they are not shouting. Research into classic conditioning suggests that the conditioned response will weaken over time if the association is not present and that even after long periods of dissociation, there can be spontaneous recovery. For us this is important as it may be that we have associated certain conditions or specific people with successful performance or high confidence and so feel enhanced or decreased confidence in their presence.

Operant conditioning

Around the same time as John Watson was working on classic conditioning, Edward Thorndike, another American psychologist, contributed to learning theory by introducing what he called the 'law of effect'. Thorndike suggested that behaviours followed by positive consequences are more likely to be repeated, whilst those resulting in negative consequences are less likely, hence people learn how to behave because of negativity avoidance. The concept of classic conditioning will become extremely important as we move through the book and look at how the confidence appraisal process and self-efficacy spirals work. For now, it is worth recognising that if a lot of our early learning is done through unconscious association, then it is possible that our confidence is also created that way.

Information Inequity

The quality of the information that we use for our 'cognitive appraisals' of confidence is vital to the accuracy and value of the confidence judgement that comes out the other end. Sadly, the volume and quality of the information that individuals have access to develop confidence varies wildly, and so creates an unfair playing field for confidence creation. As we will see later in the book, our past experiences, the modelling we have seen and the feedback we have been given about our capabilities, are all like seeds that get sown in the ground waiting to be harvested when they are needed.

Experience

As we move through our lives, we are all subject to varying frequencies and depths of experience, which are in turn affected by individual, social and cultural influences. Some children are more curious than others and seek out new experiences, while others shy away and pull back from life. We also naturally gain the capacity to engage in more experiences as we grow, and we gain more physical, intellectual and social resources. Our parents or carers play a pivotal part in our access to experience as their values and attitudes towards things directly affect our exposure and engagement. Our socioeconomic status can put a very real limit of the breadth and quality of our experiences through access to travel and extra-curricular activities. Where we live can be another freeing or constricting influence on our experiences with varying levels of access to libraries, parks, museums, and other community resources. Additional factors that create this experiential inequity include access to technology, cultural traditions, and norms and most significantly the impact of our peers which we will explore more next.

Modelling

The role of experience in building confidence is undisputed, but another key category of information that we use for confidence creation is what we see and sadly is another area where some get more than others. Two key researchers that we will meet later in the book are Julian Rotter and Albert Bandura, who were both fascinated by social learning and the idea that we can acquire new beliefs and behaviours by observing and imitating others. Growing up we are almost constantly observing the actions of others, and it's the success and consequences of the things we see that make a difference to our confidence. It stands to reason that observing someone successfully complete a task gives us confidence that we could do the same, and observed failure may do the opposite and develop hesitancy or fear instead. As with experience, the inequality comes from our access to this information and specifically, access to successful models. The presence of positive role-modelling is not resigned to physical demonstrations of skills, though as the presence of alternative viewpoints may give people the confidence to think in different ways, and the achievements of others may raise expectation and aspiration.

Feedback

Another vital type of efficacy information which is variable between people is feedback and is defined as 'information about a person's performance that is used as the basis for improvement'. Day-to-day, this is the information we receive from others or ourselves about how well something has gone. As we will see later, feedback is a tricky and complex beast and alongside the obvious positive or negative categorisation, there are intricacies woven into its source, purpose, subject, and tone. Much like experience and modelling, the frequency and value of feedback varies wildly between individuals and contributes to this idea that most of us probably develop our confidence at different rates. One person may get regular positive feedback from a parent or their peers and thus their confidence gradually grows whilst another receives the opposite and then experiences a sustained downward spiral of confidence. Our third individual receives very little feedback at all and so is confined to their own perceptions of confidence with little opportunities for validation.

As we reach the end of this chapter, I want you to take a minute to think about your own confidence curve and what kind of mess you and those around you are in. Are you currently as confidence as you would like, and more importantly are you as confident as you need to be to achieve your personal and professional goals? What have been the milestones or who have been the people in your life that have shaped your confidence level and has the curve been a passive or proactive one? Wherever you are on the confidence curve, I would challenge you to open your mind and lean in as the rest of the book is full of knowledge and activities that help you and those around you reach completely new heights.

Nuggets

- You can't just expect to be confident; it takes purposeful action.
- The power of confidence is underestimated, and this ignorance breeds apathy.
- Many believe that the future is fixed, and they will be who they will be.
- It is common to 'inherit' the confidence levels of your family and peers.
- People often develop their confidence passively.
- Subtle reinforcement cues either build or destroy confidence over time.
- Confidence levels vary because levels of past experience vary.
- Confidence levels vary because exposure to successful modelling varies.
- Confidence levels vary because the frequency and focus of feedback varies.
- Confidence levels can always be improved, and this book will show you how.

Next Steps

✓ Reflect on your current level of confidence and how it was created.
✓ Complete your own confidence curve graph.
✓ Get members of your team to create confidence curves and use the results as a stimulus for discussion.

CONFIDENCE CURVE

WHAT

Our confidence curve is a visual representation of our general confidence over time. The curve maps out the general shape of our confidence journey, highlighting the highs and lows and periods of stagnation.

The curve also identifies the key elements or experiences of our lives or work that have triggered increases or decreases in our confidence, showcasing the important focus points for exploration.

Confidence curves can span varying timescales but are often best kept discrete so that the detail of confidence changes can be best highlighted.

WHY

Creating a confidence curve can provide a range of benefits:

- Guides our reflection on personal confidence creation.
- Provides an overall sense of confidence fluctuations.
- Identifies the current level of confidence.
- Highlights key confidence creation triggers.
- Provides stimuli for further reflection or exploration with others.

HOW

Step 1 – Draw a set of axes showing confidence (Y axis) against time (x Axis).

Step 2 – Add titles so that your axis starts with January of this year and ends with December of the same year.

Step 3 – Sketch a rough curve to highlight your starting point, the peaks and troughs and the final finishing level of confidence.

Step 4 – Place dots or markers at key locations along the curve to represent significant triggers to either confidence increases or decreases.

Step 5 – Add annotations to describe each trigger point and its impact. (optional).

2

STUDYING OURSELVES

If you lead a team, interact with young people or are in a romantic relationship, then you know acutely how complex people are, and so it won't come as a surprise that academics and philosophers have been studying 'the self' for a very long time. Before researchers like William James introduced the term self-esteem in the late 1800s, philosophers and poets like Aristotle and Virgil were interested in the self and its impact on human behaviour. This popularity continued into the early 20th century through researchers such as James, Charles Horton Cooley, Sigmund Freud, Geroge Herbert Mead, Lev Vygotsky, and Kurt Lewin. The emergence of behaviourism saw researchers such as Ivan Pavlov, Edward Thorndike and B. F. Skinner take a difference perspective, but in the 1950s and '60s interest in the self re-emerged in the form of humanism and cognitivism through researchers such as Abraham Maslow, Lewin, Carl Rogers, Jean Piaget and Jerome Bruner.

To begin to understand a phenomenon called self-efficacy, which will be the main focus for the rest of the book, we first need to position it amongst other, probably more familiar constructs such as self-concept, self-esteem and confidence.

DOI: 10.4324/9781003558934-3

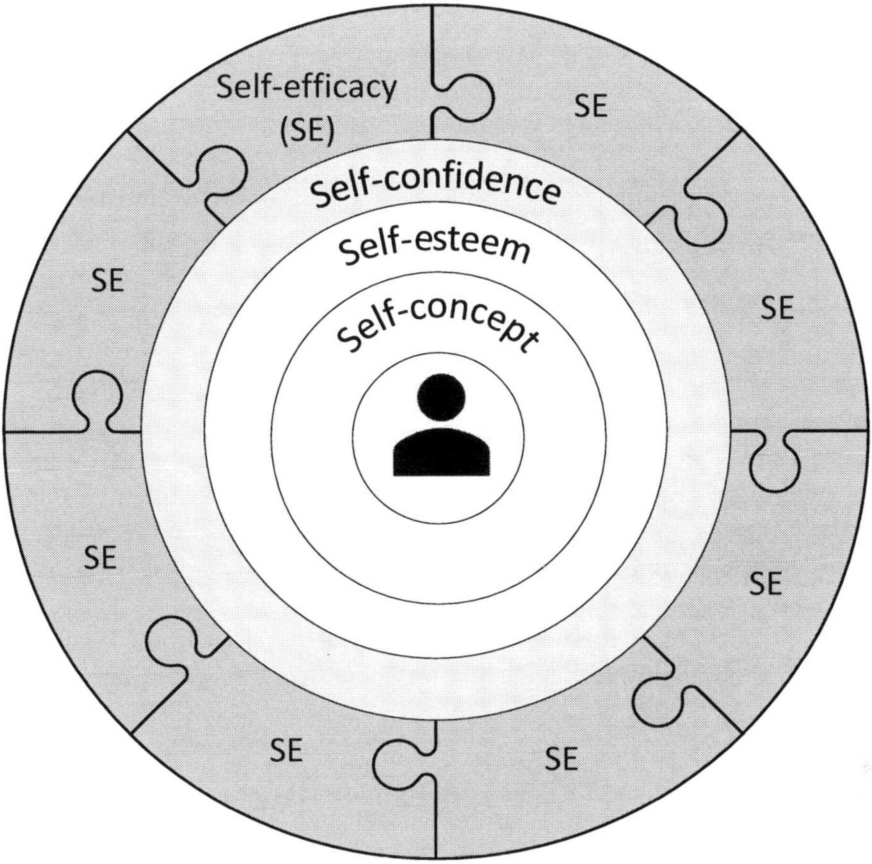

Figure 2.1 The different theoretical constructs of self

Self-Concept

If we start at the centre of the model, we come across something we call our self-concept which is arguably the foundation of all the others. Our self-concept is typically described as the way we see ourselves and includes our physical, emotional, and spiritual selves. Each of us has a unique self-concept, which is different from the self-concept of others and from their concept of us. The key characteristics of our self-concept include the following:

1. It displays uniquely with each person.
2. It varies on a continuum from very positive to very negative.
3. It carries emotional, intellectual and functional dimensions.

4. It changes with context.
5. It changes over time.
6. It influences the individual's life.
7. It dynamically interacts with other constructs of self.

One of the key people linked to the work on self-concept was American psychologist Carl Rogers. Rogers started in the 1920s working with troubled children and developed a client-centred approach to therapy that emphasised empathy, genuineness and what he called unconditional positive regard. Self-concept was a central theme in his research and in the 40s and 50s he explicitly introduced the idea that our self-concept is made up of three things: our self-esteem, which we will explore in more detail later, and what he called our self-image and our ideal self. As the name suggests, our self-image is the way that we see ourselves and includes our physical appearance like height and attractiveness, our social roles like brother or leader and our personality traits like kind or adventurous. Our self-image is a personal perception and so can be over or under inflated and often is not perfectly matched to reality. Rogers also suggested that we have an ideal self that describes the way we would like to be or be seen as by others. The interplay between these two elements is what links us to our next layer, our self-esteem. Rogers suggested that the level of perceived congruence between who we are and who we want to be can directly impact our levels of self-esteem.

Self-Esteem

Self-esteem is the next part of our model that we need to explore and is more focused on how good we are rather than who we are as with our self-concept. Typical descriptions include things like 'an inner evaluation of our worth and abilities', 'our own emotional rating of ourselves' or 'how much we value and appreciate ourselves'. Like self-concept and the other constructs, it is personal to each individual, changes over time and dynamically flows from and into the other areas. The now famous, 'Hierarchy of Needs' pyramid created by Abraham Maslow, which described five levels of human need, prominently displayed the importance of what he called 'esteem needs' by placing it almost at the top of the original model. Maslow placed it within the 'deficiency needs' category where the motivation to fulfil these needs increases the longer they are unmet. Over time, these esteem needs have been separated into 'inner esteem' which describes our desire for achievement, adequacy, independence and freedom, and 'outer esteem' which includes the pursuit of recognition, attention, importance and appreciation. Levels of self-esteem are important to human functioning because of their links to mental health and their impact on things like stress, depression, mood and overall happiness. Our self-esteem can also have a substantial impact on our relationships as it helps us set healthy boundaries, communicate effectively, and promote assertiveness. Our levels of motivation and even the goals we set for ourselves have been linked to self-esteem because of its close links to our confidence, which we will look at next.

Self-Confidence

So now we reach probably the most familiar term in the set, our 'self-confidence', which describes the general level of assurance that we have in our ability to be successful. Most people can describe their self-confidence when directly asked about it, but are less conscious of the ways that it is visible to others and the impact is has on their lives.

Table 2.1 Signs of low confidence

Category	*Sign*
Communication	Negative self-talk
	Apologizing excessively
	Avoiding expressing opinions or ideas
Body Language	Anxious behaviours (biting nails, crossing arms, etc.)
	Avoiding eye contact
	Poor posture
Social Interactions	Avoiding social situations
	Taking criticism poorly
	Difficulty saying no
Behaviours	Procrastination
	Perfectionism
	Self-comparison

We won't explore these in much detail at this stage as the next section on self-efficacy or task-specific confidence will do that much more justice. It is, however, worth highlighting the substantial impact that our general confidence can have on us, and studies have continuously found links between it and most aspects of our lives. High levels of confidence tend to increase happiness, satisfaction and general well-being. It enhances our relationships through better communication and the building of trust and creates greater opportunities by enabling us to step outside our comfort zone. Our confidence levels tend to have a direct impact on our performance and boost levels of motivation, focus and perseverance, leading to better outcomes. So, if we are all in agreement about the importance of confidence then why are the levels so variable and why is it so hard to develop. The answer might lie in its broadness and the volume of things that is encompasses which is why we need to go even deeper and explore something called self-efficacy.

Self-Efficacy

We have now reached our outermost circle and the focus of the rest of this book—self-efficacy. Self-efficacy is defined as a 'person's belief in their own ability to succeed at a particular task or goal' and could be seen as a sub-set of general confidence. Our level of general confidence is made up of the varying levels of self-efficacy for individual elements of our lives or jobs. You may have higher self-efficacy for written communication than verbal, for soccer rather than basketball, or for strategic versus operational leadership. This level of granularity is what makes self-efficacy so interesting to explore and what makes it more easy to develop, which of course is the aim of the book.

The godfather of self-efficacy was psychologist Albert Bandura who in the 50s and 60s became fascinated with the role of observational learning and its impact in shaping behaviour. This focus on what he called 'social learning' continued into the 70s when he published a landmark paper introducing the concept of self-efficacy and identifying it as a key determinant of human behaviour. Bandura's continuing work (1977, 1986, 1997) on self-efficacy led him to develop the very first measurement tool and to expand its reach into a wide range of fields such as education, healthcare and most relevant to us, leadership.

Studies of self-efficacy in education have naturally focused on either teachers or students which both strongly support its role in effective practice and successful outcomes. A study by Margolis and McCabe in 2006 indicated that students with strong self-efficacy tend to take on challenging tasks, are intrinsically motivated, apply high degrees of effort, attribute failure to things within their control and recover quickly from setbacks. Other research has highlighted its links to resilience during problem-solving tasks, engagement and more effective self-regulation. Schunk and Pajares (2002) found that highly efficacious students monitor their work time more effectively, solve problems more efficiently, work harder, evaluate their progress more frequently and engage in more self-regulatory strategies. On the teacher side, self-efficacy studies have suggested that high levels lead to greater levels of commitment, less job-related stress, improved classroom management and the ultimate goal, improved student grades. Mirroring the findings of the student studies, researchers have found links between self-efficacy and teacher resilience and motivation, but interestingly also to burnout and reduced levels of effort.

In terms of leadership, we have to look a little closer to find specific studies, but if we view the word confidence as a related, albeit more colloquial term then the research opens up. One of the most commonly reported findings in the literature on effective leadership is the relationship between levels of self-confidence and successful leadership. A major review of leadership literature by Bass and Stogdill (1990) highlighted self-confidence as an essential element of effective leadership, even suggesting that the idea that self-confidence is a necessary trait for successful leadership is undisputed. A more recent study by Maurer (2001) found that effective leaders share many of the characteristics of efficacious people in that they are motivated, persistent, goal-directed and resilient. Hannah et al. (2008) found that positive psychological states such as efficacy directly promoted effective leader engagement, flexibility and adaptability.

To further strengthen the importance of self-efficacy and why it is the focus of our work together in this book, let's pull together the research on self-efficacy and uncover some common characteristics of people with high or low levels.

Individuals with high levels of self-efficacy

- Accept challenges.
- Demonstrate intrinsic interest and deep engagement with activities.
- Show resilience during difficult tasks.
- Recover quickly from setbacks and disappointments.
- Experience lower levels of stress.

Individuals with low levels of self-efficacy

- Have low aspirations.
- Avoid challenging tasks.
- Lessen their efforts during difficulties.
- Demonstrate weak commitment to goals.
- Focus on personal failings and negative outcomes.

As we reach the end of this chapter, I want you to take a minute to think about your own self-concept, self-esteem and self-efficacy and that of those you work with most closely. How would you describe yourself and what you are? How much do you value and appreciate yourself and how has this changed over time? Can you spot a disconnect between the ideal self that you have in your mind and the actual self that the world sees? Finally, as we ready ourselves to delve much deeper into our core topic of self-efficacy, could you assign a perceived confidence level for yourself and every member of your team against each of the core components of their roles. If not, then there is work to do because this granular level of awareness is what we need to have if we are going to develop confidence by design.

Nuggets

- We are complex and all see ourselves in different ways.
- How we see and feel about ourselves has a big impact on our lives.
- Our self-concept or 'who we are', sits at the root of our beliefs about ourselves.
- Our self-esteem or 'how much we value ourselves' flows from our self-concept.

- Our self-confidence is a general feeling about our capability.
- Our levels of self-efficacy are task- and context-specific levels of confidence.
- Self-efficacy has been shown to be a key determinant of success in life and work.
- Self-efficacy has been directly linked to effective leadership.

Next Steps

✓ Reflect on your own self-concept, self-esteem, general confidence and self-efficacy.
✓ Complete your own SD (Self-Definition) Grid.
✓ Get other people in your team to complete SD grids and share their insights.

SD GRID

WHAT

SD Grids or 'self-definition' grids are a way of reflecting on and then describing the different elements of yourself. The grid is made up of the key constructs of self that we have discussed in this chapter.

Self-concept + Self-esteem + Self-confidence + Self-efficacy

WHY

Awareness and acknowledgement are the first steps to any personal change, and these often come about through personal or guided reflection. This exploration can be uncomfortable and challenging, but the result is often a greater level of clarity and understanding which can then lead to action and improvement.

Sharing SD grid information with others can be a great way of increasing inter-personal understanding, building relationships and creating stronger links within teams.

HOW

Step 1 – Define your self-concept by listing who you are *(parent, artist, teacher, etc.)* and your attributes *(calm, brave, curious, etc)*.

Step 2 – Define your self-esteem by exploring the difference between your ideal self and your current self in terms of attributes, behaviours, etc.

Step 3 – Define your overall sense of confidence using a 100-point scale, with 100 being extremely confident and zero being extremely unconfident.

Step 4 – Define your self-efficacy by listing the elements of your current role that you feel the most confident in and the elements that you feel the most unconfident in.

References

Bandura, A. (1977). *Social learning theory*. Englewood Cliffs, NJ: Prentice Hall.

Bandura, A. (1986). *Social foundations of thought and action: A social cognitive theory*. London: Prentice Hall.

Bandura, A. (1997). *Self-efficacy: The exercise of control*. New York: W. H. Freeman.

Bass, B. M. (1990). *Bass & Stogdill's handbook of leadership: Theory, research, and managerial applications*. New York, NY: Free Press.

Hannah, S. T., Avolio, B. J., Luthans, F., & Harms, P. D. (2008). Leadership efficacy: Review and future directions. *The Leadership Quarterly, 19*(6), 669–692.

Margolis, H., & McCabe, P. P. (2006). Improving self-efficacy and motivation: What to do, what to say. *Intervention in School and Clinic, 41*(4), 218–227.

Maurer, T. J. (2001). Career-relevant learning and development, worker age, and beliefs about self-efficacy for development. *Journal of Management, 27*, 123–140.

Schunk, D. H., & Pajares, F. (2002). The development of academic self-efficacy. In A. Wigfield & J. S. Eccles (Eds.), *Development of achievement motivation* (pp. 15–31). San Diego, CA: Academic Press.

3

BACK SEAT DRIVER

Okay, so now that we know what we are talking about, let's go a little deeper and examine the idea that our levels of self-efficacy or 'contextual confidence' have a massive impact on our day-to-day lives and very little of it is not in some way affected by it. I want you to think back to a day this week and walk yourself through its key moments and events. I would imagine that it started fairly habitually, you went through your morning routine without any fuss or worry, you successfully made it to work, and the day was suddenly in full flow. During that day you probably made lots of decisions both personally and professionally and also encountered numerous challenges along the way. You will have felt varying levels of energy and enthusiasm for the different parts of the day, and had lots of thoughts and feelings that you intelligently filtered in order not to upset people. The day will have ended as it started with a low stress, low thinking set of habits that set you up for the next day and sent you off to sleep.

What you won't have realised during the day is that in the background of all of that, you perceived levels of self-efficacy and they directed the way

DOI: 10.4324/9781003558934-4

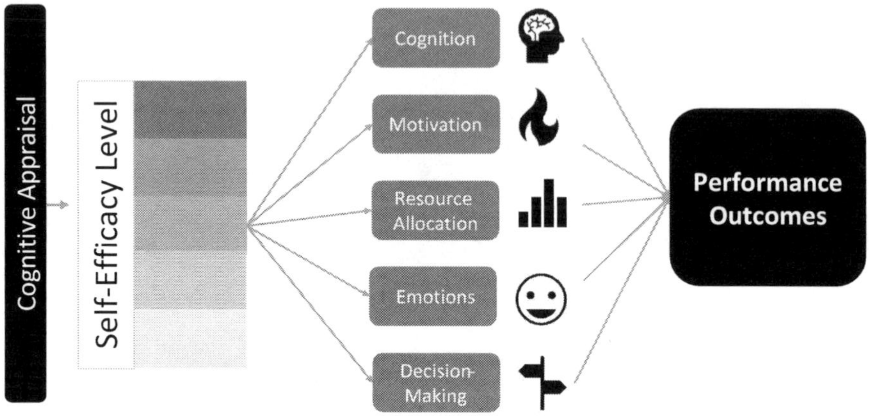

Figure 3.1 The impact of self-efficacy

you perceived situations, how those translated into emotions, the decisions you made because of that and the subsequent levels of energy and commitment you showed.

Cognition

Lots of what we will talk about in this section and throughout the book will probably be a little unsettling in terms of the magnitude we attach to self-efficacy and no more so than the suggestion that it affects how we think. Our perceptions of confidence act on how we process information, the inferences we make and the analysis we do to then take action.

The earliest sign of this impact is through the way that we process information from the environment and what we pay attention to. As we will see later in this chapter, simple models of memory suggest that we can't learn or store what we don't pay attention to, and our ability to think about the right stuff in the right way is a big deal. Our levels of self-efficacy towards a task affect how well we can focus and filter out distractions as well as selectively attend to information that is relevant to the success of the task. Highly efficacious people are more able to ignore redundant information because of their confidence in their ability to accurately and efficiently scan situations. This reduces their level of cognitive overload and smooths out the path of information through the short- and long-term memory. How we interpret information is also linked to our self-efficacy. Typically we see things in a much more positive light when we feel confident than when we don't. We see challenges as opportunities and failures as temporary setbacks, all leading to less anxiety and clearer thinking. Another key element of our thinking that is affected by self-efficacy is our anticipation of impending events and our thoughts about them even before they have happened. The level of confidence we attach to an event often directs our levels of excitement and the expectations that we form around how it will go and how it will end. We naturally look forward to events where we are likely to be successful, and of course feel the opposite about the likelihood of failure. Our ability to cognitively rehearse how an event or a decision may play out allows us to protect ourselves from anticipated issues by planning mitigation strategies for them or by withdrawing altogether. As we will see later in the book, the impact of self-efficacy on the way we think also plays an important role in our learning, metacognition, our beliefs around agency and our role as leaders.

Motivation

Our levels of motivation towards something naturally impact on our behaviour towards it, which then of course affects the quality of our performance and its impact. For this reason, motivation is definitely something worth exploration and is closely tied to our levels of self-efficacy. When we think about how our motivation for something is formed, we need to consider both our forethought and afterthoughts about the goal or task. In most situations we will approach a task which some form of goal in mind and this represents our conscious aim, desire and aspirations for the situation. Edwin Locke, a psychologist we will learn more about later in the book, suggested in his 'goal theory' that the way we set goals and their levels of specificity, challenge and possible success directly affect how motivated we are towards them. Self-efficacious people typically set themselves ambitious goals, and those with low levels of confidence often set goals that are too high, so the expectation of success is lower or set at overly easy goals so that success is guaranteed.

Another element of foresight which affects motivation and is affected by self-efficacy is what we call our 'outcome expectancies', or what we believe the outcome of a task or challenge will be. This sits at the core of our confidence, as we rarely feel confident about things we expect to go badly, and this then has a negative impact on how motivated we are and how much effort we apply. In Bandura's self-efficacy theory, he suggests that the strength of the expectation and the value of the outcome directly affect our levels of motivation. If we strongly expect to succeed and the reward is something we value like recognition, enjoyment or tangible prizes, then we experience higher levels of motivation to complete it. On the flip side, we also feel strong motivation not to complete tasks when we strongly expect to fail and the failure leads to things like embarrassment, decreased social status or formal losses of responsibility. It is often the strength of the expectancy that plays the biggest role in motivation, and people with high levels of self-efficacy typically have strong positive expectations of situations and themselves.

Another factor that affects motivation comes after the event and is linked to Bernard Weiner's work on something called attribution theory. What we attribute our successes and failures to can have a big impact on our levels of motivation and self-efficacy towards any future attempts. We will explore this in more detail later in the book when we look at locus of control. but at the most basic level, we typically attribute outcomes to either ourselves or others and to controllable or uncontrollable factors. We gain the most motivation when we attribute success to our own ability and any failure to controllable factors. An example would be linking a successful promotion to our intelligence or skill level (internal) and a lack of promotion to not having enough qualifications (controllable). In the same situation, gaining a promotion because of insufficient competition (external) or luck (uncontrollable) would not have as big a positive impact on our motivation. Self-efficacy also has a part to play here, and people with high levels tend to attribute success to internal, stable factors and failure to things they can control, meaning that they have the power to avoid it in the future. Individuals with low levels of self-efficacy tend to blame it on external, unstable things in order to protect themselves and unwittingly rob themselves of the ability to change the outcome of any future attempts.

Resource Allocation

Closely linked to our levels of motivation is how we decide to use our personal resources and judiciously allocate our time, thinking and effort. We initially feel it in the level of preparation that we do for tasks or challenges with the two extremes of very high or very low confidence resulting in the lowest levels of effort, time and thinking. When we don't expect to succeed, preparation feels pointless, and when we feel like success is guaranteed then preparation feels unnecessary. This pattern continues into the task where we are noticeably reserved, distracted or lethargic when our confidence is low and we feel like the outcome of the task is already decided. Thoughts and comments like "what's the point" or "I can't be bothered" are often signals of a deep-rooted link to confidence which plays out as variances in resource allocation. What we do with our time, thinking and effort during resistance or setbacks is also affected by our levels of self-efficacy. Highly efficacious people tend to apply themselves more in these situations because of their belief in their ability to overcome adversity and their desire to complete the task. Individuals with low levels of task-specific confidence typically give up when they face difficulty and either scale back their resources or shut them off completely. The impact of this resource moderation is significant and speaks again to the reciprocal and cyclical nature of self-efficacy and performance. When we don't feel confident, we don't try very hard and give up easily which then negatively affects the outcome of the task or challenge, which then reinforces our low confidence. This spiralling is something that we will look at in more detail in chapter 11.

Emotions

Another big and unsettling suggestion about the importance of self-efficacy is that the literature shows it even affects how we feel, with levels of it being linked to stress, anxiety and even depression. One of the early impacts of self-efficacy is how events are perceived in the first place and how emotionally disturbing they are thought to be. The level of threat attached to an event is not a fixed trait but is rather an individualised perception by the person experiencing it. A setback in a project may feel inconsequential to someone with high self-efficacy but paralysing to another team member with lower levels. This accounts for different people's reactions to the same stimulus and in some way is directed by their levels of self-efficacy. As we see right at the end of the book, confidence is closely tied to coping, and when we are confident about our ability to cope, then we are more able to moderate our emotional responses to events. Highly self-efficacious people don't magnify threat levels or catastrophise by imagining extreme consequences and generally have a muted response to threat because of their confidence in their ability to cope.

Self-efficacy levels are also thought to impact the way that we express our emotions and our levels of confidence to express them, the modulation of their intensity and our choice of expression channel. How confident we feel about being authentic and assertive about the emotions we are feeling is important to our feelings of agency, acceptance and something called psychological safety, which we will explore in more detail later in the book. When we have high levels of self-efficacy, we trust in the value of our feelings and trust that we can handle the reactions of others and any consequences. When we don't feel confident, we tend to suppress our emotions and hide them because of a fear of negative judgment or unwanted outcomes. Our confidence levels also play a part in how we moderate the intensity of the emotions we express. People with high self-efficacy are more capable of avoiding extremely high and low emotional states and express themselves in a healthy and measured way. When we have low levels of task-specific confidence, we often overreact or under-express ourselves leading to frustration on our part and negative reactions from others. This often results in behavioural outbursts, spiralling meltdowns or withdraw from situations and responsibility. Low confidence often creates anxiety and perceptions of threat and so it is common for these individuals to choose negative pathways for emotion like passive-aggressive behaviour, confrontation or avoidance. When confidence levels are higher, emotional control is also typically higher, and so these individuals are able to use additional channels such as art or physical activity to manage and express their emotions.

The final piece of the self-efficacy emotion puzzle is the power it holds over the way that we act during emotional experiences and again is closely linked to our coping confidence. What we do in emotional situations strongly affects both the outcome of the event and the strength and duration of the emotions that we feel. People with high levels of self-efficacy actively adopt strategies and produce actions that reduce the level of hazard in situations. They regulate their stress and anxiety levels by taking action and using their knowledge of themselves and their calmness of mind to evaluate possible cause-effect links and select the most appropriate behaviour. On the flip side, those with lower self-efficacy tend to passively allow the situation to affect them and therefore delay any emotional or outcome resolution. The boldness of the response to threat is often linked to its outcomes and is also thought to be linked to self-efficacy with low levels leading to superficial actions and high levels leading to substantial efforts and greater success. This, like lots of relationships we will come across in the book, is a reciprocal one in that greater self-efficacy leads to more effective action, which then leads to more success and then even greater levels of confidence.

Decision Making

As we will see in the next chapter, our self-efficacy beliefs are a constant companion in our lives and have the power to significantly change its direction. This course-altering effect is largely due to the idea that our perceived levels of confidence direct our decision making and our choices. It is frightening to think that we are in the jobs that we are in, have the interests that we have and have achieved what we have achieved in a large part due to our levels of self-efficacy. The role we didn't apply for, the country we never visited, the person we never asked out on a date or the challenge we never signed up for are all possibly due to a lack of confidence.

We typically select activities which we have strong levels of efficacy in, and avoid those that we perceive could end in failure. These selections extend from the subjects we study at school, to the hobbies we take part in and the career choices we make later in life showcasing just how dramatically self-efficacy can alter the course of our lives.

As we reach the end of this chapter, I want you to take a minute to think about how much control self-efficacy has over your life and the lives of those you work with most closely. How positive is your thinking and what's your default response to challenges. Can you recognise a link between your levels of motivation towards tasks and your self-efficacy levels? Do you place the blame for failure elsewhere and pass off success as just luck? Can you see a link between your confidence level and the time and effort you apply to tasks? How good are you and your team at coping with the emotional roller coaster of work, and what part does confidence play in the emotions they feel and show? Finally, what decisions did you make today which might have been affected by your levels of self-efficacy?

Nuggets

- Self-efficacy affects almost every aspect of our day-to-day lives.
- It affects how we think about impending, current and future events.

- It plays a key role in the regulation of our motivation levels.
- We are more motivated for things that we feel we will be successful in.
- People with high levels of self-efficacy are more intrinsically motivated.
- Self-efficacy plays a big part in how we feel and the emotions we experience.
- It predisposes people to feel positively or negatively about events.
- People with high levels of self-efficacy typically experience less stress.
- Self-efficacy plays a part in what we pay attention to and what we remember.
- It affects our choices, which in turn directs the course of our lives.
- People with high levels of self-efficacy more readily take on challenges.
- Self-efficacy directs how much time, thinking and effort we apply to tasks.
- We don't tend to fully apply ourselves to tasks we don't think we can succeed in.
- People with high levels of self-efficacy are resilient in the face of setbacks.

Next Steps

✓ Explore the impact of your own self-efficacy by completing a BSD (back seat driver) analysis.

✓ Get members of your team to complete BSD analysis and share the insights.

BSD ANALYSIS

WHAT

A BSD or 'Back Seat Driver' analysis is a method of exploring and evaluating the influence of self-efficacy beliefs. The process involves systematically working through the established impacts of self-efficacy, judging their level of influence and locating examples to justify each evaluation.

WHY

Self-efficacy's role in our lives is often hidden and largely unconscious. Increasing our awareness of its influence can be a key step in the process of improving it and can also develop our sense of agency and readdress an external locus of control.

As with the SD grid, getting others to complete and share insights from their BSD analysis can improve inter-personal relationships, build belonging and increase levels of empathy and psychological safety.

HOW

Step 1 – Reflect on the way that your self-efficacy levels affect your

- Thinking
- Motivation
- Effort and resilience
- Emotions
- Decision making

Step 2 – Give each element an influence rating with ten being an extremely strong influence and zero being an extremely weak influence.

Step 3 – Add some explicit examples of where your self-efficacy levels have affected each of the influence areas.

4

SELF-EFFICACY OVER TIME

As we said in the first chapter, confident people are not made over night and our levels of self-efficacy are long in the making. If we assume that every interaction we have with the world either increases or decreases our confidence, then we start to acknowledge the importance of consciously developing it from a young age. You probably had early childhood experiences that will have cemented a foundation of confidence and then moved through a set of fairly common experiences during adolescence and early adulthood that decided its development. What you will not have recognised is the constant course direction effect that self-efficacy has and that at any one point in your life, your self-efficacy levels probably had a hand in directing the next step and the next in a reciprocal and amplifying dance.

Early Childhood

Our self-efficacy curve begins as soon as we start to interact with our environment with each stimulus – action – result cycle either adding or

DOI: 10.4324/9781003558934-5

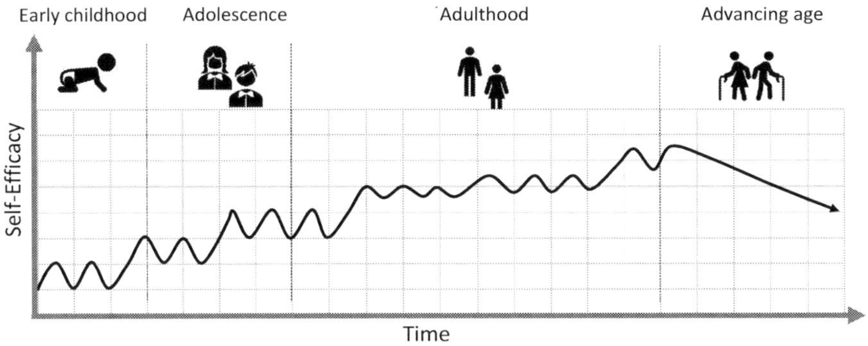

Figure 4.1 Self-efficacy levels over time

subtracting from our confidence in our abilities. A key stage in this early formation of self-efficacy is when children start to move from what we call 'action causality', where they know that they are doing the action, to 'personal causality', where they realise that they are the cause of outcomes and begin to believe in their ability to make things happen. A child making a tower out of blocks starts to see that it's not the blocks themselves that determine the success of the tower but how they stack them and it's their decisions that make the difference. Even the process of crying to get more food strengthens the idea that something they did brought about an outcome that they wanted.

The high levels of dependency associated with early childhood place an even greater importance on the role of the parent in terms of self-efficacy development. Our parents initially act as the gatekeeper to our involvement in activities and experiences, and it is our success in these that either develops or erodes our feelings of confidence. The nuances associated with self-efficacy development through experience are complex and something that we will cover in the next chapter. Parents also play a key role in self-efficacy development through the messages they send about the likelihood of success and the reasons behind outcomes. Positive affirmations from our parents ahead of and during events tend to boost our confidence, and feedback afterwards has the power to make or break the confidence creation process.

Another element of our early lives worth thinking about is the impact of our siblings, which due to their sustained presence, have a particularly big influence on us at this early stage of life. Siblings play an important role in self-efficacy development through the modelling they do both in their attitudes to risk, their responses to stimuli and their successful completion of tasks. Seeing someone else complete a task not only shows you that it is possible but also provides a blueprint on how to do it which can then be followed. This observational learning or vicarious influence is another key type of efficacy information that we will delve more deeply into in the next chapter.

Adolescence

As we move further into our lives our self-efficacy curve hits more milestones and is affected by a range of new internal and external stimuli. One key development is that we get better at appraising our efficacy levels, we use a wider range and deeper set of information, our judgements become more objective and our ability to make accurate inferences improves. These improvements typically lead to more success as we make better choices about what challenges we take on and how to organise ourselves and others to perform effectively.

Now sadly, childhood and especially adolescence is not always an easy ride, and many of us experience different types of adversity along the way. These can present in the form of socio-economic challenges such as poverty, discrimination or displacement and situational issues like divorce, bereavement or abuse. The negative side of these causes an obvious decrease in levels of confidence and the associated loss of ambition, motivation and general well-being. If there is a plus side to adversity, then it is linked to the potential increases in coping efficacy which we will explore later in the book and improved levels of resilience and resourcefulness.

A final element of adolescence which impacts heavily on our levels of self-efficacy is the widening of our peer group, our access to role models and the frequency with which we can make comparisons and receive feedback. Increases in self-efficacy at this stage often occur because we typically choose friends who have attributional similarities in terms of interests and values which serve to validate and strengthen our confidence. Sadly, of course the breadth of our peer group and the necessity to interact with different people because of schooling and residential neighbourhoods mean that we also encounter negative influences. Explicit discrimination and internal negativity and self-doubt can cause significant damage to our levels of confidence and lead to insecurity, ostracization and choices that affect the rest of our lives.

Adulthood

As we move into adulthood, our self-efficacy levels are again subject to change and affected by a range of factors due to the newly acquired demands of things like relationships, parenthood and career progression. These elements cause levels of instability in our self-efficacy levels due to the volume of situations that require cognitive appraisals of confidence. Starting relationships is fraught with social comparisons, and the act of even asking someone out on a first date requires a level of confidence that lots of us don't readily have.

Another frighteningly important impact of self-efficacy is our choice of career, which can probably be tracked back to the confidence-related educational choices we made in school. It stands to reason that students who don't feel confident in subjects like history or chemistry don't choose to continue their studies and thus don't then find themselves in related careers. This impact doesn't stop there though as career progression is no doubt affected by our confidence and plays out in situations where people stay in jobs that they don't enjoy and shy away from opportunities to change role or even sector.

If you have been fortunate enough to become a parent or carer, then you will no doubt be aware of the crippling sense of self-doubt that regularly washes over you as you recognise the enormity of the task. Parenthood seems to come with a never-ending number of challenges and reasons to question our confidence with varying access to support or successful modelling. To further complicate the story, we also become responsible for the self-efficacy development of another human being which we will explore more in chapter 8.

The middle years of adulthood typically bring an increase in self-regulation and control, and so often result in a period of relative stability in terms of our self-efficacy levels. Our peer groups selectively shrink and bring greater alignment of values and interests, reducing our need to evaluate or validate ourselves. We actively manage the levels of challenge in our lives through the interests that we keep and the goals that we set for ourselves, protecting ourselves from any chance of confidence decline. The only blip in this part of our story is the infamous mid-life crisis where we experience a period of emotional turmoil and self-doubt brought about by increased levels of reflection and often regret. During this time, self-efficacy levels can take a hit due to negative perceptions of personal accomplishment, incongruence between our actual self and our ideal self, comparison to peers and confusion about our purpose or identity.

Advancing Age

The final part of our self-efficacy story takes us into the final chapters of our lives and is sadly associated with a general sense of decline. Decreases in our physical and intellectual capabilities create regular self-efficacy appraisals about success and comparisons to previously held abilities and accomplishments. Our inability to maintain levels of effectiveness and usefulness can dramatically affect our confidence levels. Advancing age also often results in a further reduction in peer group size and involvement in social activities and previously held hobbies. This lack of involvement robs us of many of the things that once supported our self-efficacy development like successful experience, role modelling and positive feedback and persuasion. The accompaniment of negative efficacy information in the form of mental health issues like stress and anxiety and physiological signals such as pain and reduced function all contribute to a sub-optimal level of self-efficacy.

For some and probably many people, the later stages of life result in a loss of agency which further dents their levels of self-efficacy. Alongside the loss of physical capabilities, we often perceive a drop in the control we have over our choices, decreased opportunities to express ourselves authentically and a reduced ability to influence our environment. The combination of these factors and the ones previously mentioned can have a cumulatively negative effect on self-efficacy levels and cause us to spiral downwards into lower and lower levels. There are however a range of different strategies that we can use to reverse the direction of what we call 'self-efficacy spirals', which we will explore in more detail in chapter 11.

As we reach the end of this chapter, I want you to take a minute to extend the thinking you did in chapter 1 when you created your confidence curve. What were the key milestones in your early childhood and adolescence that shaped that early foundation? Did your journey follow the typical path outlined in this chapter and how have you been affected by life events like career, relationships and parenthood? Finally, how much of your team's stories do you know and how might knowing more help you develop their confidence?

Nuggets

- Our self-efficacy development begins in early childhood.
- The way that we are parented and interact with siblings makes a difference.
- We get better at accurately perceiving self-efficacy as we move into adolescence.
- Our confidence is strongly shaped by any adversity.
- Peer modelling and feedback play an ongoing role in self-efficacy development.
- The demands of employment, relationships and parenthood create instability.
- As adults, we create more stability and protect ourselves through our choices.
- We often hit a self-efficacy wall during mid-life as we reflect on past choices.
- Self-efficacy levels drop as opportunities and status decrease.
- Advancing age is typically linked with a decline in self-efficacy.
- As we lose our physical and mental capabilities, so do we lose our confidence.
- Our inability to continue with work or hobbies causes further reductions.
- Self-efficacy levels can be boosted by new interests and positive social comparisons.

Next Steps

✓ Map out your own confidence journey using the SE (self-efficacy) life tracker.

✓ Get the members of your team to complete a SE life tracker and discuss key milestones.

SE LIFE TRACKER

WHAT

A Self-Efficacy Life Tracker is an activity used to gain a wider perspective of confidence or self-efficacy development over time. Much like the confidence curve we completed after chapter 1, the SE tracker attempts to describe our self-efficacy highs and lows but does so through the key stages of life.

The tracker indicates significant increases, decreases or periods of stability in a person's life, and importantly, highlights their comparisons to the established norm. The tracker also provides opportunities to describe the details of events that led to those patterns.

WHY

The SE Life Tracker is another tool for raising awareness and locating key stimuli, which in turn can help us better understand our confidence journey and the roots of our current levels. As with the other reflective tools, an increased understanding can be useful for change management and emphasising with others.

Tracking self-efficacy across a wider timescale can highlight patterns and common triggers as well as add a predictive function by hypothesising about future changes and comparisons to the norm.

Sharing SE Life Tracker information is a useful activity for developing relationships, increasing inter-personal understanding and creating a sense of belonging.

HOW

Step 1 – Create an SE tracking grid with separate sections for the key life stages of early childhood, adolescence, adulthood and advancing age.

Step 2 – Reflect on your confidence journey over the stages you have completed so far.

Step 3 – Indicate broadly whether SE levels increased, decreased or remain stable.

Step 4 – Add comments to explain the triggers for key SE changes.

5

SELF-EFFICACY IN THE MOMENT

So, we now know that we have been involved in this ongoing construction project for the whole of our lives and we will have had key events that have shaped our confidence along the way. What will be more surprising is how dynamic those changes have been and how many of what we call 'cognitive appraisals' you have gone through and still complete on a day-to-day basis. The often-unconscious nature of these self-efficacy judgements means that they probably go unnoticed (which of course is part of the issue and the reason for the book), but we are all checking our confidence throughout the day in order to manage our motivation, emotion and decision-making.

But what are we doing during one of these cognitive appraisals?

Let's take a physical challenge as a first example and imagine that you have been asked to take part in a 10-kilometre run for charity in a months' time and need to confirm your enrolment by the end of today. Figure 5.1 shows how we use a range of what we call efficacy information to complete an appraisal and arrive at a level of self-efficacy for the task in question and in our example, whether we say yes to the event or not.

DOI: 10.4324/9781003558934-6

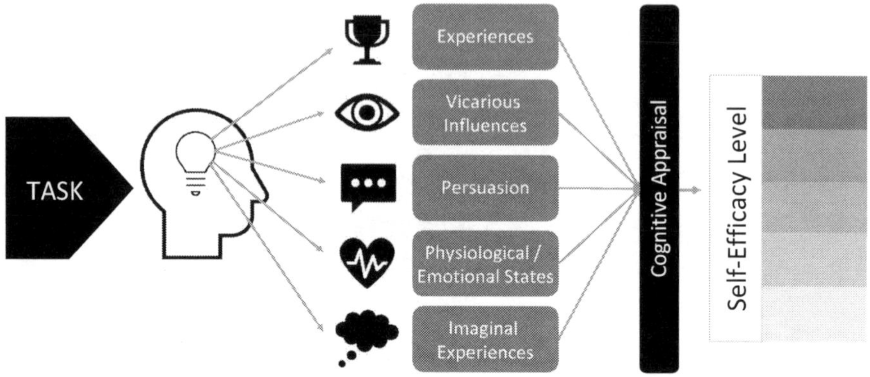

Figure 5.1 The self-efficacy appraisal process

The information that we use to appraise our task specific confidence levels can be separated into five key categories, and is accrued throughout our lives and constantly refined and updated. It is the variance and dynamism of this information that makes self-efficacy so personalised, temporally specific and most importantly for this book, developable.

Experience

Past experiences have been shown to be the most influential source of efficacy information (Bandura, 1977) with experiences viewed as successful serving to increase confidence and the contrasting attribution of failure serving to reduce it. At its simplest level, this reflection on previous attempts creates an inner dialogue of "I've done it in the past, so I can do it again" or "I'm not so sure as I've never done this before or it didn't go well last time". The influence of past experiences is complex, and the literature cites a range of contributory factors that we must be aware of during our efficacy appraisals and when we think about the self-efficacy development of others.

Recency

The first factor associated with past experiences that we will look at is time and how far in the past they occurred. If in our example we had run a 10K twenty years ago, then it would have a less positive impact on our current confidence levels than if we ran one last week. The impact of time on self-efficacy is magnified as when we reflect back, we also naturally compare our physical and mental states at the time of completion with how they are now and also add that to the mix.

Difficulty

The level of difficulty attached to past experiences also subtly contributes to the appraisal process with the successful completion of difficult tasks strengthening our confidence the most. In our example it may be that the terrain and weather conditions of the previous attempt made it a particularly difficult or easy challenge. It is the comparison between past and current events that again dictates the impact with the best situation being that the events were similar or the past experience was more difficult than the current one.

Support

The levels of support or assistance we had during past experiences also plays a part in our use of this type of efficacy information with independently successful tasks strengthening our confidence the most. In our example it may be that we had the use of a pace runner or a coach that ran with us during the race which supported our success and would soften any confidence boosting reflections. Again, it is the difference in support between the past and current experiences that makes the difference. Our self-talk can suddenly take a negative turn with the addition of a "but I had a lot of support the last time I did it".

Effort

Closely linked to the difficulty of past experiences is the level of effort we had to apply to be successful with low effort – high success situations strengthening our confidence the most. If in our example we had completed multiple 10 kilometre runs in the past with very little effort, then it stands to reason that we would feel more confident about entering the charity race.

Before we finish this section on past experiences, we need to acknowledge that when we talk about cognitive appraisals, we are often using information from our own memories and that this information store is often subjective. What we remember about past events is rarely a perfect recording and is based on our own personal interpretations at the time. It is also true that memories can fade and distort over time with us regularly creatively filling gaps and conflating different events together. A final thing for us to remember about the accuracy of the information we use for self-efficacy judgements is the influence of emotion on our memory storage. We typically store highly emotional experiences more strongly than others, as the emotion amplifies our attention and even causes the release of hormones like cortisol which enhance their consolidation in the long-term memory. The subjectivity of memory is particularly important to us, as we can only use the information that we have stored and if that information is flawed then so will our levels of self-efficacy.

Vicarious Influence

Comparisons with others are another source of efficacy information and can have a powerful influence on self-efficacy beliefs, as they provide a standard against which our own performances can be evaluated, and they confirm the message that skills are learnable and difficult tasks are surmountable. The idea that we learn things from observing others dates back to early philosophers like Aristotle who explored the idea of mimetic learning and how children learn from adults. The concept of social facilitation or the impact of others on an individual's learning took this further and was studied in animals by researchers like Edward Thorndike and Wolfgang Kohler in the early 1900s. The creation of 'social learning theory' by Albert Bandura marked a significant jump in our understanding and famously showed the dark side of modelling. Bandura's bobo doll experiment in 1961 took 36 children aged 3–6 years old and divided them into three groups. One group observed an adult modelling aggressive behaviour towards a doll and punching, kicking and even hitting it with a hammer. The second group observed an adult calmly playing with the doll and the third, control group, did not observe any model. After the observation, the children were left alone with the bobo doll and the results were probably what you were expecting. The children who observed the aggressive adult then displayed much more violence towards the doll, indicating that even aggression can be a learned behaviour and caused concern about the power of vicarious influences like parents, peers and the media. The research into observational learning continues and researchers are increasingly interested in the brain mechanisms that are involved in imitation and the role of technologically mediated learning and social media. Before we move onto the intricacies of this type of efficacy information, we need to recognise that alongside the observation of others, our confidence is also affected by just being compared to others. Being told that you rank in the top or bottom 1% of your class or year group or feeling like you are superior or inferior to others around you can have a significant impact on your self-efficacy.

Much like past experiences though there are a range of factors that we must consider when we use observational learning experiences in our confidence appraisals.

Contextual alignment

The first and most important consideration is the contextual alignment between you and the observed model. The closer you are in terms of demographics and expertise, the more powerful the observational impact, but this is true for both confidence growth and decline. If we see others who are very similar to us succeed, then our confidence to produce similar results is boosted, but if they fail, then we may see that as a limiting factor for our own performance. The less similarity, the weaker the impact. The impact of this alignment is of course at its highest when we are viewing recorded footage of ourselves or 'self-modelling'. Viewing our own successful practice can be especially powerful because of the trust we place in observations of ourselves and the recollection of past experiences that is then possible.

Previous experience

Our amount of previous experience is another key consideration when we use vicarious efficacy information as the research suggests that the less previous experience we have in an area, the more we rely on modelling and comparisons. This is particularly important for novices, and as leaders we must recognise the impact that our comments and role modelling may have on others in those early career stages. Another consideration when using observational efficacy information is the possibility of inattention or misperception during the observation process. There is a possibility of interpersonal variance in the information that people take from models and the inferences and attributions that they make, and so often the presence of a guide like a mentor or coach can be beneficial. The final thing we need to think about is the potentially hidden information within the modelling or influence of others. At the simplest level, models demonstrate whether something is achievable or not but there is often much more to learn and therefore to integrate into our self-efficacy appraisal processes. If we look closely enough, we can also find benefits in the way that people break down specific skills and techniques, how they motivate themselves verbally, what they do in the face of difficulty and the information we can gain about the nature of the environment and the task itself.

Persuasion

A third type of information we typically use during self-efficacy appraisals is the information we receive from others in the form of feedback or internally in the form of self-talk. This source varies in its impact between people depending on the strength of their self-concept and esteem and how much weight they place on the opinions of others. As with the other efficacy information sources, persuasion has a number of characteristics that users must consider.

Source

A key element that affects the power of the persuasion is its source and where the information is coming from. Our perceptions about the other person doing the persuasion or the validity of the persuasive information strongly affects whether we receive it in the first place, how we interpret it once we have it and if we actually use it to drive future thinking and actions. Feedback has the strongest impact, both positively and negatively, when it comes from sources that we feel are credible and trustworthy. In our example of the charity run, receiving affirmations from our running coach, who themselves hold the national record for the 10K distance, would have a much greater impact than those we get from our non-running spouse or children.

Attribution

Another consideration for us when we use persuasory information during self-efficacy appraisals is what the success or failure is attributed to. We will talk more about our locus of control in the next chapter, but for now it is relevant as the impact of feedback on confidence is affected by whether it is attached to things inside or outside of our control. We typically find that confidence levels rise if success is attributed to factors in our control such as motivation, effort and resilience, and protected when failure is attributed to external factors out of our control such as luck, our environment and other people.

Frequency

Formal persuasion is often variable in its frequency, and you are probably struggling to remember the last time you had any written feedback on your leadership. More frequent is the steady stream of informal feedback that we receive from all kinds of people on a day-to-day basis. This feedback comes in the form of verbal comments, non-verbal gestures and implicitly in the outcomes of the tasks we complete. The frequency with which we receive this persuasory information affects how stable our self-efficacy levels are and also how reliant we are on our own perceptions. As previously mentioned, a lack of external feedback is often as damaging as negativity, as it forces us to rely on our own beliefs which are questionably accurate.

Congruence

The wide range of feedback sources presents potential issues with congruence and consensus which then alters its impact on our confidence levels. Where there are conflicting messages about our ability to perform successfully, we tend to ignore or dismiss either both sources of information or more dangerously just the source that we don't want to hear.

Self-talk

We can't finish this section on persuasory information without considering the invisible but significant impact that our internal self-talk has on our levels of task-specific confidence. We all have an inner dialogue with ourselves which ticks along in the background, helping us to understand the world and then raises its head and shouts at times like pre-task appraisals and post-task evaluations. We will explore self-talk in more detail in chapters 7 and 8 when we talk about self-efficacy development and the work of Professor Steve Peters, but for now it is useful to briefly outline its types and influences. Broadly, self-talk is divided into positive, which plays out as affirmations such as "I can do this" or "I am ready for this", or as negative, critical and often judgemental comments like "I'm not good enough" or "I am never going to be able to do this". As you would imagine, it is the positive comments that boost confidence, motivation and general well-being the most, and the negative elements that can create anxiety, undermine confidence and hinder progress.

Physiological and Emotional States

The way we feel physically and emotionally can also be used during self-efficacy appraisals as states such as fear or anxiety and symptoms like sweating and increased heart rate can be indicators of deeper, often unconscious feelings and thoughts. This efficacy information often presents itself both prior to a task when we carry out the confidence appraisal and during the task itself and thus has a power of whether we take on the task in the first place and whether we continue with it once we have started. In our example of the charity run, feelings of anxiety or worry during the appraisal would, for lots of us, signal a lack of confidence and any physical symptoms like pain or extreme rises in heart rate during the event would lead us to question our ability to finish. Like the other sources of appraisal information though, there are discrete considerations that need to be made if want to arrive at an accurate level of confidence.

Social labelling

Social labelling is where a group of people or society itself associates two things together and thus creates a stereotype which is then used by the people in that group to make sense of the world. This social labelling often has negative connotations which of course we see play out in forms of discrimination, prejudice and preferential treatment. For confidence, these social labels can mean that we misinterpret how we are feeling and what that means for our chances of success. A good example is the feeling of anxiety you may have because of your social grouping or upbringing and learnt to see anxiety as a negative emotion or associate it with failure. Alternatively, you may have learnt that the feeling most people call anxiety, you call focus or excitement which is a positive thing and one that improves your chances of success. The trick of course is being able to make accurate inferences about the way you feel, and we will look at strategies to do this later in the book.

Task characteristics

The characteristics of the task itself can also play a part in whether physiological and emotional efficacy information can be trusted and it's mostly to do with levels of expectedness. There are some tasks and conditions where we would expect certain physiological symptoms like increased heart rate like in our charity run, and others where it would feel abnormal like writing a magazine article. The degree of expectedness indicates its normality, and then we use past experiences to interpret how the feeling will affect our performance and possible success. A classic example is what most people call 'butterflies in their tummy' or a low-level feeling of anxiety prior to a task. For most of us this feeling is seen as normal, goes away quickly and has not in the past caused any major dips in performance, and so the feeling is largely ignored and does not impact on our confidence. The same is true for moderate levels of pain for which we know the cause and again do not persist for long. I get pain in the right side of my knee for the first 5 minutes of every run I do, and this has a limited impact on my confidence, and probably unwisely I choose to ignore it and do not interpret it as a signal that I should stop running.

Imaginal Experiences

A final category of information that has been shown to be regularly used during cognitive appraisals of self-efficacy is what we can see in our minds. Visualisations of being successful or working through the steps of a process can help us believe more about our ability in the real world. The use of visualisation is of course not new and has been used since ancient times in rituals and ceremonies as well as in practices like meditation and contemplation. Philosophy and literature are full of references to people like Marcus Aurelius using it to prepare for challenges and heroes like Beowulf visualising his triumph over monsters to gain more confidence. More recently we see it used widely in sports by athletes striving to increase focus, reduce anxiety and prepare themselves for important game winning tasks like penalties. Its use in therapy is something we will explore later in the book when we look at its ability to re-align negative self-talk. The information we get from imaginal experiences continues the trend of the previous sources in that it is as much to do with its quality and the way we do it as it just doing it.

Specificity

The level of detail that we include in our visualisations plays an interesting and important role in their effectiveness and varies between individuals, goals and contexts. Detailed visualisations can increase levels of engagement due to their vivid and realistic nature, and can help create an emotional connection which strengthens confidence. High levels of detail also increase levels of clarity which improves our understanding of things like the success criteria, key decision-making opportunities and potential blind spots. Both of these combine to make the task feel more tangible and attainable, and positively impact on the amount of preparation we do and our resilience to challenge during the task. On the flip slide, detailed visualisations can cause anxiety by overwhelming the individual, creating unrealistic expectations of perfectionism and reducing flexibility and creativity.

Positivity

Another element of visualisation which needs to be carefully considered and is not as clear cut as it seems is its level of positivity. Logic would dictate that the more positive our mental rehearsal is, the better our confidence becomes, but there are some downsides. Highly positive visualisations can trigger the release of dopamine and other neurotransmitters linked to confidence as well as reduce anxiety by replacing negative thought patterns and therefore have a general calming effect. There is, however, a chance that the extreme positivity sets people up to experience dissonance and disappointment when the reality does not match their mental model, which then of course dents their confidence. Extremely positive visualisations can also have a negative impact on our levels of preparation and an underestimation of the challenge and obstacles inherent to the task.

The potential for visualisation to go wrong and to have a negative impact on confidence points to the need to take caution when either carrying out the process or interpreting the information we get from it. Done poorly it may well result in the rehearsal of poor practice, the creation of unrealistic expectations and ultimately serve to reduce self-efficacy levels. For this reason, we need to become skilled in the use of the technique both through training, self-development and experience, something we will look at in more detail later.

As we reach the end of this chapter, I want you to take a minute to think about what drives your perceptions of confidence and which sources of information you use the most. Do you always think about past successes and failures first, and how heavily do they weigh on your judgement? How sensitive are you to the words of others and your own inner voice? Can you remember any crushing pieces of feedback that still haunt your confidence now and have you been the provider of those to others? When you close your eyes and think about challenges, can you summon pictures of success and achievement, or does you mind wander straight to barriers and mistakes? Finally, how can you get into the heads of your team to find out what drives their confidence and how you can you alter this for the better?

Nuggets

- We carry out confidence appraisals more often than we think.
- We use a variety of information to decide how confident we feel.
- The biggest factor in our confidence is our success in previous experiences.
- Independent success in difficult things creates the most confidence.
- Observing success in ourselves and others is another key lever.
- Models that are not similar to us do not have as much of a positive impact.
- What we are told and what we tell ourselves strongly directs our confidence.

- Positive and specific feedback from trusted sources has the biggest impact.
- Feedback that clashes with self-talk has limited impact.
- How we feel physically and mentally before and during tasks plays a role.
- We often have fixed mental states that hijack the appraisal process.
- Being able to visualise success can improve self-efficacy levels.
- Any mental images need to be detailed and positive to add value.

Next Steps

✓ Create a self-efficacy information chart.

✓ Get your team to create their own self-efficacy information charts and compare results.

SE INFORMATION CHART

WHAT

Self-efficacy information charts are a method for reflecting on the different influences that affect your SE levels and how strongly they affect you. Creating the chart firstly involves rating the strength of the influence of past experiences, vicarious influences, persuasion, physiological and emotional states and imaginal experiences. The next step is to identify key examples from each information source which have or continue to have an influence on your SE fluctuations.

WHY

Different people are affected by different efficacy information sources and to different degrees and so the exploration of their impact can provide us with clues about how to better manage our SE levels.

Knowing which sources have the greatest influence can help us rationalise their past impact and help us moderate and manage their impact during future self-efficacy appraisals. This awareness can also enable us to seek out particular sources of information if our goal is to fast track our SE development.

HOW

Step 1 – Reflect on the varying influences of each of the self-efficacy information sources.

Step 2 – Assign an influence rating with ten being an extremely strong influence and zero being an extremely weak influence.

Step 3 – Add some explicit examples of where specific self-efficacy information has affected your confidence.

Reference

Bandura, A. (1977). *Social learning theory.* Englewood Cliffs, NJ: Prentice Hall.

6

ANTECEDENTS

You would think that managing our self-efficacy information store and filling it with lots of successful past experiences, positive feedback and daydreams about winning was the key to confidence creation, but there are some other factors that deserve attention as well. Sadly, as leaders, none of us is able to live in a bubble or ignore the external factors that affect us and our performance. Nor can we or should we ignore the fundamental elements of ourselves that also sit below the water line and form the foundation of what we think and do.

These antecedents, as we will call them, also play a big part in our self-efficacy appraisal process and thus are worth discussing and examining in our own contexts. These internal and external factors can and do affect how the self-efficacy information we spoke about in the previous chapter interact with each other and contribute to our confidence levels.

DOI: 10.4324/9781003558934-7

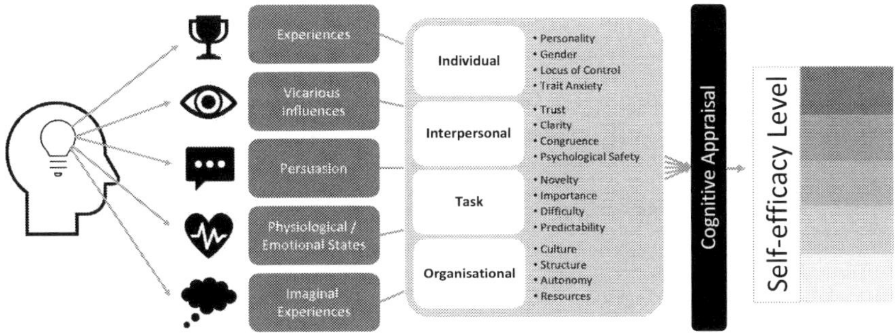

Figure 6.1 The antecedents of self-efficacy appraisals

Individual

The natural place for our exploration to start feels like with ourselves and how our characteristics and demographics can add an often hidden but powerful filter to our efficacy appraisals. The inherent and often fixed nature of these individual factors makes them pervasive to most of our lives and also resistant to change.

Personality

Our personality is thought to play a part in our general confidence levels and our task-specific levels of self-efficacy with most of the research centred around the five-factor personality model. The model began its life in the 1930s and '40s through research by Gordon Allport and Raymond Cattell who identified over 4,000 personality traits and then worked to narrow those down, resulting in an early personality assessment of sixteen core dimensions. Further work by Lewis Goldberg in the 1960s reduced that even further, and through extensive data analysis was able to present the five overarching dimensions of personality shown below, which all sit on continuums from low to high:

- **Openness to Experience:** Willingness to explore new ideas and experiences, valuing imagination and creativity.
- **Conscientiousness:** Focus on organisation, achievement and self-control, emphasising order and responsibility.
- **Extraversion:** Preference for social interaction and stimulation, characterised by sociability and energy.

- **Agreeableness:** Tendency towards cooperation and trust, valuing kindness and empathy.
- **Neuroticism:** Susceptibility to negative emotions and stress, prone to anxiety and mood swings.

In terms of self-efficacy, studies have shown openness to experience to have a positive impact due to the links with willingness to explore new possibilities and learning from mistakes. On the flip side, individuals who are closed to experience can develop low levels of confidence due to their reluctance to move outside their routines and not accept opportunities for challenge and growth. People who demonstrate high levels of conscientiousness tend to be organised, disciplined and goal-orientated, which leads to effective planning and consistent effort, which in turn boosts confidence. Levels of extraversion are another key personality dimension and one that also has a positive impact on confidence. Extroverts tend to be optimistic, outgoing and sociable, which enables them to build communities of support and bounce back from setbacks, both contributing to self-efficacy development. On the negative side, there is a belief that agreeableness can lead people to sacrifice their own interests and goals in place of others and to underestimate their capabilities, which in turn have a negative impact on confidence levels. Our final dimension, neuroticism is closely linked to negativity, self-doubt and anxiety, and so naturally has been linked to individuals with low levels of self-efficacy. Neurotic people tend to hold back from risk-taking, demonstrate limited resilience and experience dramatic changes in feelings which limit their confidence development.

Gender

The psychological differences between genders have almost become the source of comedy with phrases like "Men are from Mars, women are from Venus" pointing to the significant difference in the way that we often think, feel and behave. Research into work-related performance has found that women are more orientated towards interpersonal elements of roles, whereas men tend to prioritise task-orientation, and that women are usually less aggressive and competitive. Women have also been shown to underestimate their performance during assessments and to recall more failure than actually occurred, which of course has relevance to us in terms of their self-efficacy appraisals. Specific research into self-efficacy and gender has typically found that men are significantly more confident, both in their self-reports and the perceptions of those around them. As we look deeper though, we find that the self-efficacy–gender relationship is closely tied to the specific domain in which its measured and the tasks that people are appraising against. There are rare instances where the physicality of gender plays a part in the moderation of confidence such as certain sports or labour-intensive tasks, but generally the differences exist because of stereotypes and social labelling. Unhelpful and inaccurate messaging throughout our lives about the limits of our gender-related abilities can act as a strong antecedent during appraisals, and often stop the process before it really gets started. Negative or stereotypical messaging around career choice is particularly damaging for self-efficacy and leads to faulty selective processes that decrease early participation, educational choices and job applications.

Locus of control

"Are you a puppet?" and "Who is pulling your strings?" are questions that start to explore a psychological phenomenon called locus of control (LOC), which describes where an individual believes the control of their life rests. The research started back in the 1950s when people like Julian Rotter pioneered this idea of internal and external control and a scale for measuring our LOC beliefs. The basic premise is that there are two main dimensions of control. The first is an internal locus of control where individuals attribute their successes and failures to their own actions, abilities and effort. These individuals see themselves as in charge of their lives and believe that their feelings, thoughts and actions have a significant impact on their outcomes. On the flip side, individuals with an external locus of control tend to believe that any success or failure that they have is due to external factors such as luck, fate or the actions of others. Before we look at its impact on confidence, it is important to recognise that people are rarely at the extremes of the locus of control continuum and that individual and situational differences mean that not only do they sit somewhere in between, but they also move dynamically during their lives and from task to task. As with the other antecedents we have looked at, locus of control and self-efficacy have a complex relationship. Broadly, individuals with an internal locus of control have higher levels of confidence as they feel a greater sense of empowerment and use that to set ambitious goals and persist through challenges. This of course works in the opposite way with an external locus of control, which drives feelings of helplessness and an inability to influence their levels of success or failure. What is interesting though is that in some situations and especially those where there is the presence of a recognised professional like a doctor or a builder, an external locus of control can be helpful. In this situation, individuals may find greater levels of confidence in handing over the reins to someone who they perceive as more highly skilled.

Trait anxiety

Linked closely to the neuroticism dimension of personality is the concept of trait anxiety, which describes a chronic tendency to experience negative emotions and has been shown to act as another key filter in the self-efficacy appraisal process. Unlike what we call state anxiety, which is situational and temporary, trait anxiety as the names suggests is a more enduring and stable disposition. Due to its persistent nature, trait anxiety forms an almost foundational level on which other more typical stress builds on. Its persistence comes from the breadth of impact that it has on individuals, invading their minds and leading to overthinking, rumination and catastrophising. In terms of symptoms, it shows itself as prolonged susceptibility to negative emotions such as stress, frustration and irritability, and physical signs such as sweating, muscle tension and disrupted sleep. It won't come as a surprise to read that trait anxiety has been linked to reduced self-efficacy levels and the associated avoidance of challenge, inhibited decision-making, self-doubt and excessive control.

Interpersonal

As we have spoken about before, people and most certainly leaders don't work in a vacuum and so we need to consider the interpersonal factors that affect our appraisals of self-confidence. The relationships we build and the interactions we have with our superiors above us, our direct reports who work below us and our peers who follow alongside can have a significant impact. It is important to recognise before we go into more detail that the lines of efficacy impact flow in all directions with each group of people both impacting on the other's confidence levels and being influenced by them at the same time.

Trust

Our first interpersonal consideration is the level of trust that exists between people and within groups. As a leader, the amount of trust we place in the ideas and actions of those we lead directly affects how they feel about themselves and their chances of success. Interestingly, the levels of trust we instil in others through our credibility can also play a part in their self-efficacy development. So, let's start with those we lead whom we will call our followers. We can see the impact of levels of trust between leaders and their followers within acts like delegation which is a key skill for leaders and done well with lots of preparation and autonomy can increase an individual's confidence. Done poorly, involving high levels of prescription and micro-management, it can actually communicate a lack of trust and therefore dent the confidence levels of those involved. Trust between individuals also plays a part as we saw earlier, in the impact of feedback and persuasory information. If we trust the source of the information and feel that it is authentic and accurate, then we are more likely to believe it and include it in our appraisal process. I am sure you will be able to think about a time when you believed or second guessed the feedback you were given because of how much credibility you felt the other person had in that area. So, in terms of self-efficacy, high levels of interpersonal trust help to build confidence by enhancing an individual's sense of security in their own competence and judgement, and security in their leader's values and decision-making.

Clarity

As humans, we like things that make sense, and trying to make sense of the world is a fundamental human action. We typically feel anxious and doubtful when things don't make sense, which is why clarity is another element of interpersonal lives that can affect self-efficacy levels. Let's use the idea of delegation from the previous section and focus in on the instructions and information we have been given about the task. The combination of how that task is communicated to us and how it is processed by us will lead to varying levels of clarity and understanding. This level of understanding then becomes part of the confidence appraisal process with uncertainty leading to reduced confidence levels. We also see the impact of clarity within the observational learning that we might do through others and the persuasory information that we get from them. We highlighted the importance of vicarious influence or observation earlier in the book, but it is the clarity of this information that can act as a filter to its usefulness. Observed practice or feedback that is vague in its detail or loosely matches our own context is typically less useful and can actually drive performance and confidence development in the wrong direction.

Alignment

Whether something makes sense often has to do with how closely it matches our current thinking and so alignment is another important interpersonal consideration during self-efficacy appraisals. There is a psychological phenomenon that we are all subject to called confirmation bias, which describes our inclination to seek out and interpret information in a way that supports our existing beliefs. We tend to do this because we typically tie our beliefs to our identity and self-worth, and reject anything that clashes with those because of the uncomfortable cognitive dissonance that it causes. We also find it hard to change the way we think about something because of the time that we have usually spent learning it or believing in it, which is often called the sunk-cost bias. Both of these biases are probably in play during confidence appraisals and can act as powerful filters to the information that we are using. Information that closely aligns, causes a validation effect which then increases our levels of confidence.

Psychological safety

The final interpersonal antecedent of the cognitive appraisal process that we will explore is the level of psychological safety a person feels between them and those involved in the task. The concept started back in the 1960s with Edgar Schein and Warren Bennis who emphasised the importance of creating safe climates for learning within organisations. The research and interest have been taken further during the last twenty years and now closely linked to Amy Edmondson (2018), a professor at Harvard Business School. Psychological safety is often described as 'how safe people feel being vulnerable' and points to how confident people feel doing the following things within groups or one to one relationships:

- Raising issues and concerns.
- Disagreeing.
- Giving and receiving feedback.
- Asking for clarification.
- Asking difficult questions.
- Asking for help.
- Offering solutions.
- Admitting errors.

In terms of the appraisal process, how psychologically safe we feel can affect how confident we feel both prior to a task and during it. Feeling safe or unsafe to raise concerns, disagree or ask questions during the planning stages can have a direct impact on the levels of clarity that we spoke about earlier as being key to our confidence. Not being able to do these things also limits our ability to create alignment between any new information and our existing beliefs which can also have an impact. During tasks when we are re-appraising our self-efficacy levels, it is important that we feel confident to deal with issues and setbacks by being able to admit errors or ask for help. An inability to do these things because of a perceived lack of psychological safety can and will have a negative impact on our levels of confidence. The good news for us as leaders, is that psychological safety is able to be developed, and we will explore that in more detail in the next chapter when we look at self-efficacy development.

Task

So, it's not just the people involved that affect how confident we feel about completing a task but also the task itself. Each task will have a set of characteristics that either contribute to greater levels of self-efficacy or send our appraisals the other way.

Novelty

When we are children, the world is regularly new, and novel experiences and situations are commonplace. This slows down for most people as we mature and slot into a familiar way of living, but either through choice or circumstance we are still presented with a variety of novel tasks on a regular basis. The novelty of a task affects our confidence judgements because of the lack of information that we have available for the appraisal process. If we have never tried something before, then we naturally don't have any past experiences to draw on or any feedback to use. The unknown is a powerful creator of self-doubt and anxiety, and so novel situations and tasks can cause a decrease in confidence levels.

Importance

The importance of the task is another key consideration and antecedent of the self-efficacy appraisal process. Linked to the people involved and the possible impact of success or failure, a task's importance can create varying levels of pressure and stress for individuals. Tasks for the CEO of your company or another member of staff whom you hold in high regard naturally steal your attention more and force you to interrogate your confidence beliefs more deeply in fear of letting them down. Tasks that hold the possibility of significant financial loss or unemployment again force you to pause longer during the appraisal process, which in turn can drive an increase in self-doubt and a reduction in perceived confidence.

Difficulty

A task characteristic that springs to mind almost immediately during the appraisal process is its level of difficulty. It stands to reason that we feel less confident about difficult tasks than easy ones but there is some nuance involved. Although there are some tasks that are clearly difficult like getting to Mars or running an ultramarathon, for most tasks it's our perception of the task's difficulty that makes a difference. We often link task difficulty to how complicated a task is and how many steps or moving parts are involved in its successful completion. Tasks that require high levels of resourcing are often seen as difficult and especially if that resource is in the form of people who need to work together in order to achieve success.

Predictability

The final task-related antecedent we will explore is its level of predictability. As we saw earlier, uncertainty can cause self-doubt and anxiety which then affects our confidence and tasks that have unpredictable outcomes create similar feelings. The lack of predictability within a task often comes from its level of complexity, with highly complex tasks being less predictable. The number of parts in a complex task and their levels of interconnectedness mean that the behaviour of single components cannot be relied on or trusted to interact with other components in the way that we anticipate. To add to this complexity, it is rare to find a task that is not affected by the environment around it and with which we typically have even less control. Tasks themselves change in response to their environments which although is often in subtle ways, adds an unpredictability that can affect self-efficacy appraisals both before and during the task itself.

Organisational

As we reach the end of this chapter on the additional elements that fit around the core sources of efficacy information, we need to consider the influence of the organisations that we work and lead within. These characteristics often sit the furthest out of our control and thus are magnified in terms of their impact.

Culture

Organisational culture is scary in terms of its influence on how people think, feel and behave and complex in the way that it drives these things but is also simultaneously developed by them. Most models of culture point to the idea that there are elements of it we can see and others that sit below the waterline and this echoes its role on self-efficacy. Edgar Schein developed a now famous model of organisational culture in the 1980s which positioned various levels of consciousness in terms of layers that were subsequently modified over time by others into pyramid and iceberg images.

Schein's model highlights the important, foundational role that an organisation's underlying assumptions can have on relational power, the nature of reality and truth, and how the organisation interacts with the outside world. At the next level up, Schein highlights how culture also describes

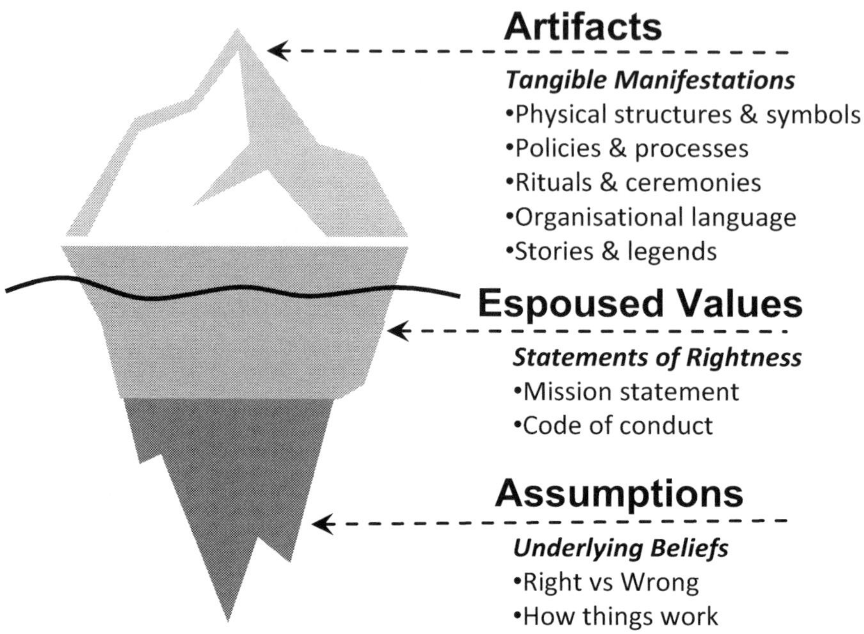

Figure 6.2 Schein's iceberg model of culture

the more visible, espoused values that the organisation has. These are the stated beliefs that are often found in mission statements and public pronouncements, communicating what the organisation claims to uphold. The final level of the model describes the most visible and tangible elements of organisational culture and typically includes things like its physical environment, policies and processes, rituals, language and stories. When we look at self-efficacy appraisals through the lens of culture, we can see how basic assumptions about levels of control, power and autonomy can affect how confident people feel about their chances of success. We can see that an organisation's public declarations about innovation and risk-taking may impact an individual's decisions about challenge acceptance and resource allocation. Finally, an organisation's artifacts, to use Schein's language, describe the most visible parts of its culture and therefore the elements that act most closely on observational efficacy information. These artifacts also act as a filter to efficacy information because of the existence or non-existence of support systems, the complexity of those systems and of course the visible behaviour of others.

Structure

Organisations are often structured in different ways in terms of lines of reporting and where the responsibility and accountability lie, and this can have a big impact on self-efficacy levels and how confident people feel doing their jobs. Some organisations have a hierarchical structure, much like a pyramid, where there is a clear chain of command and decisions flow from the top. This creates multiple layers of leadership and multiple filters that knowledge and decision making must move through. A hierarchical structure typically offers more direction than other models but with less autonomy and flexibility. In terms of self-efficacy, this type of organisation helps create clearly defined roles and lines of reporting, which can provide a sense of stability and safety for some staff and therefore boost their confidence. The lack of decision-making can, however, lead to feelings of powerlessness which then leads to frustration and reduced confidence because of delays and a lack of clarity.

Some organisations have a flat structure where hierarchy is kept to a minimum and employees have more autonomy and more power to make decisions. Flat organisations typically create more opportunities for collaboration, support and information sharing between colleagues. They also create higher levels of ownership and perceived control which in turn help develop belonging and agency. In terms of self-efficacy, flat structures boost confidence because of the trust that is given to its staff, coupled with the knowledge that support from other people is ever present. The ability to learn from others can significantly improve expertise which as we know is a key determinant of task-specific confidence. On the negative side, flat structures can leave some staff feeling overwhelmed because of the lack of direction and guidance which can decrease their levels of self-efficacy.

The third organisational structure that we will explore is called a matrix structure and sits somewhere between hierarchical and flat because of its combination of different elements. In a matrix environment, individuals have a fixed line of reporting through a line manager or senior leader, but also report dynamically to the managers of projects they are involved in. This cross-reporting creates a matrix or a grid with intersecting lines of communication, collaboration and reporting. Many organisations create this type of structure because of its flexibility, dynamism, efficiency and general increases in motivation, learning and autonomy. In terms of self-efficacy, this sweet spot between direction and agency can provide the greatest improvements in confidence as people feel assured about aims and goals but also empowered by trust, learning and collaboration. The negative side of a matrix structure largely comes down to the intersecting lines we spoke about and how they can cause confusion, conflicting priorities, power struggles and unhealthy competition. These can then cause stress, anxiety and uncertainty in individuals which has a negative impact on their self-efficacy.

Autonomy

An antecedent of self-efficacy closely related to the structure of an organisation is the level of autonomy that individuals either formally have or informally perceive themselves to have. Autonomy is defined as the perceived freedom to make choices and regulate one's own actions and has strong links to psychological safety, which we spoke about earlier in this chapter, and agency, which we will explore later in the book. Finding the right level of autonomy within teams and organisations is a key challenge for leaders and is often viewed on a continuum with the extremes being full prescription and full autonomy. Each of these extremes bring with them a range of benefits which are highlighted in Table 6.1.

When we think about how autonomy affects self-efficacy we need to revisit the idea that neither extreme is particularly healthy and that there is probably a sweet spot between the two where performance is maximised.

Table 6.1 Benefits of standardisation and autonomy

Prescription	*Autonomy*
Improved consistency	Increased staff engagement
Greater levels of compliance (regulatory)	Increased staff motivation
Improved efficiency	Improved job satisfaction
Increased safety	Greater adaptive expertise development Increased innovation Increased confidence / Self-efficacy

The location of that sweet spot will vary between organisations, teams, people and even between different situations and will be affected by a range of factors at each level.

At an organisational level it will depend on the industry and regulatory environment in which it occurs with highly regulated industries more likely to lean towards prescription. The size of the organisation may play a role with smaller, less complex organisations able to provide more autonomy. The current performance of the organisation can affect the location of that sweet spot with a move towards prescription typically for teams that are underperforming. We can't of course ignore the influence that the senior leaders within an organisation will have on the general culture, attitudes towards risk, the leadership styles that they use and their own levels of confidence when it comes to delegation and shared ownership.

At an individual level we would expect the sweet spot to vary between people with different personalities, their comfort with complexity, their cultural background and their previous experiences of delegation and freedom. Although logic may suggest that higher autonomy leads to higher self-efficacy, for some individuals total autonomy creates uncertainty which subsequently creates anxiety and sometimes decision or action paralysis. As leaders we need to be mindful of these individual differences and seek to understand our staff well enough to responsively alter the release of responsibility in order to gain maximum performance.

Resources

The leaders reading this book will no doubt work in organisations of varying size and with varying access to resources. These resources typically come in human, financial, physical, technological, and informational forms and can create boundaries and constraints around self-efficacy levels. Access to other people and teams for support, guidance and modelling can act positively on self-efficacy levels through access to feedback, role modelling and the comfort of help when things go wrong. We saw in chapter 5 when we looked at the difference sources of efficacy information that when we have low levels of experience in a task, we rely more heavily on the observation and feedback of others. This additional information not only reassures us that success is possible but also provides useful information about how to complete tasks successfully and how to deal with setbacks.

Feedback when given carefully and from trusted sources can have a great moderating impact on both overly negative and overly positive levels of confidence. The comments we receive from others around performance can also contain the hints and tips we need to maximise our success and further boost our self-efficacy. The comfort that comes with knowing we have access to other people for support both prior to and during a task can be an important factor in confidence appraisals and growth, and give us the reassurance to begin and persist.

Not having the physical or financial resources required to be successful in a task or project is another organisational factor that affects self-efficacy levels. Any hesitation or uncertainty around the presence or sustainability of resources during the planning process can mean that individuals don't commit in the first place or that they moderate their input because of the inevitability of failure. As we will see later in the book, self-efficacy levels are intensely dynamic, and any decrease in financing or physical resourcing during a task is sure to create a confidence dip.

A related resource, which is becoming increasingly important in our professional lives, is the role of technology, and much like the other resources a lack of the required amount typically reduces our confidence. More interestingly though is the beneficial impact that access to and mastery over technology has had on our levels of self-efficacy. Tasks that were once challenging because of their repetitiveness can now be automated, those which were inherently complex have been simplified through slick user interfaces and data analysis, and visualisation has jumped from the paper to the screen. The reduction of task-related challenges through technology is one of the key mechanisms for confidence creation, and allows many of us to take on things we once would have shied away from. The almost complete dissolution of communication and collaboration boundaries that technology has allowed has transformed the ease with which these things can be achieved and again boosted our confidence towards them. We have referenced a number of times during the book the inextricable link between our perceived expertise and our perceived confidence, and technology is having a noticeably impact here as well. Access to asynchronous professional development has never been greater, and at our fingertips we have the ability to upskill ourselves in any area of our professional or personal lives. Gone are the days of inefficiently attending, poorly delivered formal courses or workshops which are only loosely tailored to our needs. The variety of providers, mediums and modes of professional development available online means that we can match the granularity of our self-efficacy weaknesses with learning that is when, where, how and what we need.

A final resource that often impacts efficacy judgements and particularly prior to a task is access to information. Sadly groups, teams and organisations share information with varying levels of effectiveness which in turn leads to varying levels of clarity. Not having the data that you need or access to the reports that define it can limit our ability to clearly understand a task and thus create levels of self-doubt and insecurity. When we have all the information we need, we are empowered to make decisions and to make them effectively. Having access to evidence, analysis and different perspectives helps us with our problem solving and typically leads to greater levels of performance. The absence of information can create dangerous blind spots both in our own thinking and in the collective thinking of our organisations leading to missed opportunities and reduced development. An element that ties both technology and information together is the rise of artificial intelligence and the potential for even further improvements in knowledge through technology. Access to online knowledge has been common for over two decades and has become increasingly easy to navigate and interact with, but the shift I feel we are heading towards is even better and one of extreme personalisation and partnership. Having access to an always on call, objective expert who understands our context and our performance will not only improve our access to information but ensure that it is always what we need. The time is not far away where an AI professional development partner improves our awareness and acceptance of our needs through guided noticing of observational footage, provides objective, reliable and valid feedback, and can analyse our developmental trends and patterns over time. Our confidence would be further boosted by the expertise development that could occur because of the targeted reflection and directed study that the AI would provide us with and the psychological safety it could provide for us to rehearse challenging elements of our roles. Our confidence curves would remain in an upward trajectory because of the ever-present guidance that the AI could give during deliberate practice cycles and the motivational support it could provide through prompts, praise and action planning. This may seem fanciful, but if hearing it made you feel more confident then it only serves to strengthen the impact that resources like knowledge, collaboration and time can have on our self-efficacy.

As we reach the end of this chapter, I want you to take a minute to think about how strongly your own confidence and that of your team are affected by personal factors like personality, gender and relationships with control. How does the dynamics of the teams you work in or lead affect individual confidence? Do you feel more confident in some teams than others and why is that? How does your organisation help or hinder confidence, and can you spot cultural or structural things that dent confidence? Finally, what do you do as a leader to either build or erode the confidence of your team and is it by design or just by chance?

Nuggets

- A range of internal and external factors also affect self-efficacy appraisals.
- Our personality, gender, perceived levels of control and anxiety all play a part.
- Extroversion, agreeableness, agency and low trait anxiety support self-efficacy.
- Links between gender and self-efficacy depend on the task and context.
- Who we are working with makes a big difference to our confidence.
- High levels of trust, clarity, belief, alignment and psychological safety all help.
- The characteristics of the task itself play a part in the self-efficacy appraisal.
- Tasks that are new, important, difficult and unpredictable reduce confidence.
- The organisation and environment we work in can have an impact on confidence.
- Cultures of trust and sufficient resources support high levels of self-efficacy.
- How confident we feel about the teams that we work in affects our self-efficacy.

Next Steps

✓ Complete a self-efficacy antecedent review.

✓ Get members of your team to complete SE antecedent reviews and discuss the commonalities and differences.

✓ Review your learning from section 1 on the impact and development of self-efficacy.

SE ANTECEDENT REVIEW

WHAT

A self-efficacy antecedent review involves reflecting on the impact of the often-hidden self-efficacy influences. The review focuses on the individual and organisational antecedents as these are more commonly the biggest influence and most easy to change.

The process involves systematically working through each of the antecedents, reflecting on the influence of things like our personality and gender, and the culture and structure of the organisations we work in, assigning each one an influence rating.

The process then requires the participant to describe the positive and negative impact each antecedent has on their SE levels.

WHY

Self-efficacy development is a complex phenomenon, and behind the more obvious influences like experience, modelling and persuasion sit a deeper, more hidden set of influences. This set of antecedents often go unnoticed and so require purposeful reflection to uncover their impact and power.

As with the other reflective activities we have completed, awareness and acceptance are the first steps to change and completing the review can lead to a greater understanding of how to improve confidence by design.

HOW

Step 1 – Reflect on the varying influence of each of the individual and organisational self-efficacy antecedents.

Step 2 – Assign an influence rating with ten being an extremely strong influence and zero being an extremely weak influence.

Step 3 – Describe the positive and negative impact of each antecedent on your SE levels.

SE IMPACT AND DEVELOPMENT SUMMARY

HOW

Step 1 – Write a reflective paragraph that describes the impact that your self-efficacy levels have on your role as a leader, considering the following (thinking, motivation, effort & resilience, emotions, decision-making).

Step 2 – Write a reflective paragraph that describes the key factors or events that have affected your self-efficacy levels during your life, considering the following (parents, siblings, adversity, peer groups, relationships, parenthood, career, health, agency).

Step 3 – Write a reflective paragraph that describes the key factors that affect your self-efficacy levels on a daily basis considering the following (experiences, vicarious influences, persuasion, physiological/emotional states, personality, gender, interpersonal factors, task factors, organisational culture, organisational structure, autonomy/resources).

Reference

Edmondson, A. C. (2018). *The fearless organization*. Hoboken, NJ: John Wiley & Sons.

7

DOING A SELF-BUILD

Now that we have a clearer sense of what this thing is and how it gets created, we can turn our spotlight onto how to develop it. This book is built around the idea that confidence can be developed, and more than that, we can consciously and purposefully do it for ourselves and others. For me, this is a liberating and exciting idea and only matched by the frustration that I didn't know all this sooner. When we think of strategies for improving levels of self-efficacy, our minds need to immediately focus on how we can collect and store as much positive efficacy information as possible.

Experience

Goal setting

The first strategy we can use for our own confidence creation is to reassess and possibly re-design our goals so that they are more achievable. Ambitious goals are important for motivation and can require large jumps in self-efficacy as we will see in chapter 12, but harder is not always better and

DOI: 10.4324/9781003558934-8

so we need to seek out and select our own difficulty sweet spot. The idea of a sweet spot is something we see across various domains from sports where arousal needs to be moderated and in education where students need to work within their zone of proximal development to maximise their learning. A broader example is the fact that planet Earth exists within something called the Goldilocks zone where the conditions are 'just right' for life to thrive. If we extend that idea to think about 'Goldilocks goals', we are thinking about goals that are not too hot and unrealistic or too cold and easy. In order to maximise our chances of success, we need to select tasks that are difficult enough to motivate us and force us to allocate sufficient resources but that also feel attainable. Sadly, our situation is even more complex and unlike the planetary zone, the 'Goldilocks goal' zone changes as we move between different domains and also over time as we develop our expertise. This means that we need to regularly reassess our goals to ensure that they exist within the zone and that we adapt levels of task difficulty or support to maximise our chances of success.

Another goal setting strategy we can use to increase our success rates and bank more positive efficacy information is to shift our perception of success away from outcomes and towards performance. The organisational psychologist Edward Locke explored the concept of goal setting during the 1950s, '60s and '70s and was one of the earliest to separate goals into performance and outcome. Outcome goals, as the name suggests, emphasise the final result of a performance and often include scores, deadlines or acquisitions. While outcome goals can provide increases in confidence once successfully completed, there is a range of downsides which shouldn't be ignored. Outcome goals typically hold greater levels of uncertainty and reliance on external factors such as luck or resources which can lead to frustration and feelings of helplessness. The sustained pursuit of outcome goals can also lead to the development of a fixed mindset where the only two options available are win and lose. This binary view of goals can damage motivation and levels of effort due to a reduced perception of agency and an individual's capacity to control whether they succeeded or not.

If the goal is to experience success more often, then a shift towards performance goals can be helpful. Performance goals focus on the how, and link more to the actions that are required to achieve the outcome, such as effort and resilience or improvement and mastery. If an outcome goal looks like "achieve an 80% client retention rate" then an equivalent performance goal might be something like "Complete more regular customer satisfaction surveys" or "Invite more customers to engagement events". Performance goals have a more positive impact on our confidence because they typically fall more within our control, and they allow for micro-improvements associated with progress rather than endpoints. Performance goals also support long-term confidence development because of the growth mindset they foster, and the continuous effort and learning involved. The shift towards performance goals also strengthens an individual's perception of setbacks that allows them to be viewed as opportunities for development and growth which then further support confidence development.

Vicarious Influence

Modelling

The second big lever for improving our confidence is to collect really clear mental models of what excellence in a task looks like and how success is achieved? The role of imitation in learning has its formal roots in early philosophy but has of course been ever present informally in the way that people and even animals mimic each other's behaviours. Between the 1920s and 1940s, researchers like Edward Thorndike and John Watson played a significant role in the academic exploration of the subject through their studies on association and reinforcement. Further developments in the '50s by a now familiar source, Albert Bandura, strengthened the view that we learn not only by experience but also by observing the actions and consequences of others, and that this is an active process that goes beyond just copying.

Before we start to explore where these observational opportunities might come from, it's important to recognise the subtle difference between active modelling in the form of observed actions and static models that come in the form of images, diagrams, or instructions. Static models of excellence are something that we should be seeking out. Although they are thought to have a lesser impact on confidence, they do hold some key advantages. Static models are typically more readily available and significantly more cost-effective that active-modelling scenarios. They enable much greater levels of self-directed study and pacing, as well as enabling users to revisit the information as often as required. Static models are much easier to standardise in terms of their content and also support the learning of large groups much more effectively.

Active modelling on the other hand is inherently more engaging and the interactivity between a person, the environment and even the audience serves to increase a learner's motivation to learn and their persistence to continue. Visual demonstrations tend to enhance our cognitive processing by increasing opportunities to direct the observer's attention, by improving the encoding of information into the long-term memory and by allowing us to see the relationships between actions and their consequences. Another benefit of active models is the tight feedback loop that is possible between the model and the observer's understanding. Observational learning that includes dialogue with either the person modelling or a peer provides opportunities to continually direct attention, check understanding, and uncover and correct any misconceptions. The authenticity of active models is another key advantage over static models. Live modelling can be tailored to the observer's context by including real-world situations, set in their natural environment and subject to typical challenges and considerations. This increased alignment, can lead to improved perceptions of relevance, usefulness and also improve the transfer of modelled behaviour back into the observer's practice.

A method for modelling which has seen a steady increase in its popularity is the use of video, and due to its powerful blend of static and active modelling benefits, it is definitely something that we should utilise on our curve to greater confidence. When we think about the use of video models, we are typically describing a situation where an individual has access to pre-recorded footage of excellence that have been selected purposefully as either part of a directed study programme or made available for exploratory self-study. Videos retain the accessibility and cost-effectiveness of static models alongside the ability to pause, rewind and replay at the user's discretion. Alongside that, video holds the dynamism and authenticity of active models as well as the explicit interactions between actions and consequences. Video models also provide opportunities to view practice in a controlled environment which minimises distractions and focuses attention on key points in a way that is difficult with live modelling. The depth of observational learning is often enhanced through video because of the multiple angles and perspectives that it can include by combining examples or by using multiple cameras. A final benefit of video modelling comes through the option to accompany it with resources like subtitles, transcripts and audio descriptions that support the learning of those with additional needs or preferred ways of working.

Before we finish this section, I guess the final word on the use of modelling to improve confidence is that it would be wise to incorporate and take advantage of a range of different techniques. If we were building the ultimate system, we might want to include all three methods and sequence the different types so that we leverage all of the different benefits. We could start with static models to introduce concepts and provide an initial overview of key points and information. We could then move to video modelling to reinforce the initial understanding and provide dynamic demonstrations of the theory in action. Finally, we could provide opportunities to observe active models so that individuals have the opportunity to see excellence in their own contexts and be able to ask questions and refine their understanding.

Persuasion

Feedback

As we move further through the sources of efficacy information that we introduced in chapter 4 we arrive at another key strategy for confidence building – persuasion. The cognitive appraisal process that creates our self-efficacy level is essentially a process of self-persuasion and one that can be either in support of task success or against it. Ideally during the appraisal process, we are using stored information to convince ourselves that we can and will successfully complete a task, but how can we make sure we have the best information?

The source that probably jumps immediately to mind and for which we typically have the most experience is feedback from peers or superiors. We collect feedback about our effectiveness from formal mechanisms like performance reviews or assessments, as well as informally through our daily interactions and conversations with others. Formal feedback is often used to document performance or evaluate progress, and so can be seen as high stakes and can create high levels of anxiety because of its perceived importance. This is further magnified by the tendency for formal feedback to be provided by those in power, which can add to its credibility and impact on confidence development. On the positive side, the formality of this feedback does mean that it is often recorded officially which can lead to greater levels of recognition when positive and professional development opportunities when negative.

Informal feedback is less structured, less explicit and less reliable in terms of when it happens, how often it happens and where it comes from. Informal feedback is the information that we get spontaneously from others or ourselves when we share ideas, ask questions or observe something. It is more organic in its nature and can be less intimidating due to the types of sources it comes from and its focus on guidance and learning rather than evaluation. When we ask for advice or feedback it is often in an informal setting, and so another positive would be the specificity of the information and the control that we have over its focus. On the negative side, the lack of structure can mean that informal feedback is highly subjective and strongly affected by personal biases and filters.

When we think about feedback as a strategy for confidence building, we need to take a proactive and systematic approach if we want to reap the most benefit. As mentioned earlier in the book, the absence of feedback is often more damaging to confidence than occasional negativity as it leaves us subject to our own perceptions and creates feelings of uncertainty and self-doubt. For this reason, we must seek out regular feedback both informally through our daily interactions and also ensure that formal feedback systems are in place, are utilised and are robust. We need to ensure that any feedback we receive is tailored to our needs and is a balance of areas we feel we need to improve and bright spots that we want to magnify. We need to protect the credibility of the feedback by selecting people whose expertise we trust and weed out any cognitive biases through the design of the feedback process and our processing of the information. Finally, if we really want to supercharge the impact of feedback on our confidence, then we need to increase our belief in its purpose and usefulness by explicitly drawing links between the information we get and the improvements we make. The first step in this process is finding a way to record the informal and formal feedback that we receive and the actions that are given to us or decided by us as a result. This might be on organisational documentation or in a personal journal, but the key is to have a record of it which can then be added to in terms of outcomes and improvements in order to create a timeline of confidence creation. The explicit demonstration of feedback leading to improvement will solidify its usefulness and systematically grow our own self-efficacy.

Self-talk

When we think about the feedback that we give ourselves, we uncover another key strategy for improving the persuasive elements of confidence creation. This inner dialogue is often called our self-talk and deserves attention because of its ever-present nature and the damage it can do if not properly managed. The study of self-talk has a long history, and some its key researchers include Albert Ellis and Donald Meichenbaum who recognised its power and explored it as part of their work on Cognitive Behavioural Therapy (CBT) and Rational Emotive Behaviour Therapy (REBT). Martin Seligman, who founded the positive psychology movement, saw it as a key tool for building resilience and well-being, and Carol Dweck famously identified it as a way to develop a growth mindset.

The first distinction people make when they think about self-talk is whether it's positive and acts as a cheerleader or negative and acts like a cynic or critic. Positive self-talk typically manifests itself in affirmations like "I can do this" or "I am ready for this" and is consciously or unconsciously used to persuade us that we can and will be successful. Links have been made between positive self-talk and improved motivation, determination and resilience which then positively affects our performance levels. Cognitively, positive affirmations have been linked to improved levels of focus and concentration as well as better decision-making due to its reductive effect on fear and doubt. Early pioneers of self-talk research like James Pennebaker and Barbara Fredrickson also discovered links between positive persuasion and our immune system with decreases in blood pressure, heart rate variability and stress hormones as well as increases in healing times and relaxation. Before we shift over to looking at negative self-talk, it's worth pausing for a second on some of the key misconceptions about positive self-talk. Positive self-talk is definitely not about being happy all of the time or completely eliminating all negative thoughts as this causes an unnatural state and creates distrust of persuasive affirmations and robs us of the benefits of negative self-talk. It is also a misconception that the process is easy and that it simply involves repeating empty affirmations. These generic statements as we will see later in this chapter hold limited power and are easily ignored or mistrusted because of their superficiality. The final misconception that will play out later in the book when we talk about hyper self-efficacy is the idea that more is better, and that positive self-talk must be hyperbolic and spoken out loud in order to get the most benefit.

When we talk about negative self-talk, we switch from the term affirmation to words like negation and self-deprecation to describe the negative statements that people tell themselves when faced with a task. This type of self-talk typically manifests itself in phrases like "I'm not good enough", "I'll never be able to do it" or post task evaluations like "I'm useless" or "I'm a total failure". The last two comments speak to a key characteristic of negative self-talk and its generalisability. We often use small elements of failure and expand those to encompass our whole selves or the whole of time. Linked closely to this, we are also easily drawn into catastrophising and allowing our negative self-talk to get blown out of proportion and extend to the worst-case scenarios. Another characteristic is personalisation which is more typical with negative than positive self-talk and drives us to take responsibility for things that are out of our control and to believe that "it's all my fault". Alongside the comments about probable success, negative self-talk also includes the labels that we assign to ourselves like 'loser' or 'idiot' which can damage confidence and become persistent beliefs if not managed. The impact of negative self-talk is understandably often the opposite of the positive benefits we saw earlier. It tends to reduce confidence and motivation and create unwanted anxiety, depression and procrastination that of course affects our performance and can even spill over into our relationships with others.

When we think about how to use self-talk to improve our confidence, it feels fairly obvious that we should reduce the negativity and supercharge the positive, but the current thinking is that it might not be that simple.

Another distinction that psychologists make with self-talk is the difference between declarative and interrogative. Declarative means 'to make a declaration' and so this type of self-talk presents itself as statements of perceived truth. These declarations are typically either affirmative or evaluative and include all of the examples we have seen so far. Declarative self-talk is the most common form that we use and can be either positive or negative in its content and used prior to tasks for motivational reasons or afterwards as part of a self-evaluation. In contrast, interrogative statements involve individuals asking themselves questions about their ability rather than making statements or declarations. This type of self-talk may manifest itself in questions like "can I do this?", "am I doing ok?" and on completion, things like "how did that go?" or "did I give my best today?"

On the question of which is better for our confidence, the thinking and research continues as they both hold strengths and weaknesses. Declarative self-talk provides clear messages, improves certainty and reduces self-doubt. On the negative side it can be overly simplistic, can feel fake if it doesn't match with our actual beliefs, and is hard to refine or modify during tasks. The benefits of interrogative self-talk come from the fact that it requires a deeper level of thinking and often further action by the individual. Questions like "can I do this" can naturally flow to "yes but how will I do it?" which in turn creates an opportunity to locate evidence and drive proactive problem solving. This additional introspection may be the difference between being successful or not. On the negative side, interrogative questions require more effort and time, and can uncover more self-doubt if no evidence for success is available. This type of self-talk is also more uncomfortable because of its level of reflection and so is a technique that must be mastered over time through practice and feedback. To close out this section of the chapter we arrive at the suggestion that all types of self-talk can be useful, and the choice often depends on a combination of the type of goal, the current confidence level and the individual's personal preference.

Coaching and mentoring

One of the best mechanisms for confidence development and especially the creation of positively persuasive efficacy information is coaching and or mentoring. In my own doctoral research on leadership development, the presence of a coach and or a mentor came through as one of the most significant influences on confidence levels and that their presence improved self-efficacy and the absence of them limited its development. Both coaching and mentoring create great opportunities to receive and even request persuasive information and to test out perceptions and self-talk with an objective other.

Before we get into how coaching and mentoring can improve our confidence, we need to add some clarity to the difference between them. Historically people have found comfort in placing them at opposite ends of a continuum and using distinctions like "coaches ask, and mentors tell",

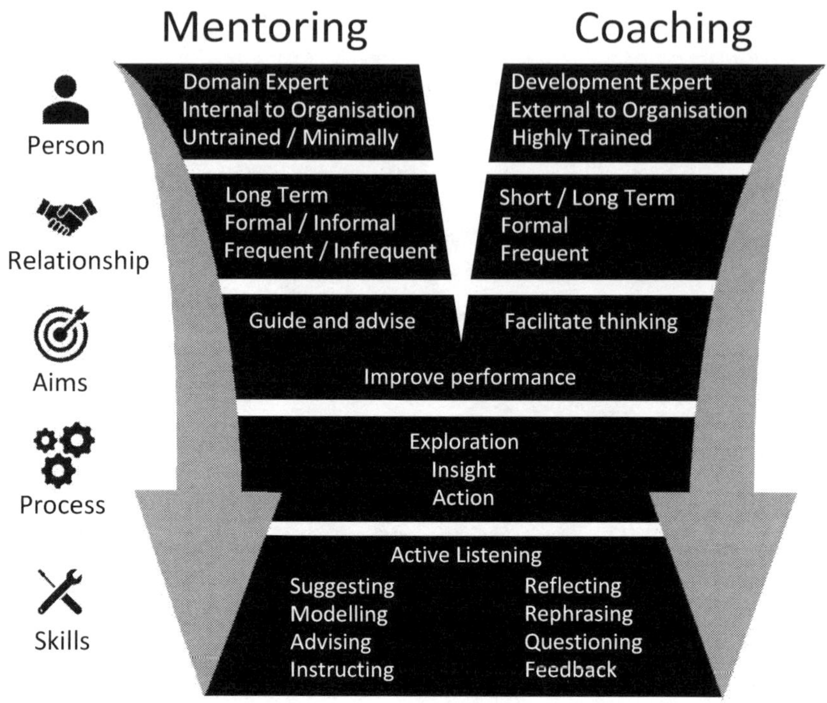

Figure 7.1 The coaching vs. mentoring distinction

"coaches pull and mentors push" and "coaches don't need to be experts, but mentors do". Humans have a strong desire to make sense of the world and to reach cognitive conclusions as quickly as possible to make their mind available for other stuff. A large proportion of the population feel uncomfortable with complexity, and so actively seek to organise information and knowledge by categorising, ranking and delineating between elements through definitions. This type of binary thinking has led to what I think is an unhelpful distinction between coaching and mentoring with no room for nuance or complexity and so let's unpick the distinction a bit more.

The diagram above highlights the need for both terms but suggests that the distinction is only helpful up to a certain point. It may be helpful to separate mentors from coaches as people and to clearly distinguish the difference in their relationships but then the separation starts to lose its usefulness. That distinction gets less helpful as we move into the aims of the two activities and almost disappears when we reach the actual process that happens and the skills that are used in order to make both of them successful. This may very well clash with some beliefs you have held for a long time and so let's unpack each level in a bit more detail.

The terms coach and mentor definitely have value and can be initially helpful in their description of the person providing the support and can be useful during the design of professional development and support interventions. The use of the titles should also be flexible enough to allow one individual to be a mentor to some and a coach to others. When it does come to distinctive characteristics, I feel like the most credible difference is the presence of domain expertise as this is essential for mentors but only desirable for coaches. The same is true in my mind for role experience and the closer this is contextually, the better. A myth that seems to be losing value is that mentors come from within the organisation and coaches from outside. Many teams are now looking to develop in-house coaching capacity, and as virtual networks connect people more easily and dissolve geographical boundaries, the option of external mentoring becomes more of a reality. Another myth that doesn't sit well with me is the idea that coaches are more highly trained than mentors. Although it may be the case that because of the volume and formality of their work, coaches complete more training, it should not be the case that we either fail to train our mentors or accept lower standards of professional development and performance from them.

Another level at which I feel the distinction remains helpful is in the description of the relationship between coach and coachee or mentor and mentee. The key differences at this level can be useful content for the initial contracting meeting where the two individuals attempt to gain a shared understanding of the mentoring or coaching process. When seeking a distinction at this level, it may be helpful to consider the length of the relationship and its formality. Mentoring relationships are typically longer than those in coaching and often stretch over multiple years. Where capacity is lacking, individuals may engage with a coach for short windows of time when the need arises. In terms of formality, we typically see more structure, policy and paperwork within coaching but as with training, this may be an undesirable difference rather than by design. When formality is low, there is also an accompanying variance in the frequency of activity. As we will see in the next section, informal mentoring action is often triggered by the mentee when a need arises and thus leads to less frequency than a formal rhythmic coaching relationship.

In the early stages of my career, I was lucky enough to have access to both a mentor and a coach, and thinking about what I wanted from them or the aim of our meetings was a clear and helpful distinction for me. In my role as a senior leader, the aim of the support has also been a useful lens when I have been designing professional development for others. When I needed some role or domain-specific support, I would contact a mentor and then use coaching sessions to explore wider issues. It's the perceived need that should drive the selection of support giver and the agenda for the conversation. Another consideration as to whether mentoring or coaching is most appropriate is the organisational agenda if one exists. Superiors may perceive the development needs of the individual to be role-specific or more general and so choose an intervention to suit.

As we move further down the proposed image, the distinction becomes less helpful, and although many will still be able to find various differences, the focus should remain on how helpful these distinctions are to the person wishing to increase their confidence.

By process, I am describing what the individuals actually do when they meet, and I feel like at its most basic level, this is the same in both coaching and mentoring in that it is a conversation or dialogue that can be enhanced through the use of reflective or practical activities. The nature of the dialogue, its structure and content will shift of course between individuals and indeed between sessions, but as suggested by Garvey (2010, 2014) it is always essentially a 'developmental dialogue'.

As we reach the bottom of the image and the skills that coaches and mentors use, I think we reach the least helpful level of distinction and sadly where the most ingrained differences lie within peoples' minds. The directive–non-directive continuum of skills is popular within coaching and mentoring literature, and historically mentoring has always fallen at the directive end leaving coaches to occupy the non-directive position.

At its most unhelpful, a perceived distinction between mentoring and coaching skills limits the range available to the person providing the support and thus their effectiveness. It may be that mentors, because of their domain and role experience, are sought out for advice and guidance and the opposite true for coaches but ideally, they remain flexible in their use of skills so they can responsively support the needs of their coachee or mentee.

So now that we've explored the distinction or non-distinction between the two types of support let's switch to their benefits for confidence development. Coaching and mentoring are uniquely placed in the professional development toolkit in that they are typically carried out on a 1:1 basis. This level of personalisation is rare as organisations are often pushed towards large scale training and development because of efficiency or resource management. The small scale, focused nature of coaching and mentoring mean that the person receiving it has much more control and responsibility over the focus of sessions, and therefore the support is instantly more relevant and useful. In terms of confidence building, this means that the client is able to address specific elements of self-efficacy as and when they become relevant. Coaching and mentoring usually take place over longer timelines than traditional training interventions and so there is a consistency and rhythm to the support that adds real value. The ongoing nature of coaching and mentoring supports the inherent dynamism of self-efficacy that we spoke about earlier in the book. The ability to make continual tweaks to our confidence can create what we call a self-efficacy spiral which we will explore in more detail in chapter 11.

Another key benefit of coaching and mentoring is the flexibility that the coach or mentor has in the way that it is delivered. We spoke earlier about the varied set of skills that can be used to meet a client's needs, and this is further enhanced by an almost infinite range of activities and tools. This flexibility means that they can adapt the way that they build confidence between different clients but also between sessions with the same client as they themselves develop and require different levels of challenge and support. The final benefit of coaching and mentoring that we will address is the focus on capacity building and the long-term development of individuals. It has been said that a coach or mentor's aim should be to make themselves progressively unnecessary and not to create a dependency that stifles life-long growth. The process of coaching and mentoring if done well will itself teach the client to take greater ownership over their own development and build the confidence and skills to do it successfully. When clients reflect, problem-solve and action plan regularly, guess what, they become more confident in and better at reflecting, problem-solving and action planning.

Physiological and Emotional States

The next strategy or set of strategies we can use as self-efficacy builders is linked to what we do with the physiological and emotional states that we experience prior to, during and after tasks and which we then link to our confidence levels.

Awareness

The first step to any change or improvement is often an increase in awareness and we need to step back from the unconsciousness that allows us to run on autopilot in order to get started. The idea that we have different levels of awareness or even levels of consciousness has been wrestled with by philosophers and researchers for a very long time. In the '60s a group of management professors at New York University started looking at levels of teaching which in the '70s was adapted by Noel Burch into stages of learning and the creation of the now well-recognised ladder of learning or ladder of consciousness. Although not typically linked to confidence or physiological/emotional states, we will use it to highlight the importance of awareness.

The ladder model which has also now been adapted by various other people has four or in the image above five levels of consciousness. The first and lowest level of consciousness is called 'unconscious incompetence' and is where individuals have no awareness of any issues or gaps in their knowledge or ability. In this stage people tend to experience overconfidence, a lack of motivation, resistance to feedback and an inability to problem solve. The next level up is called 'conscious incompetence' and is where individuals become aware of their lack of ability or in our case aware of their physiological and emotional symptoms. It is here where people start to feel

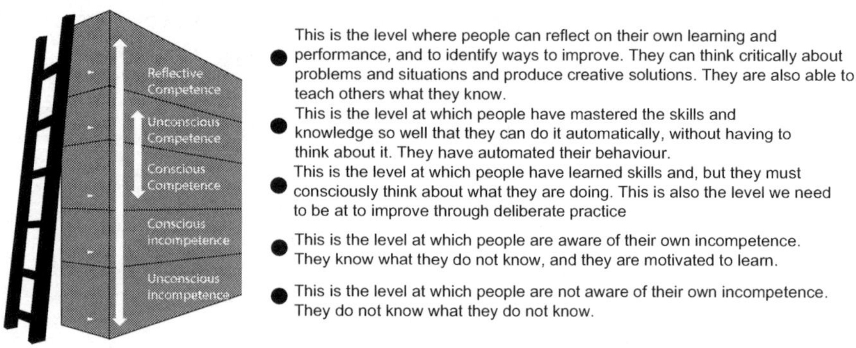

Figure 7.2 The ladder of consciousness/awareness

self-doubt but also become open to learning and receptive to feedback. For efficacy builders this is the key step of recognising that their heart or breathing rate is higher than normal or that they are feeling anxious or stressed. The next level of the model describes how we typically then move into 'conscious competence' where we have acquired knowledge and skills, but we need conscious effort to perform effectively. The final stage in the original model describes 'unconscious competence' where successful completion is on autopilot because of high levels of ability or familiarity. An additional level has been added to the ladder by some researchers that describes a level of 'reflective competence' where we are aware of why we do certain actions and the results that each one produces. At this level, our knowledge about what we choose to think, feel and act in order to achieve success and why we do it that way then allows us to develop others.

The important takeaway from the ladder model for self-efficacy builders is the importance of consciousness or awareness in learning and change. The arrows on our image also clearly highlight the dynamic nature of consciousness and suggest that we can control to a degree our levels of awareness. Although for some situations, autopilot is beneficial, in terms of efficacy building we need to know whether we are experiencing abnormal psychological or emotional states to deal with them. Reaching the reflective competence level is important for us if we are looking to build confidence in others and be able to provide guidance and support reflection.

Attribution

If being aware of our physiological and emotional states is the first step in building confidence, then the next step is to know why we have them and what they are attributed to. Attribution theory is a recognised branch of social psychology that seeks to understand how people explain to themselves and others, the causes of events, feelings and behaviours. Its roots can be found in Kurt Lewin's work in the 1940s on the concept of 'psychological field' and his focus on how individual perceptions are used to explain behaviours. Its development continued through work by Fritz Heider on the 'Naïve Psychologist' concept, Harold Kelly's covariation model and Bernard Weiner's achievement motivation theory. Some common elements of attribution theories and ones that are useful to us for confidence building are the impact of causality, distinctiveness and consensus.

Causality

We talked about locus of control in chapter 3 and described how we typically seek to attribute the outcome of a task's success or failure to either internal or external factors. We recognised the importance of this for levels of self-efficacy and suggested that individuals with high levels of confidence usually have a strong internal locus of control. Closely linked to our locus of control is our locus of causality and our beliefs about where our behaviours come from as opposed to where outcomes come from. Our locus of causality can also be internal where we believe our behaviours stem from our own desires, intentions and values or external because of things like rewards, punishments or social expectations. The important decision making and thinking that self-efficacy builders need to do is whether the physiological and emotional states they find themselves in are due to internal or external causes. At a superficial level we need to manage our perceptions of causality so we can rationally decide whether us sweating is an indicator of anxiety and low confidence or just because we are in a hot room, and if our low mood or negativity is due to a lack of confidence or just the gloomy weather. The self-efficacy research highlights a reciprocally amplifying relationship between confidence and locus of causality with effects going both ways and increasing each other. An internal locus of causality has been linked with higher levels of self-efficacy because individuals see themselves as the change agents of their behaviour and the opposite for those who feel a lack of control. Working the other way, high self-efficacy is said to strengthen our internal locus of causality because of the attribution of success or failure to internal, controllable factors and vice versa. All this information comes together to recommend that if we want to build more confidence, we need to attribute our behaviours more closely to internal factors and resist placing their ownership and cause elsewhere.

Distinctiveness

Another element of attribution theory that we need to be aware of if we want to use physiological and emotional appraisal information effectively is its level of distinctiveness. The question for self-efficacy builders is whether what they are experiencing or feeling is unique and uncommon for them or not. Do they commonly sweat a lot or get butterflies in the stomach or are those things specifically linked to the confidence appraisal they are completing and a signal of anticipated failure? The more distinctive feelings are, the more likely we are to pay attention to them and add importance to their influence. On the flip side, physiological states or emotions that are commonplace can easily be chalked up to normality and either ignored or rationalised away. The complexity occurs when we examine what non-distinctive states or emotions have led to in the past. If we have felt anxious before a presentation in the past, then we can see it as normal, but if that normally leads to us messing up our words or failing to even complete the presentation then the result will be a dip in our self-efficacy levels. If on the other hand it normally leads to increased focused and alertness to the audience, then it can drive up our confidence.

Consensus

The final piece of the attribution puzzle is the level of perceived consensus between what we are experiencing or feeling and whether others would be doing the same. Levels of consensus affect where we attribute the physiological or emotional states that we feel during self-efficacy appraisals and then our resulting confidence levels. Feelings that are common amongst the population and so have high consensus, such as feeling slightly nervous before an important interview, are typically attributed externally to the interview process itself rather than internally to some personal weakness or trait. Conversely low consensus situations like vomiting before an interview because of nerves are rare and so may be attributed internally to a personal weakness and may cause reduced confidence. There is however a positive side to low consensus if the resulting behaviour is positive. Situations where an individual is not experiencing states like anxiety where most other people are can actually boost their confidence because of their ability to overcome a seemingly common issue.

Imaginal Experiences

So, we have reached the final type of efficacy information that we typically use in our confidence appraisals and so the final set of techniques that we can use to boost our confidence.

Visualisation

Our imagination is an incredibly powerful tool and has been explored and utilised throughout time in early tribal rituals through to modern treatments for phobias and improving sports performance. A key tool for those of us wanting to improve our confidence, visualisation involves creating vivid images and sensory details of desired outcomes. An example might be visualising the audience standing to clap after your big presentation and how that would make you feel or what you would like team members to say in a staff voice questionnaire after a big announcement. It's a way of seeing success before we have even started a task, and its impact has been explored across a wide range of organisations and domains.

In sports, researchers have found strong links between it and golf putting, basketball free throws and archery performance. In healthcare, research into the power of visualisation has been linked to reduced stress and anxiety, improvements in confidence linked to phobias and a range of studies into its impact on pain management. Of most interest to us is the work that has been done linking visualisation to leadership and organisational performance. Studies in the early 2000s found that visualising the successful outcomes of negotiations improved the confidence of those involved and the confidence of teams who collectively visualised successful outcomes. Later studies by House (2010) highlighted the important role of visualisation on vision creation and showed how vivid, multi-sensory visualisations can improve the communication of and engagement in mission statements or presentations.

Mental rehearsal

Before we move into how to make visualisations or mental imagery successful, we need to explore a closely related but subtly different technique called mental rehearsal. If visualisation is seeing the desired outcome, then mental rehearsal is seeing the actions and processes that will get us there. It is thought to be a more active process than visualisation as it involves mentally practicing and importantly refining the different elements of the task ahead. If we go back to our presentation and staff voice examples, mental rehearsal would include rehearsing the different stages of the presentation, what you would say, what you might show and the reactions you would hope for. It would involve you rehearsing the structure of and content of the email announcement and refining it as you imagine staff's reactions to each part. Similar to visualisation, research has found links between mental rehearsal and a range of positive benefits including boosts to confidence, focus and motivation and reductions in anxiety and self-doubt.

So how does it work and what steps do we need to take to start using it as a technique for building our confidence? The first step is to clearly define your purpose and the goal of the visualisation or mental rehearsal. Are you trying to envisage a successful outcome to boost your confidence or is it a process that you need to practice and refine in your mind? This of course will steer you towards visualisation or rehearsal, and the next steps share common characteristics. Both techniques are best done in distraction free environments, so finding a quiet room or an outside space is key to building a strong foundation to work from. The lack of distraction will enable you to find the deep levels of focus required to maintain attention and produce the vivid mental pictures needed for maximum impact. This next step sounds a bit fluffy, but you also need to engage all of your senses and tap into the ability to visualise sights, sounds, smells and even textures. The richer the sensory experience, the more detailed you can make your mental images and the more likely you are to remember them when you need them. The rest of the process will of course depend on each situation, but it is always better if you can include the emotions you want to feel, any obstacles that might get in your way and anticipate the feelings and actions of any other people involved. The end of either process should be positive regardless of the ups and downs that may have occurred during, and the final word so to speak should always be in the affirmative. Visualisation and mental rehearsal are both thought of as skills and so are both learnable and improved through practice. This is important to recognise for efficacy builders as they require a commitment to understanding each process and resilience over time as expertise develops.

Foresight

The last imaginary technique that we will talk about, which leaders can use to build confidence, rests on the suggestion that low levels of self-efficacy come from not being able to fully understand how a task might go. It is this lack of foresight about possible barriers and the unexpected that can cause self-doubt and reduce confidence levels. A strategy that has its history in the military is something we call a 'premortem' and can be a useful tool for raising confidence levels before a task begins. The war gaming exercises that military leaders have used throughout history involved the creation of 'worst-case scenarios' which explore the potential outcomes of planned strategies to improve levels of preparedness. In the late 1980s researchers like Mitchell, Russo and Pennington introduced the concept of prospective hindsight where future failures are prevented by imagining that we are looking back on a failed task and identifying its root causes. Psychologist Gary Klein is often credited with developing the premortem technique and used it to improve air safety by analysing pilot decision making in aviation accidents. Since then, it has been used throughout business organisations, healthcare, education and professional development to improve decision making, implementation and confidence. The typical premortem has three stages: describe the failure, identify the causes and then create solutions, but we are going to amp that up and include five distinct stages.

Stage one is to gather the team and set the stage. During this step it is important to ensure that all relevant stakeholders are involved and there is a diversity of perspective. You need to clearly articulate the aim and process of the pre-mortem emphasising its predictive nature rather than any attribution of blame. It is vital at this stage that you create high levels of psychological safety so that participants feel comfortable speaking openly and admitting to concerns, errors and disagreements. Stage two involves imagining the failure, and much like visualisation and rehearsal, this needs to be done vividly with as much detail as possible. The participants need to reflect on questions like "What does failure look like in this project/task?", "What are the worst possible outcomes for this project/task?", "If this project totally fails, who is affected and how?" Everyone involved should be encouraged to be as creative as possible and explore unlikely and even humorously improbable outcomes. All contributory factors must be considered and recorded so that effective solutions can be identified in the next stage. A relatively new addition to this stage is something called the 'Triple Filter' method and adds a prioritisation element to the failure identification process. For each potential failure, participants need to consider the impact and severity, the reversibility and ease of recovery, and finally the likelihood or probability of it occurring. These triple filters then allow participants to assign an overall threat level to each of the possible failures so that resources can be focused, objectivity increased and efficacy improved.

Step three of the premortem process involves identifying the possible causes of the failure and is where teams need to feel most safe. As we mentioned before, the process is not aimed at assigning blame but for some it can be an uncomfortable experience and especially when it uncovers possible weaknesses in their areas of responsibility. Each potential failure identified in stage two should be analysed in terms of its contributing factors and the why behind them. The analysis should include an exploration of the actions, decisions and events that may have led up to the failure and what resources, information or actions were missing to cause it. Participants need to consider both the internal and external factors that may have played a part and broaden the timeline to include foundational elements created way in the past that may be impactful. Once the group has exhausted their list of possible causes, they should look for patterns and themes as failures rarely occur in isolation and there may be systematic vulnerabilities that require broader solutions. The final step in this stage is to bravely question any underlying assumptions that may be driving the identification of certain causes. We are all subject to a wide range of unconscious biases which affect our thinking, and the first step to avoiding them is acknowledgement.

Step four of the pre-mortem process is focused on finding solutions to the failures that have not even happened yet and so actually results in a set of mitigation strategies. Participants in the process should again be encouraged to think creatively and share their ideas bravely in order to explore all possible options. It is important that all solutions have a strong evidence base and there is a consideration of their resource cost in terms of people, finance and time. Time and energy in stage four should be directed toward the most significant causes of failure identified in stage three so as to be efficient. Once key mitigation strategies have been selected, it is then important to assign levels of accountability and responsibility and to consider lines of communication. A useful process for this is the completion of a RACI matrix which emerged from the field of project management and is used to gain this type of clarity. For each element of a project or in this case, each selected solution the team identifies who is Responsible, who is Accountable, who needs to be Consulted and who just needs to be Communicated with. The clarity that this process brings can drastically improve the implementation process of any solution. The fifth and final stage of the pre-mortem process is what we will call the confirm, communicate and control stage and is where the team records the learning and insights that the process has created, the agreed and prioritised causes and the chosen solutions. This stage then involves using the completed RACI matrix to communicate that information to all relevant stakeholders. The control element of this stage highlights the ongoing nature of the process and requires those responsible for each solution to monitor, assess and refine so that the mitigation strategies are successful.

As we reach the end of this chapter, I want you to take a minute to think about how conscious and purposeful your confidence creation has been so far. What have you actually done this week to build your self-efficacy levels in your core tasks and what will you do differently next week? How can you experience success more often? Do you need to move your goals more into the Goldilocks zone? Who could you go and see to observe excellence in action? Could you get access to a coach or a mentor to help you sustainably manage your self-talk and confidence creation? How are you currently managing your physiological and emotional states linked to challenges and finally how can you put a plan together that ensures that all future confidence creation is by design?

Nuggets

- We can structure our own confidence creation by focusing on the development of each type of self-efficacy appraisal information.
- Setting Goldilocks goals is key to achieving success by design.
- Seeking out models of excellence either in literature or real-life is key to uncovering where we are and what our next steps should be.
- As uncomfortable as it is, we need to watch and analyse video of ourselves.
- A lack of feedback is often worse than negative feedback.
- Interrogative self-talk may be more useful than empty declarations.
- Coaching and mentoring are the clearest routes to improved confidence.
- Attribution is what guides the impact of emotional and physiological states.
- If we can't see it, then we can't be it and so mental visualisation and rehearsal are key to confidence creation.

Next Steps

✓ Create a self-efficacy KISS plan.

✓ Get the other members of your team to create self-efficacy KISS plans and explore opportunities for support and collaboration.

SE K.I.S.S. PLAN

WHAT

A self-efficacy KISS plan is an activity that involves the identification of explicit actions that can help to manage the various sources of efficacy appraisal information. The exercise requires the user to systematically work through the sources of self-efficacy information and identify the immediate actions that they are going to Keep, Improve, Start and Stop.

WHY

Knowing more does not guarantee improvement as change almost always requires action. Understanding your own self-efficacy journey, your cognitive appraisal process and some techniques for management only gets you so far.

Real change and improvement by design requires detailed action planning and the creation of explicit action steps that can be immediately set in motion. Sustainable change also requires the creation of unconscious habits that allow us to continually build our confidence despite the unpredictability of our personal and professional lives.

Sharing the contents of self-efficacy creation plans within groups can also be useful for teams looking to be more personalised, efficient and collaborative with their professional development.

HOW

Step 1 – Reflect on the SE management techniques from this chapter that you already use effectively and would like to KEEP.

Step 2 – Reflect on the SE management techniques that you believe in but use ineffectively and would like to IMPROVE.

Step 3 – Reflect on the SE management techniques from this chapter that you don't currently utilise and would like to START.

Step 4 – Reflect on the SE management techniques that you feel are damaging and need to STOP.

Reference

House, R. J. (2010). Leadership visualization: Exploring the cognitive bases of effective leadership. *The Leadership Quarterly*, 21(4), 633–655.

8

DEVELOPING OTHERS

Alongside the liberating idea that we can manage our own confidence creation is the equally exciting and challenging thought that we have a direct impact on the self-efficacy of those around us and especially the people we work with most closely. As you think about the confidence levels of the members of your team or your bosses and the ways that these play out in the real world, spare a thought for the part you may have played in their development.

If we return to the key sources of self-efficacy information that we spoke about in chapter 3, then we find a useful starting point for understanding how we impact the self-efficacy of others through the efficacy information we provide. This information flows between us and our peers, upwards to our managers and most importantly down to those we lead. The upward impact is arguably less but still worth a brief examination if we want a clear understanding of the whole picture.

If we view self-efficacy as a representation of trust in ourselves, then we can also think about interpersonal confidence as the amount of trust

DOI: 10.4324/9781003558934-9

someone else has in us. Our impact on the self-efficacy levels of our superiors is largely due to their perceptions of trust in us and our ability to make them more successful. Tasks that require joint action or rely on our expertise for their success provide the important efficacy appraisal information that we have spoken about so much in the book. The upward impact therefore feels less like an influence on their self-efficacy and more like the creation of a 'collective self-efficacy', which we will explore in the next chapter.

In terms of our direct impact upwards, we don't tend to provide experiential efficacy information for our superiors as we rarely set them goals or tasks, but we do have a small role in the modelling process. If you assume that superiors perceive themselves to have more expertise than those below them, then our completion of a task may support a superior's belief that they can complete it. The knowledge and observation of someone perceptually lower than them in terms of knowledge, skills or experience can create feelings of "well if they can do it, then of course I can do it". Feedback is another piece of efficacy information that typically flows down or side to side, but in brave forward-thinking organisations where leaders elicit feedback from below, it can be a powerful thing. As we have spoken about before, the balance of positive and negative within the feedback has a direct impact on whether confidence grows or declines, and this is also true for upward feedback.

More significant and the focus for the rest of this chapter is the impact that we as leaders have on the confidence levels of those whom we lead, and it's a role that we should not take lightly. To add a bit of structure to the chapter, we will use the lifecycle of an employee from recruitment to promotion to explore the different strategies we can use to construct confidence and affect thinking, feeling, behaviour and performance.

Recruitment

It sounds strange but a leader's impact on the confidence of those in their team actually starts during the recruitment process by simply ensuring that they don't employ the wrong person. This starts by creating accurate job descriptions which clearly outline the role's specific duties, expectations and required skills. Any misalignment between the information in the recruitment pack and the actual role may lead to the employment of underqualified people who are then ineffective in their role and instantly doubting their confidence. If we think back to chapter 5 when we looked at the confidence appraisal process, this is exactly what is happening when someone is looking at a job description and considering whether to apply. Potential employees are using their past experiences, observational and persuasory information and imaginal experiences to judge themselves against the individual elements of the role. Inaccuracies in the job description may lead to the overconfident people applying above their actual expertise and the underconfident and potentially effective people not applying at all.

The Society for Human Resource Management (SHRM), which represent 350,000 members across 575 worldwide chapters, encourage those looking to develop strong job descriptions to break it into three key steps. Step 1 is to perform a job analysis, gathering and interpreting data about the role from current employees, superiors and other key stakeholders. The analysis should result in a key understanding of the knowledge, skills, physical characteristics and experience required for the job as well as the relevant working conditions. Step 2 involves establishing the essential functions of the role so that they are prioritised in any recruitment information or process. Leaders need to ensure that the prioritised elements are truly essential in that they have a high frequency, serve consequences and cannot be redesigned or reassigned. These are the things that mean the most to successful performance and must be part of the advertised role. Step 3 recommended by the SHRM is to organise the findings concisely into a job description document and recruitment pack. Table 8.1 highlights some of the elements that need to be included.

The design of the recruitment process is equally important in ensuring that we select the right person for the job, and leaders must commit significant time and energy to its design if they want to employ already confident individuals. Recruitment or assessment days often include a range of group exercises, like discussion and role-play, assessments such as psychometric and competence tests, and individual elements such as presentations and interviews. Much like the job description element of recruitment, the focus at this stage in terms of confidence is ensuring that you accurately measure the suitability of each candidate. Any weaknesses in the activities may also lead to the successful person showing competence on the day but actually being underqualified and underconfident from the outset. As leaders we need to ensure that all recruitment processes collect valid and reliable information, in that they directly assess the core competencies and

Table 8.1 Common elements of job descriptions

Element	*Description*
Job title	Name of position
Salary information	Pay range, band, grade, etc.
Hours of work	Full/part-time, hrs, and overtime information
Reporting information	Supervisor information
Supervisory functions	Direct report information
Role objective (s)	Summary of the core objective(s)
Essential functions	List of required tasks
Competencies	Required knowledge, skills and abilities
Required education	Job-related educational requirements
Required experience	Job-related experience requirements
Work environment	Role specific and relevant environmental information
Physical demands	Role specific and relevant physical information
Travel	Frequency, locations, compensation

are standardised enough to produce consistency across candidates. We need to ensure any instructions and scoring systems are clear and consistent and use a diverse and well-trained set of assessors to reduce any bias.

Another interesting element of the recruitment process is how authentic candidates are when under the inevitable pressure of selection. Recruiters can never be 100% sure that what they see for better or worse during the process is a true reflection of how the candidate will behave and perform in the real-world work environment.

Cognitive impairment describes how anxiety can negatively affect how well we can recall information, think clearly and articulate those thoughts afterwards. The impact of anxiety on recruitment processes has been a common interest amongst researchers with the predominant finding being that it causes negative consequences.

Another consideration for leaders looking to make their selections as accurate as possible is the presence of poor proxies for recruitment. Proxies are things that act on something else's behalf and as it is rare to be able to authentically test work performance during a recruitment process, we must often use alternative measurements. Common recruitment proxies include an individual's level of education, their appearance, and ironically their confidence during the recruitment process. The point here is not to dismiss these indicators but to make sure we don't lean too heavily on them or design recruitment processes that magnify or preference them. The overall goal for leaders looking to start the confidence creation process well is to recruit the right people.

Induction

The next phase of an employee's lifespan where leaders can have a significant impact on confidence is the induction period and in particular the training that staff receive. It is rare that a new employee will have all the requisite knowledge, skills and experience required for a specific role, and so it is important that leaders provide a robust period of initial training to boost confidence. This training is important as the frequency of self-efficacy appraisals is much higher during the induction period as employees face an onslaught of things that they have not thought about or done before. The specificity of self-efficacy makes induction training a difficult challenge for leaders as the volume of systems, processes and tasks that employees must master can be overwhelming. This means that training must prioritise what's immediately required or what is more pivotal to role effectiveness. Getting the induction period wrong and not maximising the possible learning can extend the natural self-efficacy dip that people feel when they take on a new role, and so leaders must invest time and energy in the design and delivery of high-quality training.

The field of training and development is vast, and the complexity of learning has been studied by lots of people for a very long time. You may have already heard of 'pedagogy' in relation to learning and development as it describes the method and practice of teaching, but a much smaller percentage of people have come across the word 'andragogy', which is closely related but specifically relates to the study of teaching adults. A prominent American educator in the 1970s called Malcolm Knowles brought the term back into popular use with the publishing of his book *The Modern Practice of Adult Education: Andragogy Versus Pedagogy*. In the book, Knowles (1970) suggested that alongside the established knowledge about the process of general learning, there were a set of assumptions regarding adult learning that must

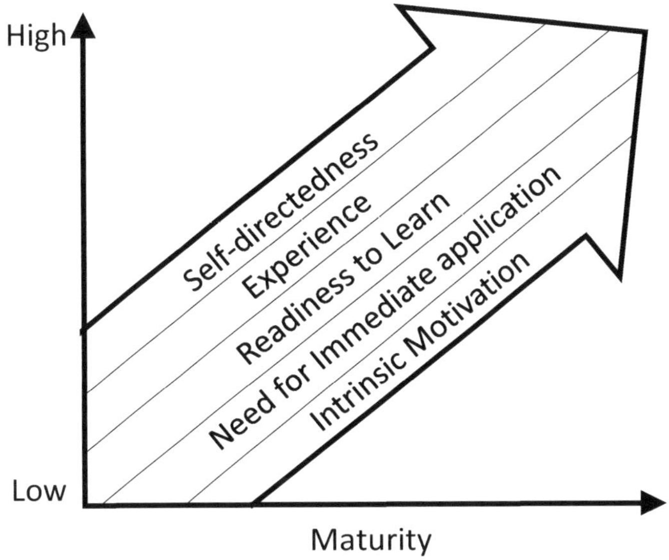

Figure 8.1 Knowles' andragogical assumptions

be considered by professional development providers. The figure below identifies these assumptions and outlines the basic premise that as learners develop maturity, their need for certain learning conditions increases. This knowledge is essential for leaders who want to design training which maximises learning and confidence creation.

Knowles' first assumption is that adults are self-directed learners, and as a person matures their self-concept moves from dependent to self-directed. Unlike children who often just have the singular role of student, adults wear multiple hats (parent, spouse, employee) and must actively decide to become a learner. It is also often the case that adult learning is optional, and although attendance at professional development activities is enforced, the acquisition and application of knowledge and skills remains within their control. It is therefore important that those teaching adults recognise this and involve them in the learning process wherever possible as partners, tapping into and developing self-awareness and self-directedness. Leaders looking to utilise this assumption need to consider:

- How much involvement do staff have in the design of their training?
- How much choice exists for staff within their training?
- What self-study materials do staff have access to?

The second assumption is that adults have a wealth of experience, and it becomes increasingly useful for learning as a person matures. A key difference between adult and child learners is the amount of experience they have developed and how influential that is to their learning. Adults bring a wealth of life experience and varying levels of domain specific experience to their learning. It is therefore important that those teaching adults recognise the presence of this experience and actively seek to utilise it. Creating activities that engage with learner experience naturally increases levels of involvement, engagement and possibly learning. Leaders looking to utilise this assumption in training design need to consider:

- How can they assess and understand the experience of their learners.
- How can they link session content to that experience.
- How can they facilitate the sharing of experience between learners.

Knowles' third assumption is that adults must be ready to learn, and as a person matures their readiness to learn becomes increasingly orientated to their roles. Developing the motivation to learn and to apply that learning is a key challenge for any training provider, and a staff member's perceptions about the relevance of content is a key driver of that motivation. Adults more readily engage with content which is directly related to their current or desired roles. It is therefore important that those teaching adults recognise the importance of accurate participant selection and clear communication of the why behind each activity. Leaders looking to utilise this assumption need to consider:

- How do they identify and understand the role-specific demands of their staff?
- How do they ensure the highest levels of relevance within the training content?
- How do they prepare staff to maximise their engagement with training?

The fourth andragogical assumption is that as a person matures they increasingly seek learning that is immediately applicable. Closely related to the readiness to learn is the perceived applicability of professional development content and the sense that adults are progressively more interested in learning that helps them solve problems. In contrast to child learners where there is the promise of future use, adults typically seek knowledge and skills that will improve their immediate performance. It is therefore important that those teaching adults recognise the importance of contextualising concepts, using real-life scenarios and guiding learners to reflect on how they can apply new learning. Leaders looking to utilise this assumption need to consider:

- How can they identify and understand the current challenges of their learners?
- How can they break training down into easily applicable chunks?
- How can they make training as contextually specific as possible?
- How can they support the transfer of training to the work environment?

The final consideration for leaders wishing to create the most effective training for their staff is that adults are more intrinsically motivated, and as a person matures the motivation to learn becomes more internal. Linking with the self-directedness of adult learning is the sense that motivation to learn increasingly must come from inside as opposed to external reward or recognition. Adults look more towards the higher levels of Maslow's Hierarchy of needs and the pursuit of self-actualisation, personal growth and fulfilment than stickers or prizes. It is therefore important that those teaching adults recognise the need to generate a sense of purpose and joy within learning activities and leaders looking to utilise this assumption need to consider:

- How well do they know their staff and their motivations?
- How can they tie training to the needs and personal goals of their staff?
- How can they facilitate the growth of intrinsic motivation?

Development

The next step in the confidence journey of a member of staff is the longest, as it describes everything after induction and represents the ongoing professional development that they need. This stage is often more complex than induction, as the focus moves away from the training they need to be successful in their role to the training they want and the incremental improvements that will allow them to maximise their impact. It is also plagued by a perceived lack of time and even the rejection of the need for further development which affects staff engagement and their transfer of training into their practice.

One of the first steps for leaders trying to develop the confidence of others is to therefore support them to acknowledge that there are elements of their role for which they have low self-efficacy. The clinical psychologist and author of 'life strategies' Dr Phil McGraw suggests that "We can't change what we don't acknowledge" strengthening the idea that the acknowledgement acts as the first step in any professional or personal development. When we pick apart the process of acknowledgement, we find two distinct actions which need to be completed to move onto any behavioural change. Firstly, we must become aware of the need to improve and identify the specific area or areas of weakness through personal reflection or with the help of a peer, a coach or a mentor. This can be a key role for leaders as either the person guiding the reflection or the one who brokers the services of a professional coach or mentor. The second part of the puzzle is often trickier, as we then need to accept that information driving the change is credible and the outcomes are desirable. Acknowledgement is therefore a process of awareness and acceptance and is a brave thing to do as it involves admitting weakness and confronting some of the cognitive dissonance we previously spoke about.

Coaching and mentoring

In the previous chapter, we identified access to a coach or a mentor as a key strategy for our own confidence creation. As leaders we may need to widen our view of this to include the large-scale implementation of these processes for our staff.

Professional development and confidence creation in large organisations is a challenge for multiple reasons including resourcing, coherence and most importantly personalisation. For many organisations the need for efficiency and the centralised selection of training foci results in large scale training activities that lack personalisation and negatively impact on relevance, engagement and application. One of the most personalised forms of professional development is a key tool for leaders looking to build confidence in others. Engaging in formal coaching or mentoring processes can be seen by some as a sign of weakness or an admission of incompetence,

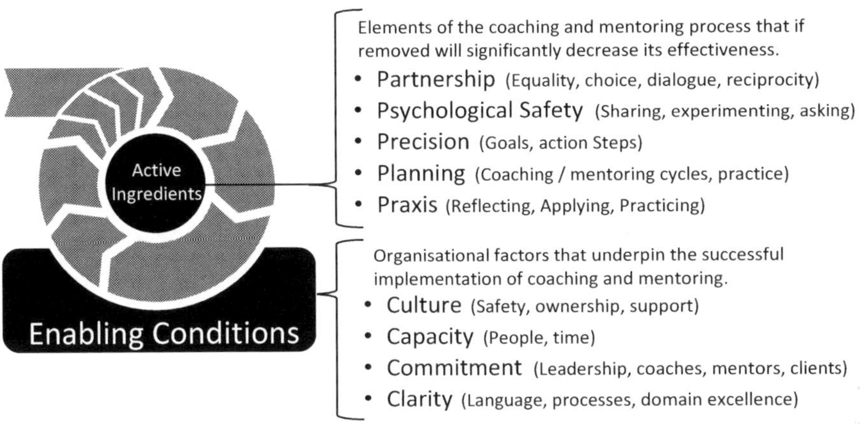

Figure 8.2 The enabling conditions and active ingredients of effective coaching and mentoring

but luckily the growth of coaching and mentoring in organisations is starting to turn the tide on that way of thinking. As leaders our job is to promote the mindset that we need support and development not because of a deficit but because we can all get a little better all the time. If coaching and mentoring are strategies that we do want to employ on a large scale for confidence creation, then there is some foundational work to do first though. Typically, like most things they are more effective if the implementation is systematically managed, and a considerable amount of thinking and planning is put into the enabling conditions and the active ingredients.

When we reference enabling conditions, we are talking about the organisational factors that underpin the successful implementation of an initiative. The first enabling condition for coaching and mentoring is culture, and organisations must have strong levels of psychological safety for staff to engage with coaching or mentoring in the first place and then be vulnerable enough to develop within it. There also needs to be a strong culture of personal ownership of professional development in that staff see themselves as the key actors in their own confidence story and that they have the agency to change it. Capacity is another key condition that leaders must cultivate if coaching and mentoring are going to be successful for individuals, groups and the organisation as a whole. Individuals need protected time to participate and the removal of distractions so that they can deeply engage with the process. Distraction is a killer for both coaching and mentoring as it robs people of their ability to relax enough to reflect deeply and be present enough to maintain focus. Those wishing to develop their own coaching or mentoring programmes also need capacity to complete training and the often-forgotten pre and post activity tasks that maximise its effectiveness.

The third enabling condition for effective coaching and mentoring is commitment and is something that needs to be cultivated within every member of staff from the highest levels of leadership to those receiving the support themselves. Leaders need to ensure that the required resources are in place in terms of time and finance and that a developmental approach flows through all organisational systems and processes. This explicit commitment to the power of coaching and mentoring will galvanise the commitment of the participants and strengthen the message of the processes' own efficacy. Leaders also need to cultivate commitment in those receiving the coaching and mentoring and enable them to be actively engaged in sessions and motivated to take action. The final factor for leaders to consider is the level of clarity that exists within the organisation around the processes and what excellence looks like. A lack of clarity about the coaching and/or mentoring process will breed confusion, scepticism and typically result in reduced engagement. A lack of clarity around what excellence looks like can lead to paralysis or the creation of misconceptions which then become ineffective behaviour and performance.

In terms of what actually happens during coaching and mentoring in the moment and how leaders can maximise its effectiveness for confidence creation, we first need to consider their active ingredients and what at their core makes them effective. The phrase active ingredient has been borrowed from fields like medicine and manufacturing and is used to describe the elements of something that cannot be damaged or removed if we want the thing to maintain its effectiveness. If we take toothpaste as an example, the active ingredient is fluoride and is essentially what makes it work. The rest of the ingredients and characteristics like colour, consistency, flavour or smell are not active ingredients or crucial to its effectiveness. This means that we could make changes to those things and still retain the tooth protecting qualities because we retained the active ingredient. This concept is useful when we talk about techniques or tools for professional development as it helps us understand what we need to maintain fidelity to and protect. The core active ingredient of coaching and mentoring is partnership and describes both the ethos and approach that those involved should adopt and the way that actual sessions are conducted. Borrowing some of the great work done by Jim Knight (2017) on the 'impact cycle' of instructional coaching, we see that in order to achieve a partnership ethos we need to embrace equality, choice, dialogue and reciprocity.

Psychological safety is another active ingredient and something we have spoken about before as vital to effective coaching and mentoring as people rarely present their real problems or are willing to vulnerably explore them if they feel like it will lead to a negative consequence. Another active ingredient of both processes is precision and like lots of things in organisations, a lack of it leads to confusion, paralysis and reduced effectiveness. If we are going to use coaching for creating confidence in others, then we must ensure that we proactively and sustainably plan our coaching and mentoring processes, their cycles and protect time for practice and the embedding of new learning. The final active ingredient of coaching and mentoring that we must protect is the activeness that is required to create the positive experiences and success that will in turn develop the individual's confidence. The Greek philosopher Aristotle uses the word 'Praxis' to describe the process of applying knowledge as opposed to just contemplating it and so for us praxis must be a part of any one-to-one support strategies that we set up for others.

The next part of our exploration into the act of coaching and mentoring as a means of confidence creation is the skills and techniques that coaches need to master and for that we need to return to chapter 5 where we looked at the differences between coaching and mentoring. The suggestion we made back there was that although there is a useful distinction between the people doing it and the relationships they have, the aim and the skills that they use are probably less distinct and therefore less helpful to separate. If we agree that one of the core aims of both mentoring and coaching is to raise the client's confidence, then Table 8.2 highlights some of the skills that might be useful. As a coach or a mentor, the most helpful way to view these skills is as a toolbox which should be responsively used between different client's and between different sessions with the same client depending on their needs in that moment. In his book *Effective Coaching: Lessons from the Coaches' Coach*, Myles Downey (2003), one of the world's leading business coaches, positions these skills on a continuum of directive versus non-directive and emphasises the need to use them flexibly. He goes on to say that for some clients at certain times, they need a directive approach and help solving their problems, and at other times they need a non-directive approach where they are supported to solve things themselves.

Table 8.2 Coaching and mentoring skills

Level of Directiveness	Skill	Description
High	Instructing	Insisting on a specific way of thinking, feeling or behaving.
	Advising	Provisionally directing clients towards a specific course of action.
	Modelling	Providing a static model or demonstration of what excellence looks like.
	Suggesting	Providing clients with a range of possible actions or points for reflection.
	Giving Feedback	Giving client's information about themselves from observations and reflections.
	Questioning	Asking clients for information that provides more information to clarify, create or evaluate.
	Reframing	Challenging a client to see things from a different perspective.
	Rephrasing	Expressing client's words in a different way without changing the meaning.
Low	Reflecting	Playing back the words of the client as they were spoken.

Decisions about which skills to use and when to use them are down to the expertise of the coach or mentor and involve the consideration of a range of factors including expertise, time, trust, complexity and preference.

The level of expertise or experience within the person being supported can affect the initial approach. Individuals can't search for information that they don't have and so for novices a directive approach is often initially more suitable. This is seen most clearly in apprenticeship relationships where the exchange of expertise is often in the form of advice or instructions. As individuals gain more experience and expertise, it may become more appropriate to use a non-directive approach and to facilitate the exploration of existing thoughts, beliefs and understanding or recall past experiences. It is important to acknowledge that expertise is often domain or even task specific and so even very experienced colleagues may find themselves at a novice level for new skills.

Time is another consideration that can affect the coaching and mentoring approach in terms of the urgency with which the individual needs to make the desired changes. It could be that the change in performance is urgent and non-negotiable and so a more direct, instructional approach is used. The contrast to this would be where changes are enhancements to existing practice and so the urgency is less, and time allows a more exploratory, non-directive approach.

Psychological safety has been mentioned numerous times already in the book and is a key element of effective coaching and mentoring. Levels of trust and the strength of the relationship between coach or mentor and client can affect the choice of the initial approach. Honest and accurate introspection is rarely possible in environments where psychological safety is low, and clients don't feel safe to explore or share. It may be that leaders need to take a more directive approach initially whilst the relationship strengthens before being able to generate deeper insights through non-directive skills.

The final set of considerations for those wishing to develop confidence through mentoring and coaching are complexity and preference. The complexity of the intended change can affect the initial approach taken by the coach with relatively simple behavioural changes, with clear stimuli and required actions dealt with through a directive approach. More global or multi-causal changes such as beliefs, values and culture typically require more time on raising awareness and thus lend themselves to a non-directive approach.

A tricky and sensitive consideration to make for those providing coaching and mentoring is the preference of the person being supported. Most individuals will have a preferred approach to being coached or mentored, and establishing this early on can really help the coach or mentor be more effective. Some individuals are more comfortable with thinking introspectively and exploring their own thoughts and feelings, and respond well to a non-directive approach. Other individuals are more action-orientated and prefer getting to the diagnosis and goal setting stages as quickly as possible. As with everything we have discussed before, the aim is to be as responsive as possible, protect the partnership at all times and prioritise what is necessary for praxis and confidence creation.

Cognitive reframing

Before we move on to the next stage of an individual's career curve, it is worth examining in more detail a core skill for leaders looking to develop confidence in others. If we accept that self-efficacy is an individual's own perceptions of their confidence, then we need to accept a certain level of subjectivity. In terms of confidence, we can often be our own worst enemy and engage in negative thinking when there is little evidence to actually back it up. Cognitive reframing is a technique used by coaches, mentors, therapists and individuals to look at a situation, person or event from a slightly different perspective. The technique has its roots in the work of people like Aaron Beck who in the 1960s pioneered the idea that we can deal with emotional distress by identifying, challenging and restructuring negative thoughts. Further work by Albert Ellis on Rational Emotive Behaviour Therapy (REBT) and Donald Meichenbaum's work on self-instructional training all support the power of cognitive reframing as a tool for confidence development.

A more recent addition to this field is the work of Professor Steve Peters, a renowned psychiatrist and author of the book *The Chimp Paradox* (Peters, 2012). In the book, he introduces a simplified model of the brain where the logical prefrontal cortex is represented by the 'human' and the emotional centre, the limbic system, is represented by a strong, emotion-driven 'chimp' who you must learn to manage. It is this distinction that sets the scene for using the chimp model for confidence creation as it's the difference between what your chimp says and what your human says that can cause the problem. The chimp model also introduces a part of the brain it calls the 'computer' which acts a reference store for the human and the chimp but can also initiate automatic behaviours. When we think about the ongoing battle between the human and chimp, it is important to remember that the chimp is neither good nor bad but is much stronger than the human and so we often find ourselves being hijacked by our chimp and acting irrationally. The goal is to learn to manage the chimp so that it can work together with the human and the computer. Leaders can support the confidence development of their team members by helping them manage their chimp through three key strategies. The first strategy is to distract the chimp by providing an alternative activity like counting to ten, removing yourself from the stimulus or some other cognitively distracting question or prompt. This temporary solution works by softening the emotional response which usually manifests itself immediately and without conscious thought. The second strategy is to exercise the chimp and offers a more productive and sustainable solution. To exercise the chimp means to listen to and process the emotions being felt and to allow them out by vocalising them to either ourselves or another. The final technique and one that is best delivered by another person like a coach, mentor or manager is to box the chimp in. During this technique we use factual, truthful and logical information to reframe the often illogical and subjective messaging from the chimp. An example would be a direct report doubting their confidence to lead projects and meet deadlines, resulting in negative self-talk only to be reframed by their manager who presents the results of a number of past projects that have been successful and completed on time. Confidence management therefore is often a case on making sure that the computer has enough positive efficacy information in it to counteract any noise from the chimp during self-efficacy appraisals.

Performance Management

The ongoing development of our staff must always include a balance of support and challenge, and we should not shy away from the need to help people manage their performance. In the right hands, performance management (PM) can be a useful source of guidance and confidence creation. Sadly, it can also be the opposite, serving to create anxiety and weaken our perceptions of competence. The focus should always be how we as leaders can support others to improve their performance and include a collaborative exploration of its causes and creation of possible solutions. Many of the techniques we have spoken about earlier in this chapter would sit comfortably within a PM conversation and so we won't go over old ground, but there are some additional strategies that might be useful for confidence development.

Guided reflection

Confidence is not the only thing that develops unconsciously, and our need to automate much of our work to save cognitive capacity means that lots of the positive and negative aspects of our performance are outside of our awareness. The levels of psychological safety that we encounter also moderate how much information about ourselves we feel comfortable sharing. This combination of unawareness and purposeful guardedness and inauthenticity can damage confidence and opportunities for professional and personal development. A key role for leaders is therefore to shine a light on elements of an individual's personal performance and encourage the sharing of personally held knowledge.

In 1955 psychologists Joseph Luft and Harry Ingham created a tool called the 'Johari Window' to explore levels of self-awareness and how information was shared between people, and it has been used in a wide range of domains and contexts ever since. The window is constructed of four panes or quadrants, organised along two axis each representing a type of information. The open quadrant contains information that is known to the individual and known to other people. This is information that has been freely shared with others and is the area which we should seek to grow if we are to maximise individual and group effectiveness. The blind segment contains information known by others but not by the individual and so represents their blind spot. We actively want to shrink this area so that we have all the information we need to maximise individual or group effectiveness. In the third quadrant we keep the hidden information which is known to the individual but not shared externally and so remains

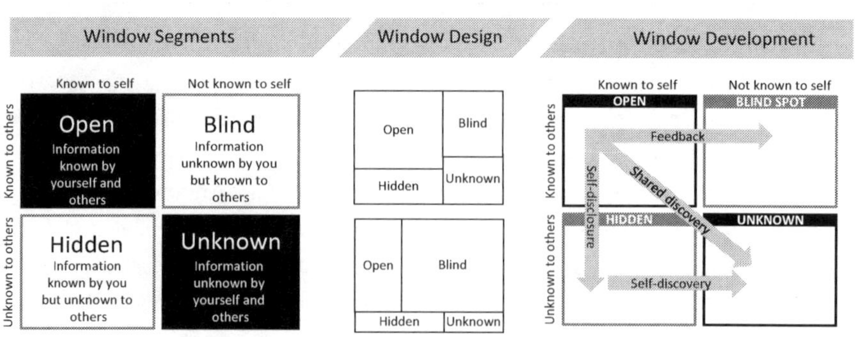

Figure 8.3 The Johari Window

unknown to others. We also want to actively shrink this area so that we enable better understanding, trust, cooperation and productivity between individuals and groups. The final quadrant is called unknown and contains information that both the individual and other people are not aware of. As with the hidden quadrant, we want to reduce this so that we can use the increased understanding to improve effectiveness.

As a tool for confidence creation the Johari Window does a great job of raising awareness, and although uncomfortable at times it can also help with cognitive reframing when the individual has a lot of information in the blind quadrant. The first step in using it is to populate each quadrant with information related to a specific focus which can be anything but typically centres around personal attributes, aspirations, anxieties or values. The volume of information in each quadrant dictates its initial structure which in itself communicates some strong messages to the individual completing it. The final part of the process is to explore and put into action strategies such as feedback or reflection to improve the balance of the window segments.

Feedback

Another tool in our leadership locker for developing confidence within performance management is feedback. As we saw in chapter 3 it is one of the key sources of efficacy appraisal information. Feedback is essentially the information we get from or give to others about actions, behaviours or performance in order to improve them. The importance and benefits of feedback lie within its ability to enable individuals and systems to adjust and improve and so has been a key strategy for leaders since time began. Over that time, research and the world of work have produced a wide range of techniques for delivering feedback. Table 8.3 shows just a small selection.

Which technique you use will be a personal preference and a decision based on situational factors, so we are going to skip exploring each one in detail and instead return to the idea of active ingredients and what makes feedback effective.

When we talk about feedback for confidence creation, the active ingredients might start with it needing to be 'specific'. When we give vague feedback like "well done" or "could do better", we provide an initial value judgement but then leave the recipient unsure about what it was that they

Table 8.3 Feedback tools and techniques

Title
Balanced, Objective, Observed, Specific, Timely (BOOST)
Bambrick-Santoyo feedback model (PPAPPF)
Context-Examples-Diagnosis-Actions-Review (CEDAR)
Describe-Express-Specify-Consequences (DESC)
Example-Effect-Change/Continue (EEC)
Identify-Describe-Encourage-Action (IDEA)
Situation/Task-Action-Result (STAR)
Situation-Behaviour-Impact (SBI)
The feedback sandwich
The Pendleton feedback model

did successfully or unsuccessfully. This may satisfy the provider but limits development because recipients lack understanding about which bit of their practice to continue with or which area requires developmental attention. Feedback should specifically reference positive and negative elements of the performance, highlight their impact on the outcomes of the performance and where possible link to the success criteria of the task itself.

The second active ingredient that must be present in any type of feedback is 'timely' and describes when the feedback is provided. Common sense would say that we need to give feedback as soon as possible as it loses its impact the longer we wait but the picture is a little more complicated. To explore this more deeply, we must first decide if we are in the presence of the individual and able to provide live feedback or if feedback must be delayed. The later situation is much simpler, and if feedback must be delayed then it should be provided as soon as possible so that uncertainty, anxiety and confidence dips don't start to occur. If we are in their presence, then we need to decide if the mistake or ineffective practice is going to affect immediate learning or performance or if our feedback can wait. Clearly if there is a safety issue or the misconception is going to lead to further misconceptions and reduced learning, then immediate is best. There is however a subtle change that we can make which is linked to the coaching approach we spoke about earlier and the importance of thinking hard for learning and memory. Leaving staff members to fully engage with a problem on their own can sometimes be better than jumping in to rescue or provide guidance. If we do feel the need to interject, then often a better strategy is to lead with curiosity and a question which can stir their initial reflection and precede any feedback that then needs to be given.

Ensuring that feedback is 'evidence-based' is another active ingredient of feedback and is vital to the creation of confidence as it impacts on the credibility of the information and the acceptance and use of it by the individual. Feedback often comes from a single individual and is based on observation or opinion, both of which are dangerously invalid. We saw in chapter 3 that if we don't believe the feedback, then it has very little impact on our self-efficacy. If we doubt its accuracy or sincerity, then we reject it or as a minimum accept it and then take no action. Where possible we need to increase the credibility of the feedback by gathering it from multiple sources or 'triangulating' it so that it feels a like a broader view of our performance and less subjective. We also need to ensure that it does not try to do more than it is able to do and by this, I mean that feedback should be predominantly descriptive in its nature rather than evaluative and focus on what was seen, heard or felt rather than why that might have been. Phrases like "I noticed" or "I felt like" followed by "help me understand" or "what are your reflections" open the door to more collaborative conversations and increased confidence creation.

As we have seen throughout the book, self-efficacy and many of the other elements like self-esteem and general confidence are often fragile and change dynamically and rapidly. For this reason, feedback needs to be balanced in terms of its positivity and negativity. The once celebrated and now largely criticised 'feedback sandwich' technique was an attempt to achieve this and only lost impact when people doubted its sincerity. At its core, it is still conceptually sound in that a predominance of either positive or negative feedback is not good for the recipient's confidence or their professional or personal development. Sadly, for those of us who like definites, there is no agreed percentage or order for the balance of positive and negative feedback but is down to professional judgement by the provider about what would be best. As we will see later in the book, when we explore the concept of self-efficacy spirals and the sweet spot, our aim as leaders is to facilitate confidence growth and at the same time avoid discouragement or hubris. Another dimension of feedback that needs to be balanced is its focus and what it provides feedback on. The majority of feedback will be task-related and focus on which parts of the activity or process went well or not so well but there may be underlying processes that weave across tasks that also require attention. It is often the feedback on these more foundational elements and transferable skills like analysis, inference, action planning or problem solving that have the greatest impact as their influence is magnified by their importance across multiple tasks. Another useful and foundational focus for feedback is the person's effectiveness in self-regulation and their ability to plan, monitor and evaluate their work. Feedback on these areas alongside references to attributes like resilience, effort and focus can also have a deeper impact on performance because of their foundational value.

The way we communicate and the language we use in our feedback can have a significant influence on its impact on the recipient's confidence. The 'clarity' of feedback is another active ingredient and is a consideration for both the deliverer and the receiver. When we deliver feedback, we need to ensure that we are as efficient in our language as possible so that the key messages get through and the recipient's attention is not mis-directed. It may be tempting to surround a key message in a story or personal anecdote, but it is often this redundant information that reduces the feedback's impact. We also need to be aware of the vocabulary and jargon we use in our feedback and the prior knowledge of the individual. If at any point the recipient is cognitively overloaded by trying to understand what we are saying or what it means, then there is a good chance that it is not being processed effectively and may be lost or forgotten. We must always be channelling the voice of the author Brené Brown and remembering that "clear is kind" and that confidence creation rarely comes from ambiguous, poorly processed feedback.

The final active ingredient of feedback that we need to talk about is how 'actionable' it is. If the primary aim of feedback is to improve performance, then common sense suggests that it needs to drive changes in future performance and not just provide a commentary of past effectiveness. Feedback that drives the biggest jumps in self-efficacy includes concrete, actionable steps that the individual can take to either cement good practice or develop areas of weakness. These actions provide a roadmap for development and strengthen perceived confidence by allowing the recipient to mentally rehearse or visualise future improvements. The presence of actions within feedback also creates a useful opportunity for progress checking and holding people to account for their development during subsequent feedback sessions.

Advancement

The final element of an individual's career that we as leaders can have an impact on is their advancement through different roles and unsurprisingly confidence plays a significant role here as well. We spoke about the impact of self-efficacy on our decision making in chapter 4, and professionally this shows itself clearly in the way we do or don't put ourselves forward for new roles and opportunities. If you are anything like me then you will be able to think back to a variety of times where your lack of confidence stopped you from taking on new responsibilities and roles because of fear and a perceived lack of success. If we want to build sustainably successful organisations, then we need to facilitate a steady stream of talent development and succession planning, and we can't afford for confidence to get in the way. Our impact as leaders starts with our support for those considering advancement and our ability to judiciously persuade those who are ready for it to do it. Two strategies that can be used to create confidence in preparation for advancement are shadowing and secondment which we will now explore in more detail.

Shadowing

The concept of learning from another person with more expertise is an old and well established one and finds its roots in the idea of apprenticeship. The expert-apprentice relationship was common in ancient civilisations like Mesopotamia where scribes would learn the art of record keeping from more established practitioners, and in Egypt and Rome where artisans would pass down their skills to the next generation. The Guild system of medieval Europe formalised the apprenticeship model by introducing a strict hierarchy of 'Masters' who were the highest level and had their own shops, to the 'journeymen' who had passed their apprenticeship but were not yet masters, and then 'Apprentices' who were typically young people learning the trade. Although the guild system declined in the 16th and

17th centuries, we can still see the remnants in professional organisations, licensing bodies and trade unions. In more recent times we see the model continuing to be used in the military with its formal ranking system and particular in the construction trades where 'on the job' training is a key element of an apprentice's development.

The benefits to confidence creation come primarily through the individual's increased access to experience, observational learning and feedback, three of the key types of self-efficacy appraisal information. Access to this additional information can if done successfully lead to improvements in knowledge and understanding and especially the contextual intricacies of a role. The often-practical nature of shadowing greatly increases skill development as individuals have opportunities to not only see the skill performed in its authentic environment but also how issues and challenges are delt with. When shadowing is done really effectively, it is accompanied by metacognitive narration from the expert to expose ways of thinking and decision making. This narration also extends to what we call 'guided noticing' where the expert helps direct the attention of the apprentice to the key elements of any environment or situation. The final benefit of shadowing lies in its ability to remove the fear of the unknown which so often dents self-efficacy levels and stops people from acting. Seeing that tasks are achievable and understanding in more detail what the potential barriers and solutions are can really boost levels of confidence and agency.

One of the key challenges for shadowing and a traditional apprenticeship approach in the modern organisation is the predictability of the environment and the need to build both physical and mental skills. A theory that ties both of those together and has become increasingly popular in organisations, schools and online is something called 'cognitive apprenticeship theory'. The theory, as the name suggests, extends the traditional approach to apprenticeship to include cognitive and metacognitive skills like problem-solving, critical thinking and reflection. It is still rooted in the importance of real-life experience and 'learning on the job' but recognises the importance of understanding the reasoning behind actions and decisions. Cognitive apprenticeship is typically a more interactive and guided approach where the apprentice is encouraged to ask questions, proactively reflect and actively integrate learning into their practice. The teaching methods are much the same in that they involve modelling, scaffolding and exploration, but are enhanced through a greater emphasis on coaching, articulation and reflection. Proponents of this style of apprenticeship suggest it leads to deeper levels of understanding and skill development, improved transfer of learning across different tasks and domains, and increased levels of engagement from the apprentice. They believe that learning time is reduced because of this increased engagement and that the addition of narration helps apprentices avoid common mistakes and understand the why behind the how. In terms of self-efficacy, there are obvious benefits from the deeper understanding and engagement, and confidence is naturally boosted through a decrease in self-doubt and uncertainty.

Secondment

Our final strategy for improving confidence for career advancement is more formal than shadowing and involves the full-time or part-time transfer of an employee to a different role, team or even organisation. The term 'secondment' seems to have originated within governmental groups during the 19th century to describe the movement of officials between teams but has since diversified to include almost all industries including finance, healthcare and education. As the world of work becomes more global and organisations strive to find more ways to develop and retain their staff, temporary secondments are increasing in their popularity. For individuals they provide a great opportunity to gain new skills, broaden knowledge and deepen levels of experience. They offer the chance to extend professional learning networks and often provide a welcome boost to motivation and engagement through the provision of fresh challenges. In terms of self-efficacy, although participants may see an initial dip in confidence as they encounter new contexts and challenges, with the right support, confidence levels quickly return and exceed previous levels. The rise in self-efficacy is slightly different from shadowing which has high levels of observation and feedback, as secondment is much more focused on accruing additional experiences that then boost self-efficacy levels if they are successful. Interestingly, successes in new, unfamiliar contexts such as with secondments have a greater impact on our confidence than similar challenges in our 'home' context because of the additionally challenging conditions. This sets secondments up to be one of the most impactful things we can do for our staff in terms of confidence growth as long as they are matched with enough support to ensure success.

Sadly, it's not all sunshine and roses with secondments and poorly designed or executed moves can have a significantly damaging impact on confidence levels and career progression. The relocation and travel often involved in secondments can be very disruptive for individuals and families and create an instability that ripples through both personal and professional effectiveness. Levels of uncertainty about the incoming role demands, group dynamics and how things will be 'back home' when they return can create a heightened sense of anxiety which then negatively impacts on confidence. One of the key confidence considerations linked to secondments is the almost inevitable dip in self-efficacy that comes with change, and we will explore this phenomenon in detail in chapter 11. These self-efficacy dips can be hard to recover from if support is not available but if expected and proactively managed are escapable in relatively short periods of time.

For secondments to maximise their effectiveness, the guidance from large Human Resource organisations like The Chartered Institute of Personnel and Development in the United Kingdom and Deloitte of the United States is to invest heavily in their planning and preparation. Secondment planning should start by defining clear objectives about what both the individual and the organisation wants to achieve. This should detail what skills will hopefully be developed, what knowledge will be transferred and what outcomes are expected. The next step is to select the right candidate, ensuring that any self-efficacy dips are minimised by choosing individuals with the knowledge, experience and skills to hit the ground running and succeed. Once chosen, individuals must receive training and guidance on the host organisation's vision, values and culture and the expectations and responsibilities of the role. Further thought should be put into place regarding any initial training and induction that will take place once the secondment has happened. It is important to ensure that lots of the things we have spoken about in this chapter like shadowing, coaching and mentoring are in place to avoid any deep or prolonged dips in self-efficacy. Communication issues are often the root of most resistance within secondments, and so clear and open communication must be achieved between the individual, home, host organisation and any other associated stakeholders. The final consideration required for successful secondments is to address any legal and logistical issues related to employment law, tax, finance and visa requirements.

As we reach the end of this chapter, I want you to take a minute to think about how you currently impact on the confidence of others. Would they cite you as a force of good or evil? What have you done today to boost the confidence of a team member? What did you do today that might have dented someone's confidence? How aware are you of your team's hidden confidence levels and the self-talk that goes on in their minds? Finally, what strategies have you got in your toolbox to build confidence in others, what do you need to add and how can you go about using these by design?

Nuggets

- We play a vital role in the self-efficacy development of others.
- Our impact starts with recruitment and continues through induction, development and advancement.
- Our first goal is to recruit the right people as errors here instantly dent confidence.
- Induction is more than knowing the organisation's mission statement.
- Induction training must recognise the andragogical assumptions.
- Coaching and mentoring are the keys to ongoing confidence development.
- People are often their own worst enemy when it comes to self-talk.
- We can't change what we are not aware of or what we don't accept.
- We need to be conscious and purposeful about the feedback we give.
- Shadowing provides important observational learning.
- Secondment is a great tool for widening experience.

Next Steps

✓ Assess the quality of your current confidence curation toolbox.

✓ Get your staff to complete a confidence creation wish list outlining the activities they wish they had more of or that were more effective.

SE TOOLBOX UPGRADE

WHAT

The SE toolbox activity involves the evaluation of current practices for improving self-efficacy in others. The exercise requires individuals to reflect on the state of their current toolbox in terms of what tools they have, how sharp or effective they are and which tools they need to add.

WHY

As leaders a core part of our job is developing others and as we have seen in this chapter, confident staff are effective and engaged staff. The success of individuals is also key to the success of teams and larger groups and so the pursuit of a robust programme for self-efficacy development should be a priority for all leaders.

The process of evaluation and prioritisation can help to create a mandate for change and identify key actions for strengthening existing programmes of support. Sharing the findings of personal or team SE toolboxes can also produce change on a wider scale and lead to systematic changes to recruitment, induction, development, management and advancement.

HOW

Step 1 – Identify and describe the current tools for SE creation that exist within each career stage.

Step 2 – Give each tool and stage a Red, Amber or Green rating on its effectiveness.

Step 3 – Identify additional tools that are required in each stage.

Step 4 – Add a priority rating to each stage in terms of need for change.

References

Downey, M. (2003). *Effective coaching: Lessons from the coaches' coach* (2nd ed.). New York: Texere.

Knowles, M. S. (1970). *The modern practice of adult education: Andragogy versus pedagogy*. New York: Association Press.

Peters, S. (2012). *The chimp paradox*. London: Vermilion.

9

CREATING COLLECTIVE EFFICACY

An element that we are yet to talk about is the role that a group's level of confidence or what we call 'collective efficacy' can have on its individuals, the group and the organisation as a whole. It will come as no surprise that the origins of research into collective efficacy come from Albert Bandura and his initial observation that a group's confidence in its abilities seemed to be linked to its levels of success. Definitions of collective efficacy typically centre around the idea that it describes a group's shared belief in its capability to be successful. Since that initial research by Bandura, collective efficacy has been studied in a wide range of different domains adding weight to its importance and usefulness for us as leaders. Robert Sampson is a prominent figure in the field of criminology and well-known for his research on collective efficacy and its relationship to crime rates. John Hattie, an influential education researcher, identified collective efficacy as the single most impactful factor influencing student achievement and other studies have focused on its role in healthcare, community building and organisational development.

DOI: 10.4324/9781003558934-10

The similarities between collective efficacy and self-efficacy continue into the way that it is created through shared appraisals of past experiences, observation, persuasion, physical and emotional states, and imaginal experiences. It also seems to serve similar functions in that it affects the group's thinking, motivation, emotions and decision-making. Most techniques and strategies for developing collective efficacy follow a similar trend as we saw in the self-build chapter in that they seek to improve the quality of the recognised self-efficacy information sources. It is for this reason that we will take a slightly different approach to thinking about its development. For our exploration we are going to assume that on top of the standard efficacy appraisal information sits a layer of evaluation linked to the characteristics of the team or group itself. The following chapter therefore focuses on what these characteristics might be and how we can develop them so that collective efficacy can increase.

The Characteristics of Effective Teams

People have been thinking about what makes an effective team for about as long as teams have existed, and so the history of this area of research is considerable. Not forgetting the work of philosophers, monarchs and military leaders from the past, the early formal development of team effectiveness understanding came from Elton Mayo's work on the Hawthorne studies back in the 1920s and then the work of Kurt Lewin on group cohesion in the 1930s. In the '40s American businessman Armand Vallin Feigenbaum strengthened the importance of effective teams through his work on 'Total Quality Control' and the idea that the production of quality was the responsibility of all members of an organisation. The 1960s and '70s saw industrialists recognise and invest in the power of collaboration and recognise the benefits and significance of interdependence. The technology boom in the 1990s and early 2000s facilitated greater levels of collaboration and efficiencies in communication and organisation which further fuelled interest in team effectiveness. Since then, there have been a vast number of iterative attempts to codify effective team performance resulting in the discovery of new phenomena and models. Models that have made a particular impact are included in Table 9.1.

As with the models of feedback that we looked at in the last chapter, the choice of a team effectiveness model will be a personal choice. For the purposes of this chapter we will focus our attention on the range of

Table 9.1 Team effectiveness models

Name	*Creator(s)*	*Date*
Team Performance Model	Allan Drexler and David Sibbet	1970
GRPI Model	Richard Beckhard	1972
Hackman Model	Richard Hackman	1983
The SDCT Model	Salas, Dickinson, Converse, and Tannenbaum	1992
Katzenbach and Smith Model	Jon Katzenbach and Douglas Smith	1993
T7 Model	Michael Lombardo and Robert Eichinger	1995
Robbins & Judge Model	Stephen P. Robbins, Timothy A. Judge	1996
The LaFasto and Larson Model	Frank LaFasto and Carl Larson	2001

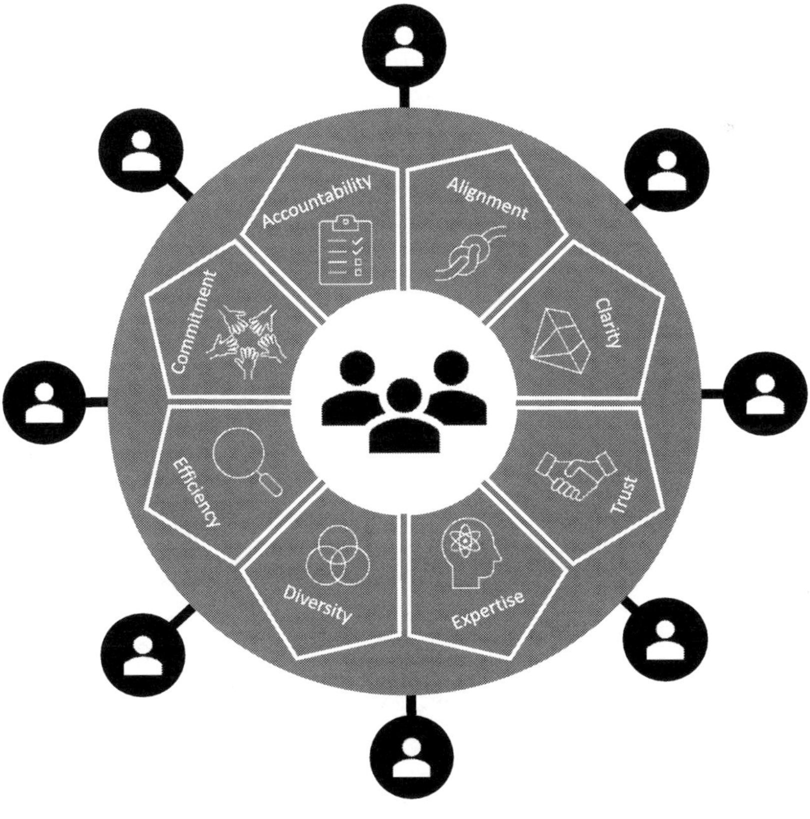

Figure 9.1 The characteristics of effective teams

characteristics that seem common to most team effectiveness models and ones that might be used by individuals to make confidence judgements about a group and thus contribute to collective efficacy.

Alignment

The first characteristic we will explore is alignment, and when we talk about this we are focusing primarily on the levels of shared understanding of a group's purpose and goals. When all members of a team are rowing in the same direction, it creates less confusion, less duplication of effort, fewer misunderstandings and quicker decision-making. Feeling part of a collective endeavour and having a common purpose also improves feelings of belonging and the intrinsic motivation that comes with that. High levels of alignment help facilitate collaboration and creativity because of the safety that comes from collective responsibility and improves resilience because of the ever-present support that is available. An absence of alignment around purpose and goals can, as we will see with the other characteristics, foster a sense of doubt in the effectiveness of the team and thus reduce perceptions of collective confidence.

Leaders looking to develop greater levels of alignment within their teams would be wise to start with exploring whether their vision and goal setting processes are effective. Vision setting is a process for which an ocean of literature has been written, and due to its complexity is far beyond the scope of this chapter to fully encapsulate. There are business orientated approaches such as the balanced scorecard or OKRs (objectives and key results), and research backed approaches like appreciative inquiry, scenario planning and Otto Scharmer's 'theory u' all of which at their core hold a similar process. Effective vision setting involves self-reflection, envisioning the future, aligning with purpose, setting goals and then sharing and inspiring. A process with a little more structure that is well recognised and used in business and may be useful for leaders who want to redesign their vision is the 'Vision Quest' approach by James Collins and Jerry Porras. In the 1996 *Harvard Business Review* article "Building your company's vision" they described an organisation or team's vision as the intersection of core values, purpose and BHAGs (Big Hairy Audacious Goals). The vision quest process starts by clearly articulating the fundamental principles that guide decision-making, behaviour and relationships within the group or in other words, its core values. Once those are established the process moves onto defining the group's purpose and its reason for being. This typically goes beyond just making a profit by articulating what unique contribution the group hopes to make to the world. The final element of the process is a detailed description of the envisioned future through the ambitious, long-term goals it wishes to accomplish. These BHAGs, as Collins and Porras call them, are unlike traditional Specific, Measurable, Appropriate, Realistic, Time-bound (SMART) goals in that they are focused on things beyond the group's current reach and may require significant creativity and sustained effort. As with all vision setting techniques the effectiveness lies in the levels of coherence between the elements and the collaborative nature of its creation. Leaders looking to create greater alignment through vision setting would be smart to engage a diverse range of perspectives at all stages of the process and to see its creation and use as an ongoing iterative process.

Clarity

The second characteristic of effective teams we are going to focus on is clarity, and when we think about teams with high levels of this, we think about those that have clearly defined roles and open communication. When team members are clear about what is required of them and where the boundaries exist between them and others, their levels of self-doubt and team-doubt reduce. They are less worried about overlapping their efforts or stepping on other people's shoes and less concerned about being the target of any finger-pointing. Having clarity around specific responsibilities and job requirements can enhance an individual's feeling of ownership and accountability which can in turn improve levels of commitment and resilience. Not being lured outside of our lane, so to speak, also improves the efficiency and productivity of teams through greater levels of focus and more efficient resource allocation.

A good starting point for leaders looking to develop greater levels of clarity within their teams is the openness of the communication between its members. When communication is 'closed', individuals filter their messages because of biases or fear, and the culture of the team means that only a select number of voices are ever heard. Open communication, on the other hand, is transparent and honest because of mutual respect, is inclusive because of psychological safety and results in better outcomes because of a deeper level of listening. Proponents of open communication like Brené Brown (2018), the author of the book *Dare to Lead*, talk about our responsibility as leaders "to be clear to be kind" and to not feed people half-truths in order to make them feel better, talking to people rather than about them. Another key voice in this space is Kim Scott who was an executive at both Google and Apple and outlined a framework for fostering open communication in her book *Radical Candor* (Scott, 2019). A core principle of Scott's approach is the idea that leaders should combine caring personally for people and challenging them directly. In the book she introduces four communication styles which use varying combinations of this and result in varying outcomes. When care is high, but challenge is low, the outcome is what she calls 'ruinous empathy' and results in us caring so much about someone that we fail to challenge them. This often results in a lack of awareness or ignorance to the need for change. When challenge is low and

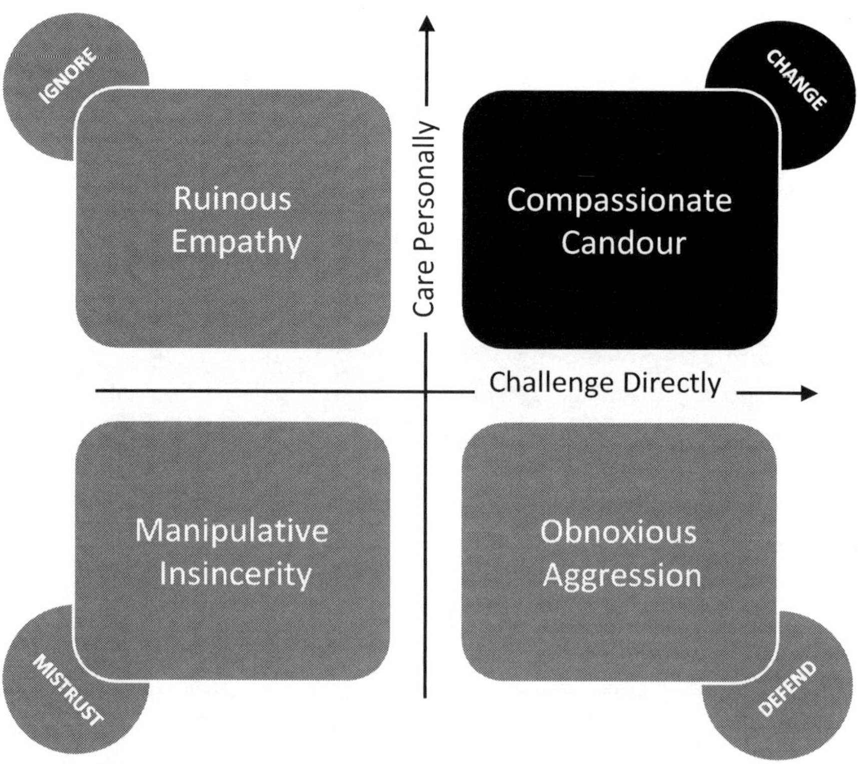

Figure 9.2 The compassionate candour model

care is low, the outcome is 'manipulative insincerity' where we communicate in a dishonest way on purpose. This often results in the development of mistrust between individuals or the group as a whole. The third quadrant of Scott's model describes a communication style where care is low, but challenge is high and results in 'obnoxious aggression' where people don't care about how the message is delivered or received. This naturally leads to defensiveness, disengagement, and a breakdown of relationships. The final quadrant and the title of the book is 'radical candour' which balances care and challenge, resulting in a communication style that enables honest feedback, tough decisions and the maintenance of high standards. Since its publication the author has been keen to soften the approach that some readers have taken from the model and rename the optimal quadrant from radical to compassionate candour highlighting the need to maintain our levels of care and kindness irrespective of how direct and challenging our communication need to be.

Trust

Trust is our next team characteristic and is often where our phrases 'collective confidence' or 'group self-efficacy' show up in team effectiveness models. When we talk about trust, we are effectively talking about how predictable we feel the thoughts, feelings and actions of a group or team are. When we trust something, we have confidence in the way that it will react to a given stimulus and we often describe those things as reliable or dependable. For leaders there are two lenses that contribute to our feelings of collective confidence with the first being how much trust we place in the expertise of the other members. Do we trust that they can and will successfully complete their responsibilities and do we trust that they will step into help us when we need them? If the answer is yes and that is true across the team, then our collective confidence grows. The less confidence we have in individual expertise, and the less coverage that exists across the team, the lower our levels of collective confidence. We are going to explore expertise in more detail later in this chapter so for now we will move onto a second lens of team trust – psychological safety.

We spoke earlier in the book about the work of Amy Edmondson on the varying levels of safety people feel being vulnerable within groups, teams and organisations. We saw that where this feeling of psychological safety is high, people trust that there will be no negative consequences when they:

- raise issues and concerns
- disagree
- give and receive feedback
- ask for clarification
- ask difficult questions
- ask for help
- offer solutions
- admit errors.

A perceived lack of ability to do these things can lead to individual reductions in well-being and performance and of course, when aggregated, a reduction in team effectiveness. Teams that don't have this often have blind spots in their thinking because people feel unsafe to speak, they make poor decisions because people feel unsafe to disagree, are less innovative because people feel unsafe to share ideas, and leverage less collaboration and professional development because people feel unsafe to ask for help.

Leaders looking to develop greater levels of trust within their teams can utilise a range of different strategies. Creating open communication channels and ensuring that everyone is transparent and open with each other even when it is difficult reduces any concerns that what people say or do is in any way disingenuous. It is also important that team members are reliable and dependable, sticking to their promises and commitments, and always being on time and committed to deadlines. In their dealings with each other, leaders and team members must be fair and consistent, avoiding favouritism or bias and making decisions based on solid principles and merit. When things are tough, leaders looking to build trust need to be empathetic and understanding, taking time to fully understand situations before launching into opinion or action. As we will see later in the chapter, accountability is key to trust building and so team members must be prepared to accept responsibility and justify their actions. When we think about developing trust by creating a safe, inclusive environment, it's worth revisiting the work on psychological safety that we spoke about before. Leaders wishing to develop high levels of this in their teams need to start by clearly explaining its benefits and modelling fallibility themselves. They need to be tentative with ideas and proposals where appropriate and reference times when they themselves experienced failure or ineffectiveness. Other strategies leaders can use include the normalisation of peer-to-peer feedback, the facilitation of all voices during meetings and the celebration of honesty and bravery when it happens.

Expertise

The next characteristic of effective teams that we need to consider is expertise which is typically one of the strongest and most visible sources of information that teams use to assess their collective confidence. When we look at dictionary definitions of the term expertise, we see the reoccurrence of words like knowledge, skills and experience and an indication that it is specifically focused within a particular field or area much like self-efficacy.

The challenge for leaders and individuals within teams is that expertise in the form of knowledge and experience is harder to see and can largely go unknown outside of formal evaluations and professional development choices. We may be able to locate small pieces of information from the

Table 9.2 Dictionary definitions of the word 'expertise'

(Oxford English Dictionary): "The special skill or knowledge acquired by experience of or deep study in a particular field of activity."
(Merriam-Webster): "Expert skill or knowledge in a particular field."
(Collins Dictionary): "Special skill or knowledge that you have because you have studied or practiced something for a long time."
(Dictionary.com): "Expert skill or knowledge; expertness; know-how."
(Macmillan Dictionary): "The special knowledge or skill that you have in a particular area because you have studied it or worked in it for a long time."
(Longman Dictionary): "Special skill or knowledge gained through experience or study in a particular area."
(Cambridge Dictionary): "The ability to do something very well because you have a lot of knowledge or experience of it."
(American Heritage Dictionary): "The skill or knowledge of an expert."
(Webster's Dictionary): "Special skill or knowledge; expertness."
(Chambers Dictionary): "Specialist knowledge or skill acquired through theoretical study or practical experience."

time we spend speaking with colleagues and whether they sound knowledgeable or experienced, but this is hardly reliable and thus makes expertise judgements and therefore collective confidence judgements based on expertise difficult.

Slightly more visible is what Peps Mccrea in his work on expert teaching calls 'expertise as action'. His suggestion is that individuals with more expertise do things differently and the first of those is the way they **perceive** situations, paying attention to more relevant information and perceiving events at a deeper level of abstraction. This enhanced perception enables them to make more accurate inferences and then make better judgements about which behaviour to employ. The next aspect of 'expertise as action' is **simulation** and describes how accurately individuals can anticipate the outcomes of situations. High levels of expertise typically come from large amount of experience which in turn enables people to play through scenarios autonomously and instantly in their minds to test out different responses. This ability shows itself visibly through a calmness and flow to actions that mean experts always look one step ahead of their audience and non-experts. The third aspect of expertise that Mccrea highlights is **execution** and simply describes the ability to do the right thing and to do that thing effectively. High levels of expertise often allow individuals to select foundational interventions that impact on the core of an issue and have a positive cascading effect which amplifies their impact. Execution also describes the high levels of flexibility, opportunities, fluency and precision that experts demonstrate through their practice. The final element of 'expertise as action' is **conservation** and is what we might call 'autopilot' because it describes the level of unconsciousness that experts can utilise and remain successful. Internally experts are able to delegate much of their day-to-day work to their subconscious and therefore use their cognitive capacity to focus on the most complex and important elements of a situation. In contrast, individuals with less expertise are often overloaded by the volume of things they must think about or are easily distracted by inconsequential information.

Leaders looking to increase levels of collective confidence by developing greater levels of expertise need to improve both their recruitment processes and the effectiveness of the professional development that their team members engage in. A key technique for expertise development which we have not yet discussed is delegation. This is a brave statement, but delegation may be one of the most important and yet widely misused professional development tools in the leader's arsenal. Badged as a builder of experience and confidence, the typical levels of abandonment and loose expectations mean that it actually has the opposite effect and for many team members, damages their self-efficacy levels. Leaders looking to successfully use the strategy should start from the premise that delegation is a process not an act and that delegated responsibility can be released gradually. The first strategy for improving our delegation is closely linked to a well-recognised technique in education called the gradual release of responsibility which in the classroom sees the teacher systematically shift the focus away from them and onto the learners. In a 2014 Inc.com article, Peter Economy wrote about the 'five levels of remarkably effective delegation'. In it he described a process where the leader assesses the team member's readiness for responsibility and then selects the most appropriate entry point. Table 9.3 shows the five suggested entry points and the different responsibilities that they include. In practice, a team member may stay at one of these levels for an entire project and progress over time or progressively move through them within the same project. Gradually releasing the responsibility of delegation can build confidence and ensure that delegation remains an act of empowerment not abandonment.

Our second strategy for effective delegation is to break the act down into separate sections and explore our role as leaders in each one. To work through these stages, we are going to use an aviation analogy and imagine the process of delegation is much like an airline flight. Prior to the start of the delegated activity (pre-flight), it is important that the leader invests in building trust with the team member and sets clear expectations

Table 9.3 Stages of effective delegation (Economy, 2014)

Level	*Title*	*Responsibilities*
1	Assess & Report	Assess a new scenario and report back
2	Recommend	Level 1 plus recommended actions
3	Action Planning	Levels 1 & 2 plus an action plan
4	Decision-making	Levels 1, 2 & 3 plus some decisions with support
5	Full Delegation	Delegation of whole project or activity

about the what, why and how. During this time, it is also important to ensure that project planning is a collaborative process which maximises engagement and proactively fills any gaps in knowledge, understanding and skill. Any concerns about expertise during pre-flight should trigger a pause in the process until deficiencies have been resolved and it is essential if the team member is going to be ready for the next stage of the process (take-off). During this brief stage, leaders need to empower the team member by being available but not stifling their leadership of the task or micro-managing their thoughts and actions. As the delegated task gains momentum, we enter the 'climb' phase of our flight analogy where leaders need to have regular formal and informal check-ins with the team member to praise and re-resource if necessary. During the ongoing 'cruise' stage of the delegation, contact with the team member will naturally decrease but progress must still be regularly monitored, trust maintained and opportunities taken to provide feedback and check resource allocation. The final stage of any delegation is of course the 'landing' and leaders should support team members to analyse the outcome and impact of the task, and locate any learning that might be useful in the future.

Diversity

We now switch our focus to the levels of diversity within a team and how that affects its effectiveness and its level of collective confidence. Rarely does one size fit all or isolation help produce the best results, and this is also true for differences in team demographics, cognition and expertise. When we think about demographic diversity we are focused on things like age, gender, race, ethnicity, sexual orientation, disability, religion, education and socioeconomic background. The most effective teams and organisations are often the ones who most closely represent the people they serve as this increases credibility and reduces blind spots. Having similar demographics to your clients creates not only an increased level of empathy and understanding but also potentially increased alignment and authenticity in the client's eyes. This of course typically leads to greater levels of engagement and commitment from their side and improved performance of individuals and the team.

Thinking the same often precedes acting the same and so can be just as dangerous for teams wanting to improve their effectiveness. Cognitive diversity describes differences in a team's thought processes, problem solving approaches and mental models about how something is or should be. Our mental models are our own personal representations of how something works and act as a sort of mental map which helps us understand and navigate the world. We have mental models for general things like restaurants or libraries and then increasingly more specific models linked to our jobs, hobbies and relationships. Our mental model of a library typically includes the need to be quiet, that books can be borrowed but not kept and that the books are organised numerically. Not having a mental model or possibly worse having an incorrect mental model about libraries being like a playground would then alter our understanding of and behaviour within them. The other elements of cognitive diversity like information processing styles, problem solving approaches and general methods of thinking are all typically products of our training and experience and so naturally evolve differently over time. Differences in cognitive diversity often sit on a continuum where both extremes can be damaging. Extreme cognitive misalignment within a team can mean that people think and behave in very different ways which can cause frustration, conflict and inefficiency. On the other hand, extreme alignment of thinking can stifle creativity, create blind spots, reduce learning and sadly in some cases, cause manipulation and control.

The final element of diversity we need to consider is the level of complimentary expertise that exists. We have already spoken about the importance of trusting the expertise of our fellow team members if we are to be collectively confident but there is also an element of trust needed in the coverage of knowledge, skills and experience that exist across a team. Highly effective teams do not seek to homogenise their members and smooth them out, they celebrate spikiness and extreme expertise and create rounded teams by pulling the right people together. A rounded team is greater than its individuals and greater than simply the sum of its parts. Knowing that there is someone on the team that can do what you can't or knows what you don't is a comforting feeling and one that supercharges collective confidence.

Leaders looking to develop greater levels of diversity within their teams can of course approach it systematically through the recruitment of their staff or the training that they provide but cognitive diversity is a little trickier to achieve and so this is where we will we focus our attention. When groups have low levels of cognitive diversity and think the same, they are in danger of suffering from something called 'groupthink' where the desire for consensus overrides each member's ability to speak their mind. Some of the signs of groupthink include the following:

- Group members believe they are superior and immune to making mistakes.
- Doubt and dissenting opinions are ignored or rationalised away.
- The group's decisions are seen as inherently good and beyond reproach.
- Disagreement is often attributed to external threats or inferior groups.
- Individual members feel pressure to conform even if they have doubts.
- Members avoid expressing individual opinions that might disrupt group harmony.
- Individuals withhold their concerns or critiques for fear of disapproval or rejection.

Groupthink can quickly lead to poor decision-making, lapses in ethics, reduced creativity and decreased morale and job satisfaction, but there are ways to combat it.

In the aftermath of the 1973 surprise attack on Israel in what would be the start of the Yom Kippur war, intelligence analysts recognised systematic flaws in their risk assessment process and their ability to predict such attacks. The subsequent inquiry highlighted a level of groupthink and overconfidence that led to the creation of what they called the '10th man' strategy which we will now call the '10th voice' technique. Although the specifics of how they used it are of course confidential, the concept has gained popularity and requires groups to assign the role of '10th voice' to an individual who then is required to provide structured dissent during discussions, contribute alternative viewpoints, voice possible risks or concerns and uncover blind spots. Since 1973 the strategy has been renamed and reused by a wide variety of businesses like General Electric, and McKinsey & Company and used within the academic peer review process as well as politics and government. For leaders of teams, it can be a great way to foster critical thinking, encourage open communication, increase innovation and build confidence.

Another technique that we can use to widen perspective and encourage open communication has its origins in early 1900s psychotherapy and its everyday use in the boardrooms of Amazon, Zappos, and Airbnb. German-born psychotherapist Fritz Perls developed a technique which involved imagining a specific person, either real or symbolic, sitting in an empty chair and then directing thoughts and feelings towards them as if they were present. Commonly used in Gestalt therapy of which Perls was a co-creator, the technique encourages the user to explore unresolved conflicts, express difficult emotions and practice open communication. Fast-forward a hundred years and the 'empty chair' technique is used by leaders to explore the perspectives of stakeholders like customers, parents, students or shareholders that can't physically be in meetings or discussions. The presence of an actual empty chair at meetings can force team members to widen their thinking and consider others during decision-making.

Efficiency

As we approach the latter part of our team effectiveness model, we uncover some arguably less glamorous but unarguably important elements like efficiency, commitment and accountability. When we think about team efficiency, we are talking about how well its members and the team itself can achieve their goals with the minimum amount of wasted resources. Efficient teams understand that sustainable success is systematic and so invest heavily in systems thinking and the creation of efficient processes. Efficient teams also embrace and integrate 'lean principles' into various elements of their organisation. The concepts of lean management, lean thinking, lean operations and even lean leadership all describe a goal to eliminate waste and optimise performance. It is the optimisation of systems, the streamlining of workflows and the subsequent reduction in waste that often improves perceptions of collective confidence.

Focus is another key element of efficiency and another core characteristic of effective teams. The ability for organisations and individuals to maintain focus helps to ensure clarity and direction, makes decision-making more accurate, boosts motivation and engagement, and protects cognitive and physical resources. Examples of how damaging a loss of organisational focus can be are rife within the leadership and business literature and played a significant role in James Collin's work on organisational effectiveness. In his book *How the Mighty Fall* (Collins, 2001), Collin's describes five stages of decline that failing companies typically go through and for which a lack of focus is a common factor. In stage 1, which he calls 'hubris born of success' companies get insulated by success and become arrogant, losing focus of their core values and what got them there in the first place. In the second stage, 'the undisciplined pursuit of more', a further loss of focus on core business and increased distraction from unaligned opportunities leads to neglect and diluted resources, inefficiency and vulnerability. A further lack of focus on the warning signs of decline is a symptom of stage three, 'the denial of risk and peril', where organisations fail to adapt to changing circumstances. Collins calls the fourth stage 'grasping for salvation' and as the decline continues, more focus is lost as the organisation desperately searches for quick fixes and silver bullets, and inefficiently uses time, energy and finances. Finally, the consequences of a sustained lack of focus finally catchup with the team and lead to their irreversible decline or irrelevance.

The last element of efficiency that teams can leverage to become more confident and effective is collaboration and interdependence. Collaboration is probably something that we would all associate with high performing teams and describes the act of working together to achieve a shared goal. The mutual respect, trust, synergy, coordination and shared responsibility that comes with collaboration provides the team with a wide range of benefits. Collaborative teams are typically more efficient and productive, they solve problems more effectively, experience increased levels of motivation and engagement, and learn and adapt quicker than other teams. Interdependence is slightly different and describes relationships between two or more things that are mutually dependent on each other. High levels of interdependence hold similar benefits to collaboration in that there are increases in synergy, efficiency, resilience and motivation.

Leaders need to be aware though that extreme interdependence can also have a negative impact on efficiency and team effectiveness. The reliance element leaves teams more vulnerable to and magnifies the impact of individual weaknesses as a failure with one person directly affects those are dependent on them. Having multiple moving and dependent parts can also negatively affect the speed and accuracy of communication and the coordination of action. Decision-making can be slowed as consensus is much harder to achieve and reduces the team's responsiveness. Having other team members that contribute to your work can lead to reduced effort by some individuals and free riding which then negatively affects the motivation of those carrying the extra load. Finally, and probably most disruptive, is the increased frequency and complexity of interpersonal conflicts due to the need for consensus of thought and the interdependence of people's action on the success of others and the team as a whole.

Leaders looking to develop greater levels of efficiency within their teams would do well to begin by improving its ability to focus and removing cognitive and physical distractions.

A strategy that is growing in popularity within organisations is the concept of a 'sludge audit' which finds its roots in behavioural economics, user experience design and the drive to remove friction from systems and processes. Sludge can be seen as anything that creates inefficiencies for individuals, teams or organisations and a range of examples can be seen below:

- Inaccessible language or jargon on documents.
- Confusing website structure and navigation.
- Complex customer service or employee systems.
- Unclear decision-making processes.
- Outdated tools and technologies.
- Overly bureaucratic approval processes.
- Repetitive meetings.
- Unnecessary data collection and reporting.
- Complex pricing structures.

Key voices in this space include behavioural scientists Dilip Soman and Cass Sunstein who are driving the importance of removing sludge and creating ways for people to manage it. One such process is the sludge audit which aims to identify where the friction is and then support the creation of solutions for removing it. Although no formalised structure exists for a sludge audit, typically they focus on processes, communication and inclusivity with the audit moving through the three stages of reflection, collection and mitigation. The first step for leaders looking to improve team efficiency through a sludge audit would be to reflect either on their own or as a team on where the sludge or friction currently exists. The result of this stage will be a list of things that cause frustration, confusion or loss of resource. The next stage involves collecting information from different stakeholders, be that customers, suppliers, regulators or employees outside the team. We are interested in hearing about their experiences and the frustration and confusion that they encounter so that we can triangulate and validate our initial reflections. The final stage is then to explore possible mitigating strategies or solutions, prioritise their implementation and then act.

Commitment

Commitment is next on our list of team elements that contribute to collective confidence, and when we think about people in our teams who demonstrate strong levels of this, we typically think about the levels of engagement, resilience and effort that they show. Its role in collective confidence like many of the others is in our perceptions of commitment levels across a team and how that makes us feel about the teams' chances of success. Engagement is the first element we will look at and is more than just showing up or being present, it's about an individual's emotional connection to their work, the team and the organisation. It has close ties to motivation and resource allocation and is therefore one of the more visible attributes of a person and a team. Engagement levels are not binary and are often represented on a dynamic continuum such as in Figure 9.3.

Individuals experience different levels of engagement at different times and in different situations which is made more complex by the influence of both internal and external factors. Typically, engagement is at its lowest and most damaging when team members are defiant and actively resist or oppose team goals or commitments. Passivity is a step above but still represents a minimal amount of engagement and often results in disinterest, indifference and a reluctance to think about or do anything. Next, we have compliance which sadly is probably the most common level of engagement in less confident and ineffective teams as it is seen as the spot between not

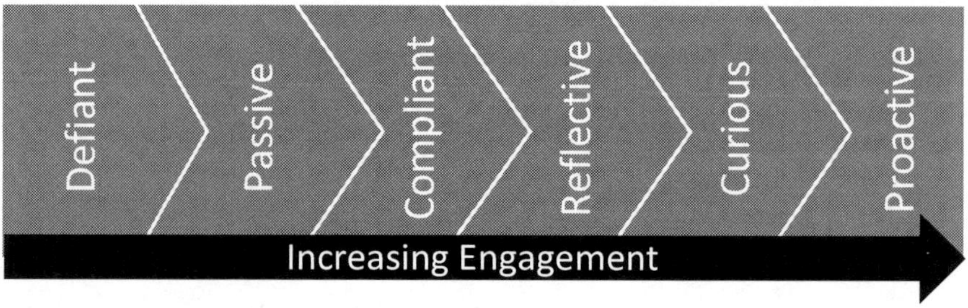

Figure 9.3 The staff engagement continuum

getting in trouble but also not doing very much. Compliance often comes from a sense of obligation to engage and a low sense of intrinsic motivation. Reflection describes a level of engagement where individuals are actively introspective and investing time and energy in questioning and analysing themselves, the team and the organisation. If reflection signals the first truly positive level of engagement, then curiosity takes that a step further and results in exploring, learning and innovation. The final level in our scale is proactivity and signals a shift in ownership from engagement being a result of something external to something that is self-driven. Proactive individuals are intensely self-motivated, able to anticipate need, take the initiative and actively make positive contributions to the team.

Resilience is another attribute often associated with commitment and describes the ability to bounce back from challenges but more than that, to adapt, thrive and grow in the face of adversity. People with high levels of resilience seem able to flexibly navigate the ups and downs of life whilst demonstrating strength and resourcefulness. In teams, the perception that "We will never give up" and "We will get through this" leads to increases in self and collective confidence. Numerous authors and researchers have explored organisational and individual resilience over time including Hugh van Cuylenburg's work on the 'Resilience Project', Brené Brown's 'Gifts of imperfection' and of course Carol Dweck's work on 'Growth mindset'. Having a growth mindset and believing that setbacks are part of the learning process feels like the foundation of resilience. A sense of agency might come next in that it imbues the individual with confidence that they can do something about the negative situation they are in. The final element of resilience may come from feeling safe to reach out for help from within the team and again builds confidence in the collective.

Levels of effort are an obvious and often explicit sign of commitment and a closely related concept that is important for leaders to understand is called 'discretionary effort' or DE. The idea that some team members give effort above what is expected is not a new concept, but it gained significant popularity in the 1980s through the work of people like Dennis Organ. Organ was an expert in organisational behaviour and management and produced a seminal piece of work called *Organizational Citizenship Behavior: The Good Soldier Syndrome*, where he defined DE as "voluntary extra-role behaviors that contribute to the effectiveness of an organization but are not formally recognized in a job description or linked to the reward system" (Organ,

1988). Discretionary effort is often characterised by abnormally high levels of altruism, courtesy, conscientiousness, civic virtue, proactivity and learning. There is a general agreement that higher levels of DE lead to higher productivity, satisfaction and performance. There is also consensus on the fact that it is affected by a wide range of factors such as organisational culture, leadership styles, autonomy, recognition and monetary factors. A final area of common thinking is that DE is not always positive and that extreme levels or an expectancy of it can lead to toxic team cultures and burn out through work-life imbalances. The presence of healthy levels of DE within a team provide assurance to its members that when times get tough, they have the capacity and willingness to go that extra round or find that extra gear to succeed. This belief is another example of how commitment can strengthen collective confidence.

Leaders looking to develop greater levels of commitment within their teams would do well to consider the different elements of the three-component model of commitment developed in 1991 by John Meyer and Natalie Allen. In the model they suggest that organisational or team commitment has three distinct parts: affective commitment, continuance commitment and normative commitment. Affective commitment which is often shown as the first component of the model describes an individual's emotional attachment to the team or organisation. It is this emotional attachment that leaders can develop more easily and have more control over in terms of confidence creation. Creating a positive work environment through recognition and appreciation, open communication, and physical and mental well-being initiatives can make the team a nicer place to be. Connecting staff to the team or organisation's purpose can also help them develop motivation, resilience and a sense of being part of something bigger than themselves. The last two parts of the model describe commitment that is driven by a fear of the perceived costs of change or a sense of obligation to a team because of social norms that have been created and so both are less desirable.

Accountability

Our final characteristic of effective teams and our last contribution to collective confidence is accountability, and is another example of something that gets very few headlines but sits under the surface as a foundational influence on team success. Definitions of accountability often include references to responsibility or being answerable for your own or a team's actions and decisions. The idea that "everyone will do their part" and "we don't make excuses around here" speak to the feelings of trust in each other that help to build collective confidence. In the day-to-day workings of a team, taking responsibility means being proactive and not waiting for others to solve problems. It involves acknowledging and learning from mistakes and following through on commitments. This requires individuals to plan and prioritise well, to communicate expectations clearly and to be open to feedback and compassionate candour from others.

Being answerable is both a feeling that people get from their cultures and often a part of formal evaluation processes. When team members and teams themselves are answerable, they can justify their actions and decisions and take ownership of any failings or lack of progress. It would, however, be wrong to think that being answerable just means taking the blame for things, as there are a number of actions that can help team members get in front of and improve how they deal with negative outcomes. Clarity and communication are key to the process with resistance or conflict often just being a lack of understanding or variance in expectations. Effective goal and outcome setting is the first piece of the puzzle and clarity at this stage can dramatically affect future success.

Leaders looking to develop greater levels of accountability within their teams should start by ensuring that they set high expectations and create robust evaluation processes. It's important to establish clear benchmarks within a team around personal and professional conduct and this can reduce ambiguity and provide a standard from which performance can be measured. High expectations can be motivating and inspiring through the challenge that they set and pushing people beyond their comfort zone and encouraging them to stretch their abilities can lead to significant increases in learning and engagement. Reaching high expectations often requires individuals to improve their competence which then of course improves their confidence and if high expectations can be maintained and even raised where possible it leads to continuous improvement. Where expectations are not consistently met, there are opportunities for feedback and learning which then further develops improvement and confidence.

Leaders looking to raise expectations in their teams need to invest time and energy in the creation of a supportive environment so that individuals believe that targets are possible and not get demoralised. Opportunities for professional development, mentoring, coaching and the provision of sufficient resources can all help with the creation of such an environment. Leaders also need to ensure that however high they set the expectations, that they remain realistic, relevant and achievable as expectations that don't directly affect team performance or that have unreachable timelines only serve to reduce engagement, motivation and accountability. The final action for leaders looking to raise expectations is the provision of regular feedback and assessment so that team members can identify and acknowledge successes and issues and to make any course corrections required to stay on track.

The process of evaluation is commonplace in organisations and teams but what is not so is the effectiveness and impact of that evaluation. Leaders looking to raise expectations need to ensure that any evaluation processes that they do use are robust in that they are transparent, comprehensive, reliable, valid and actionable. Poor processes lead to poor data, and this is not only not fair on team members but also often leads to inaccurate inferences and actions. When we diagnose poorly, we treat poorly. The metrics or 'system of measurement' that teams use varies between organisations with some of the most popular including KPI (key performance indicator), ROI (return on investment), NPS (net promoter score) and VA (value added). Rather than looking at anyone one of these in detail, it might be more useful to explore the characteristics of good metrics. In his *New York Times* bestselling book *Principles* (Dalio, 2017), the investor Ray Dalio describes the need to "build great metrics" and pushes back against the idea of collecting, analysing and acting on isolated numbers or evidence. Dailio suggests that much like goals, metrics need to be relevant so that they directly align with the team or organisation's goals and priorities. They also need to be quantifiable so that they can be measured objectively to avoid ambiguity and subjectivity. Great metrics are actionable and so should not just inform their audience but also act as a catalyst for decision-making and action. Finally, it is vitally important that any evaluation metrics are transparently understood by everyone involved. Any lack of understanding about the end goal and its measures will negatively affect planning and intervention as well as cause frustration and conflict during the evaluation process, none of which positively contribute to collective efficacy.

As we reach the end of this chapter, I want you to take a minute to think about the collective confidence of the teams you work in or lead.

Is it high, moderate or low, and how has it changed over time. What are the key levers for it being the way it is? Are there fundamental issues with levels of alignment, clarity and trust? Do people believe that the team has the required expertise, and if not where are the gaps? Are meetings full of back slapping and confirmatory nodding or do you encourage diverse thinking and rumbling? What about the unsexy stuff, how efficient are your systems and do these cause anxiety, uncertainty and low collective confidence? Finally, what about commitment and accountability, do staff go above and beyond, do they take responsibility for their actions, and do they feel like others have "got their back" when things get tough? If your answers to these feel negative, then what can you do to drive change and improve collective confidence by design?

Nuggets

- Perceptions of confidence within and about a group is called its collective efficacy.
- High levels of collective efficacy have been linked to higher levels of performance.
- Collective confidence is greater than the sum of its member's individual confidence.
- Collective efficacy beliefs have similar sources, serve similar functions and operate through similar processes to self-efficacy.
- Leaders looking to develop collective efficacy should also improve perceptions of team effectiveness.
- Leaders can improve alignment through a common purpose and shared goals.
- Leaders can improve clarity through clearly defined roles and open communication.
- A key lever for leaders wanting to develop trust within teams is the strengthening of psychological safety.
- Building expertise through effective training and delegation are key to collective efficacy development.
- Leaders should actively increase the demographic and cognitive diversity within their teams as well as celebrate differences in expertise.
- Collective efficacy increases when teams have efficient systems and can focus intensely.

- Leaders must develop strong levels of team commitment, resulting in engagement and resilience if they want to develop collective confidence.
- Collectively confident teams maintain high expectations and leverage robust evaluation processes to ensure that their perceptions match reality.

Next Steps

✓ Complete a Team Effectiveness Radar (TER) for each team that you lead and reflect on the key development priorities and action steps.

✓ Get other team members to complete a TER and compare the results.

TEAM EFFECTIVENESS RADAR

WHAT

A Team Effectiveness Radar (TER) is a reflective tool that enables team leaders and members to evaluate their team against the recognised attributes of highly effective teams. The activity requires the participant to reflect on the strength of each attribute and then assign a rating. These ratings are then transferred to a segmented circle image, which when completed creates a radar chart highlighting strengths and weaknesses.

WHY

Teams are both complex and extremely important to the effective functioning of organisations. The complexity comes from the interpersonal dynamics that exist between members and often diluted levels of accountability and fuzzy communication that are created. Levels of psychological safety dictate how openly members talk about the team's effectiveness, and so the TER is a great method for collecting and comparing perceptions in a systematic and safe way. The results of TERs can be used to drive improvement plans and form the basis of team coaching programmes.

HOW

Step 1 – Create a pie chart with eight sections and label each one with the following team attributes (Alignment, Clarity, Trust, Expertise, Diversity, Efficiency, Commitment, Accountability).

Step 2 – Reflect on the strength of your teams' attributes and rate them out of ten (0 = Very weak to 10 = Very strong).

Step 3 – Colour in each radar segment to match the rating you gave it (0 = No shading to 10 = Fully shaded).

Step 4 – Select your lowest three attributes and describe why you chose that rating.

References

Brown, B. (2010). *The gifts of imperfection: Let go of who you think you're supposed to be and embrace who you are*. Center City, MN: Hazelden.

Brown, B. (2018). *Dare to lead*. London: Vermilion.

Collins, J. (2001). *Good to great*. London: Random House Business Books.

Collins, J. C., & Porras, J. I. (1996). Building your company's vision. *Harvard Business Review, 74*(5), 65–77.

Dalio, R. (2017). *Principles: Life and work*. New York: Simon & Schuster.

Dweck, C. S. (2006). *Mindset: The new psychology of success*. New York: Random House.

Economy, P. (2014). 5 levels of remarkably effective delegation. https://www.inc.com/peter-economy/5-levels-of-remarkably-effective-delegation.html

Meyer, J. P., & Allen, N. J. (1991). A three-component conceptualization of organizational commitment. *Human Resource Management Review, 1*(1), 61–89

Organ, D. W. (1988). *Organizational citizenship behavior: The good soldier syndrome*. Lexington, MA: Lexington Books.

Scott, K. (2019). *Radical candor: Be a kick-ass boss without losing your humanity*. Fully revised & updated edition. New York: St. Martin's Press

10

DIPS AND SPIRALS

Self-Efficacy Dips

When was the last time you felt a dip in your confidence? Last year, last week, or if you are like most of us you probably have already felt one today. Dips in confidence are a natural part of our lives, but as leaders we can't afford for them to go unnoticed or unmanaged in ourselves or those we lead if we want to maximise effectiveness. Before we get into what causes them and how they can be managed, let's look at their core characteristics. Confidence or self-efficacy dips are typically temporary changes to confidence levels rather than a prolonged or chronic change. They are context specific and if managed well, only affect self-efficacy levels within the particular task that created them. The severity of them changes between people and between situations with the greatest dips coming from situations where the perceived and actual levels of success are most disparate. Their final characteristic is that they are impactful, and even the smallest and most temporary dips can negatively impact on how we think, feel and behave.

So, let's start by exploring why these dips happen.

DOI: 10.4324/9781003558934-11

Change

Change is hard to avoid in life, and we experience varying levels of it on a daily basis which have an instant and then cumulative impact on our confidence. Our brains thrive on routine and predictability, and our fondness of habits and automaticity is probably due to a balance of nature and nurture factors. Our ability to automate lots of our thinking and actions enables us to reduce the amount of cognitive load that we experience, which in turn frees up cognitive capacity to deal with the onslaught of information that we have to process and make decisions about. This adaption is probably a primal, one and a number of authors including Charles Duhigg in his book *The Power of Habit* and Yuval Noah Harari in *Sapiens* have suggested its pivotal role in human evolution. On a more temporary basis, we like predictability because it typically reduces our stress and anxiety levels, it can improve efficiency and productivity, and it gives us a sense of control.

When we think about the changes we experience as leaders, they may be as small as a last-minute increase to an audience size which makes us question our confidence or as big as a new set of responsibilities. The size of the change naturally links to its impact on our confidence levels with most changes only causing small dips that are easily overcome using the techniques we will cover later in this chapter. The larger confidence dips that occur when roles change or people acquire new responsibilities are the ones we need to be aware of as leaders. Figure 10.1 shows how individuals can acquire a high level of self-efficacy towards a specific task over time through training and experience only to be thrust back to novice status and self-doubt when a task or their role changes. As we spoke about at the

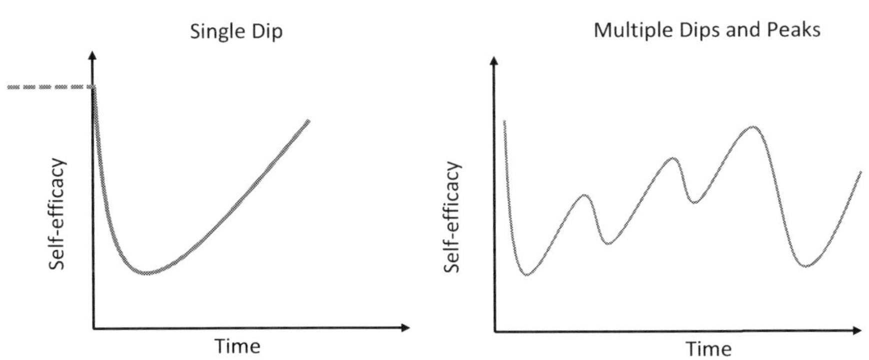

Figure 10.1 Self-efficacy dips in the moment and over time

beginning of this chapter, change is hard to avoid, and so for most of us, we are on a rollercoaster of confidence dips and peaks as the parameters of our careers and personal lives change.

Novelty

A closely related trigger for self-efficacy dips is novelty or the level of newness associated with a task. As we have spoken about numerous times in this book, often it is the unknown that causes self-doubt and the subsequent dip in confidence. When we don't know what excellence looks like or what a task involves, we question our own efficacy, and when we don't know how a peer or team will react, we question their ability to succeed. Novelty is worth speaking about separately from change in that it is often more predictable and expected. When we start a new hobby or move to a new city, we expect to have low levels of initial confidence as we encounter things for the first time, but we accept this as part of the process and carry on. The impact of novelty on confidence is similar to change in that it triggers our risk-aversion instincts, where a lack of existing knowledge or reference points leads to feelings of uncertainty and anxiety. These feelings then often manifest themselves as self-doubt which, as we will see in the next part of this chapter, can lead to reduced performance which in turn fuels a further decline in confidence and so the downward spiral continues. Before we move on, it's worth noting that there is a positive side to novelty in that its expectedness means that we can anticipate it and mitigate for it which helps us maintain resilience and lessens the duration of the dip. Novel things can also bring a great deal of excitement and boost learning, creativity, personal growth and social connections.

Resistance

Resistance is another key trigger for confidence dips, and when we think about how it shows itself during a task, we can initially break it into internal and external events. Internally our first experience of resistance is often through procrastination and the urge to delay commencement or to engage in distractions. In his book *Still Procrastinating: The No Regret Guide to Getting It Done*, Joseph Ferrari (2010) dissects the phenomenon of procrastination, insisting that it is not about laziness or that it is experienced by everyone in the same way. Procrastination and self-efficacy have an interesting relationship in that low levels of confidence cause paralysis which often leads to procrastination, but prolonged procrastination then reduces confidence because of the reduction in time to complete the task.

Another internal form of resistance that can cause confidence dips is our level of intrinsic motivation, which describes our desire to engage in activities for personal reasons rather than external rewards or punishments. Our levels of intrinsic motivation are closely linked to our innate curiosity, our need to understand, our desire to accomplish, our feelings of control and our need to be connected to a larger purpose. Dips in intrinsic motivation lead to dips in confidence because they typically lead to reduced levels of effort and resource allocation which then dents our confidence to complete tasks successfully. Motivationally focused self-talk declarations like "I can't be bothered" can quickly turn into self-doubt statements like "I was not going to be successful anyway" which then contribute to a confidence dip.

Cognitive dissonance

Another fascinating internal form of resistance that can cause immediate dips in confidence is something called 'cognitive dissonance'. American social psychologist Leon Festinger is recognised as the 'father' of cognitive dissonance and described it as the mental discomfort or tension that individuals experience when they hold two or more contradictory beliefs at the same time. Experiencing this dissonance is much more common than people think and of course, occurs almost every time we learn something new or when there is a contradiction between our beliefs and behaviours. Festinger believed that this discomfort originates from an innate desire to maintain cognitive consistency which is then disrupted by conflicting information, causing stress because of the need for dissonance reduction and the re-alignment of beliefs and actions. So how does cognitive dissonance play a role in self-efficacy dips? Well, as we have seen before, any unpredictability, novelty or change can affect the stability of our confidence in our abilities, and this is the same for the stability of our knowledge and beliefs. When we are forced to question what we think or believe because of the presence of some contradictory information, then we start to question how knowledgeable we are and how stable our efficacy is. This can increase levels of self-doubt, causing a confidence dip, and if it occurs over a sustained amount of time, even our overall integrity.

The cognitive dissonance that comes from a mismatch between beliefs and actions is also a common trigger for confidence dips because of its validating effect on our perceived abilities. For me this plays out every time I go ten pin bowling or play golf, as my perceived levels of skill are quickly unvalidated by the ball going either down the gutter or into a nearby field. The resulting reality check and dissonance between how good I thought I was and then actually how well I performed causes a dent in my self-efficacy. At work we see this every time a presentation or meeting doesn't quite go as it did in our heads or we receive unexpected feedback about our performance.

Trauma

Most confidence dips can be anticipated. Starting a new role at work, changing cities, trying out a new hobby all bring with them some initial self-doubt and a temporary dip in self-efficacy. Two further triggers that are much more difficult to predict are trauma and illness, and both of them can have significant primary and secondary effects on confidence levels. Personal trauma is described as deeply distressing or disturbing experiences that have an overwhelming impact on an individual and affect their thoughts, feelings, and behaviours. Its impact is wide ranging and often leads to self-doubt and self-criticism, hypervigilance, dissociation, isolation and a loss of identity and purpose. Organisations like the International Society for Traumatic Stress Studies (ISTSS) and national centres for the study of Post Traumatic Stress Disorder (PTSD) suggest some broad classifications of trauma which may help us explore its impact on confidence. Trauma is often described using a continuum of 'acute' and 'chronic' with the former describing single events and the latter describing repeated traumatic events. If we accept that any trauma has the power to and probably does dent our confidence levels, then what happens and how often it happens will clearly have an impact on the amount of confidence dips we experience and their depth. Another common distinction is the difference between 'interpersonal' trauma caused by the harmful actions of another person or people and 'impersonal' trauma inflicted by external events like accidents and natural disasters. Although deeply personalised, it is generally suggested that interpersonal trauma is the more complex form because it typically includes intentionality, power and control dynamics, attachment disruption and sadly is often repeated and so has cumulative effects. The complexity of trauma may have links to the scope of our confidence dips in that trauma that is multi-faceted and linked to numerous stimuli may then naturally cause confidence dips in each of those stimuli causing widespread reductions in self-efficacy.

Illness

Illness is another largely unexpected trigger for confidence dips and one that can also have immediate effects and a longer lasting impact. Illness is broadly defined as a disease or period of sickness affecting the body or mind and shares some similar characteristics to trauma in that it can be acute or chronic and vary in its magnitude. The impact of illness on confidence largely stems from the disruption it causes to the body's or mind's normal functioning. When we are ill, we often stop doing or reduce our involvement in activities like hobbies or civic engagement. Illness also has an isolating influence, cutting us of from social structures and contact with our family and community. The reductive and isolating impact of illness robs people of the vital experiential, observational and persuasory information that we know drives our self-efficacy appraisals. Our past successes get further away, our observations become out of date and feedback drifts to the back of our mind. This lack of information allows our efficacy to remain low and for our self-efficacy dips to be sustained. This is true for the business leader whose time away from the office removes them from the daily workings and decision making and for the sports person whose time away from the playing field stops them from practicing. Both of these can create increased levels of self-doubt about their ability to function effectively when they are well again because of a loss or decline in knowledge and skills. Sadly, the secondary impact of illness on self-efficacy is the effect it has on motivation and resilience which of course further reduces the individual's involvement in the very things that will get them out of the dip.

Before we move onto exploring strategies for escaping self-efficacy dips, it is worth highlighting the paradoxical impact that change, resistance, trauma and illness can have on confidence levels. The paradox lies in the fact that although these experiences are initially challenging and can cause dips in confidence, they can also hold a great deal of potential for confidence growth. Successfully managing and overcoming these triggers can lead to a renewed and even greater sense of efficacy in those areas and improved confidence about dealing with similar triggers in the future. This confidence in our ability to overcome adversity is something we call coping efficacy and is one of the big three that we will talk about in the final chapter of the book.

Escaping Self-Efficacy Dips

Escaping self-efficacy dips is essentially a combination of removing the stimuli that caused the dip and then finding ways to bring confidence levels back up to where they were or even beyond. Alongside many of the techniques for creating confidence that we looked at in previous chapters are some others also worth exploring.

Anticipation

As leaders we must be mindful of the ever-present possibility of self-efficacy dips in ourselves and those that we lead if we want to maximise effectiveness and the performance of our teams and organisation as a whole. Anticipation is key when it comes to confidence dips as we have a pretty good sense of when they are going to happen. We know that when we recruit new people, there will be a period of adjustment and typically a dip in their initial confidence. We know that when we promote someone a similar thing happens albeit hopefully at a lower magnitude. We know that if a team member has been away from work for a significant time due to illness or trauma then when they return, we will need to support them through the inevitable dip as they find their feet again. If we step outside of our leadership role for a second and put our parent, son, daughter or friend hat on then we also know that people typically go through natural confidence dips as they move through their lives. In chapter 3 we saw how the impact of peers can impact on teenage confidence and the arrival of marriage or parenthood can shake even the most secure adults. We also saw how we can often predict a dip in confidence as we move into the later stages of our lives and social circles get smaller and our level of activity and agency naturally decline. This ability to anticipate the arrival of confidence dips and a clear indication of their source allows leaders to proactively put in support in the form of the strategies we will cover next.

Acceptance

Accepting that dips in confidence are 'normal' and part of life can also be an important step in the way out of a self-efficacy dip. Acceptance is a recognised part of a wide variety of psychological models like motivational interviewing, the stages of healing as well as change management models like Kurt Lewin's freeze model and John Kotter's eight steps for change management. The reason why acceptance is such a powerful motivator for change is that it reduces resistance. Change or negative experiences often trigger a natural instinct to withdrawal, reduce engagement, limit resource allocation and protect ourselves through denial. Accepting that we are in a confidence dip enables us to loosen this resistance and take the first steps to growth.

Support and professional development

Our anticipation and acceptance of self-efficacy dips can soften the initial decrease and start the climb back up but that doesn't get us out of them and so we need to proactively seek out support and provide professional development for both us and those we lead. Any external support needs to be targeted at the source or sources of the dip, and most typically this is linked to a lack of understanding either in the task itself or the knowledge required to complete it successfully. Any lack of knowledge naturally points towards training of some type which may be formal in nature like a recognised course or qualification or may be achieved within the organisation through less formal means. We spoke earlier in the book about the power of coaching, mentoring, shadowing and secondments and all of these are great ways to increase clarity and get out of confidence dips.

Another technique that is often within the control of the team leader is the re-structuring of goals and targets, and it is often their poor initial design that caused the confidence dip in the first place. Goals that are overly ambitious, outside the individual's expertise or not accompanied by the required resources can create uncertainty, self-doubt and reduced confidence. The aim is not however to lower expectations or to artificially reduce the levels of challenge so that success is guaranteed and certainly not to remove any important individual or organisational outcomes. Tweaks to goals should be used to simply stop any further decline in confidence and start to initiate upward movement. The aim is to create a momentary increase in confidence which can then create a momentum that allows the individual to fully escape the dip that they are in. When we talk about changes to goals in this context, we are typically focusing on what additional resource or support the leader can provide to increase the chances of success. This support may come in the form of additional finance, technology, people or time, but the focus should remain on lifting people up to their goals rather than lowering the goal to them.

The PCEOS curve

Self-study is another great way to escape a confidence dip, but the individual pursuit of knowledge and understanding can be a rocky road and one that can cause additional confidence dips along the way. One strategy or set of strategies that pulls together the work we did earlier on cognitive dissonance and active processing is called the PCEOS curve and can help us out of dips caused by confusion. Cognitive dissonance as we saw earlier, is the mental discomfort or tension that individuals experience when they hold two or more contradictory beliefs at the same time. For many of us this can cause a level of stress or anxiety that then dents our confidence and can paralyse us against any further action. For me this typically happens when I have a difficult set of data that I need to analyse or a report or piece of academic writing that I need to understand. Based on David Dunning and Justin Kruger's work on how cognitive biases influence our self-perceptions, the PCEOS curve attempts to identify two key stages of cognitive dip escapism.

The first part of the curve basically describes a self-efficacy dip and suggests that often these are caused by our need to question or challenge the status quo and so the first milestone is called the 'point of critical evaluation'. It is at this point where our confidence starts to dip because of the dissonance we feel when we challenge our existing understanding and start to doubt our current knowledge. Our levels of clarity, or we could say confidence, then naturally dip until we reach our first proactive action, the 'Point of Organisation' (PO). There are a group of learning theories which collectively are called 'Constructivism' which believe that knowledge isn't passively received but rather consciously built through experiences, interactions and reflection. Key researchers in this area which we have met before include Jean Piaget, Lev Vygotsky, David Ausubel and Jerome Bruner.

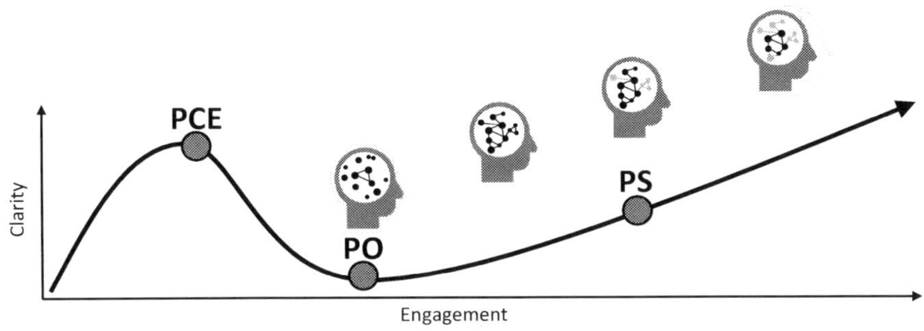

Figure 10.2 The PCEOS curve

A sub-branch of this field which is particularly important to the PCEOS curve is called 'cognitive constructivism', and as the name suggests focuses on the mental processes involved in knowledge building. The emphasis of cognitive constructivism is on how learners actively process information, make connections and build what we call 'mental models' through processes like attention, memory, reasoning and problem solving. Words like mental model or schema are often used to describe the ways that we organise information in our minds and the clarity, comprehensiveness, robustness and accuracy of these frameworks directly affect our levels of understanding.

The PO therefore suggests that our first step to increase clarity and confidence should be the active organisation or re-organisation of information and knowledge. This process often starts with breaking down or chunking the new information into smaller units that have distinct attributes and is essentially a categorisation activity. During this process, information needs to be compared and contrasted in order to challenge and then validate its position within a category. The next step is to mentally draw links between the chunks of information to start creating the web of knowledge that will form the mental model or schema. The hope is that at the end of this process, which by the way has no fixed time span is that we are starting to emerge from our confidence dip because of the increased clarity we have found through organisation.

The next step in the PCEOS curve is called the 'Point of Simplification' (PS) and is both an important and dangerous part of confidence and clarity creation. If you think about all the knowledge that you have ever collected both personally and professionally, then you can imagine that is pretty busy up there in your long-term memory. Naturally some of that information is more important and useful than other pieces and so we need to find a way to avoid the redundant and privilege the pertinent. Techniques like summarising, paraphrasing and prioritising can help us get to the core of a problem or a set of information and can be seen as a sort of 'cognitive pruning' where redundant or incorrect knowledge is removed. The use of analogy, metaphor and visual diagrams can also help simplify knowledge by helping to strengthen the organisation and tie it to prior knowledge which then offers a shortcut to comprehension. This is where we need to take caution though, as there is a danger that in our pursuit of ever-increasing levels of simplification, we lose the nuance of concepts and actually lessen our understanding. There is often a limit to how simple, complex systems and concepts can be made and so our goal should not be to lose knowledge from our mental models but just to bring it to the front of the line so to speak. Our goal should be to create a simplified gateway to the rest of our knowledge by describing the essence of the thing and its most important elements.

The Self-Efficacy Rollercoaster

At the beginning of the book and again at the start of this chapter, we spoke about the frequency at which most people experience self-efficacy dips and as life and careers progress, the graph probably looks more like a roller coaster ride rather than just an initial drop. To explore this in more detail, we are going to borrow the analogy of a sine wave which you might expect to find in the description of financial trends, audio tracks or electrical currents. When we overlay self-efficacy onto a typical sine wave, we start to see some similarities and the different measurements we might be able to make.

When we look closer at the constituent parts of a sine wave, we see some similarities in the way that we often describe changes in self-efficacy and in particular its dips over time. We often describe changes in our confidence in terms of their size which might have some parallels to the amplitude of a sine wave, and we also talk about how long our confidence dips or peaks last and so we may be able to draw in the concept of wavelength. Let's get started with those and then we can get into the fascinating area of wave interference.

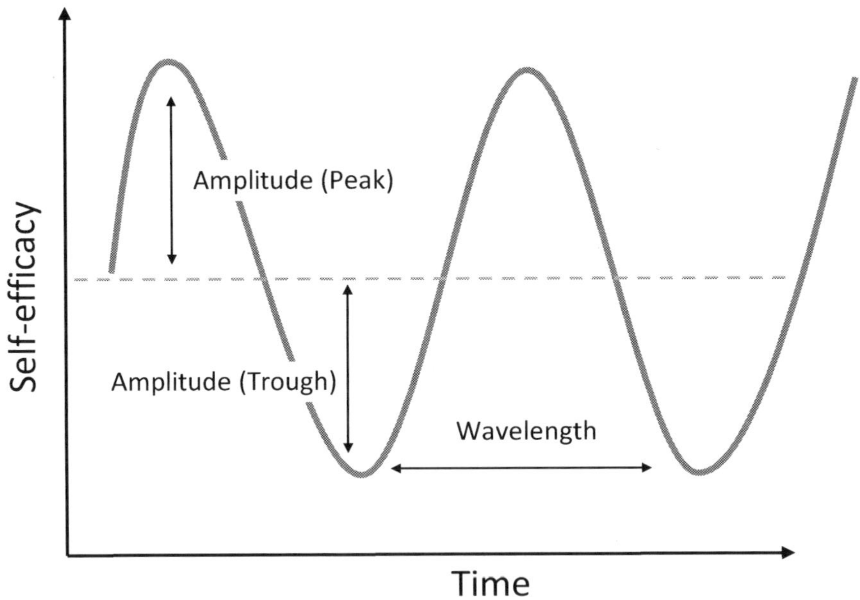

Figure 10.3 The self-efficacy sine wave

Amplitude

Firstly, let's look at amplitude and the idea that it could be used to describe the strength of the increase or decrease in self-efficacy that results from the re-appraisal process. To make the analogy work, we need to bend the science a little bit by pretending that there is a midline that represents the previous self-efficacy level and that the peak amplitude or increase can be a different value to the trough amplitude or dip below. The amplitude change would be dependent on a wide range of factors linking back to the efficacy information considerations we covered in chapter 3. The difficulty of the task would be important with success within the most difficult tasks providing the largest positive changes and failure in the simplest tasks causing the largest negative changes. Amplitude would also be affected by the level of support required to successfully complete the task with only minor peaks being felt if lots of support was used but increasing peak amplitude as the support faded. On the flip side, failure with lots of support would cause the largest dips in confidence or trough amplitude and only a minor negative impact if support was minimal or non-existent. The final consideration for amplitude would be the level of congruence between perceived self-efficacy pre-task and the resulting success level. Tasks where confidence levels were high but ended in failure are more destructive because of the jarring reality check and successful tasks where self-efficacy was low cause a more significant increase in the positive because of the unexpectedness of success.

Wavelength

If we look at the wavelength of the self-efficacy sine wave, we could use it to represent the stability of self-efficacy beliefs, but again we would need to bend the science to allow the wave to oscillate unpredictably unlike a traditional sine wave. With that in mind, certain task-specific confidences may be more stable than others and therefore be worth exploring why. Larger wavelengths and thus lower frequencies represent self-efficacy levels that are more stable and resistant to change, and of course smaller wavelengths highlight greater levels of variance and dynamism. In terms of what causes a change in wavelength, we need to first look at the task completion frequency as self-efficacy appraisals typically only happen prior to or during a task. If we use public speaking as an example and imagine that the most recent presentation was a success and efficacy levels were subsequently high, then the suggestion would be that the amplitude would remain high until the next presentation and efficacy appraisal. Unfortunately, time has an eroding impact on self-efficacy levels and so the amplitude would gradually decrease because of the increasing distance between current appraisal and the last past experience. Another factor affecting wavelength would be personality and in particular, levels of trait anxiety. High levels of neuroticism have been linked to a predisposition to negative thinking and self-doubt, and would maybe lead to greater frequencies of efficacy appraisal and therefore shorter wavelengths.

Interference

Before we stretch this analogy too far (which may have already happened), it's worth recognising that if each task has its own self-efficacy level and associated sine wave, then there are an almost infinite number of these waves overlapping each other at any one time. In physics, when sine waves overlap, a fascinating phenomenon called interference occurs and the resulting effect can be either constructive or destructive depending on how their peaks and troughs align. Constructive interference happens when the peaks or troughs of one wave coincide with those of another. When this happens, the waves reinforce each other, leading to a larger combined wave and an increase in amplitude. Destructive interference occurs when the peaks of one wave coincide with the troughs of another or vice versa. In this situation, the waves cancel each other out resulting in a smaller combined wave or even the complete elimination of the wave.

The point at which the waves overlap is important as it dictates how much of an influence, they have on each other and the degree of interference. For us this is interesting because as we know, self-efficacy beliefs are so granular and task specific that there is a very good chance they overlap. Confidence levels in leading meetings may very well overlap with confidence levels for running workshops or structured discussions. If confidence is high in these three things at the same time, then they may result in a combined increase in self-efficacy for the elements that link them together like organising people or public speaking. This would be a real-world example of constructive interference and a reason for leaders to maintain an awareness of confidence levels in similar tasks during self-efficacy appraisals. On the flip side when tasks that are similar have conflicting levels of self-efficacy, they can damage each other and result in a collectively lower overall sense of confidence. To use the same example as above, high self-efficacy for leading meetings but low confidence

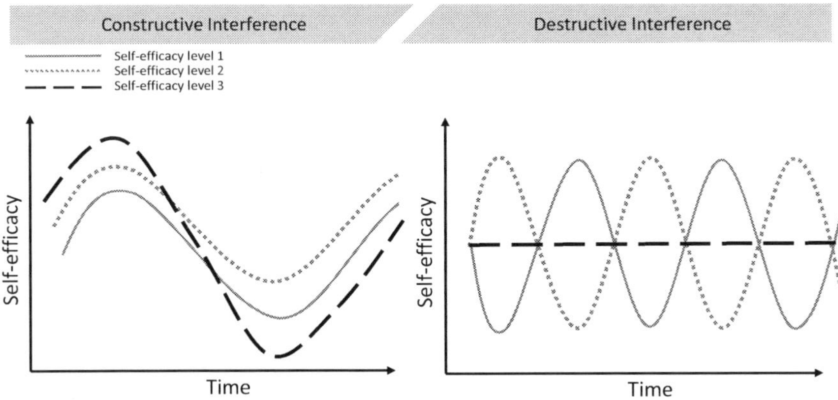

Figure 10.4 Self-efficacy interference

in delivering workshops may result in a moderate level of self-efficacy for organising people.

For those of us looking to leverage the benefits of constructive interference, we need to bring together similar tasks so that the requirements for excellence overlap, we need to successfully complete them as close in time as possible and we need to outperform our perceived pre-task levels of performance. The combination of these will give us the maximum boost in self-efficacy and get us out of any dips that we find ourselves in.

Self-Efficacy Spirals

Another self-efficacy phenomenon that leaders must understand if they are going to maximise their own confidence and that of those around them is the reciprocal and amplifying relationship between self-efficacy and performance. The concept of confidence spirals is not new, and the transformative power of belief has been explored throughout history. The Greek myth of Pygmalion has been famously connected to the power of belief through his desire for a statue to be real and then actually bringing it to life. More recently of course we have the potentially mis-attributed quote by the car manufacturer Henry Ford that "if you think you can or think you can't then you are probably right". For us we are interested in how the task performance (TP) / self-efficacy (SE) relationship can create its own amplifying effect and result in what we call a self-efficacy spiral.

If you have ever repeatedly chosen to complete a challenge or taken on increasingly difficult tasks, then you were probably within a positive self-efficacy spiral. Your performance in the first attempt was successful enough for you to have the confidence to do it again and even better to take on a more challenging task. The relationship between self-efficacy and performance is said to be a reciprocal one because they impact on each other and constantly interact in order to direct each other's characteristics. We see these relationships in nature all the time through the predator-prey connection that keeps populations stable, the fact that pollination benefits both the bee and the flower, and in symbiotic relationships between two organisms. In society we see reciprocation in trust and cooperation, giving and receiving, and teaching and learning. In business the relationships between customer and value, innovation and risk, and investment and return also highlight the interconnectedness of things. Self-efficacy spirals also experience a magnification affect where increases in one area

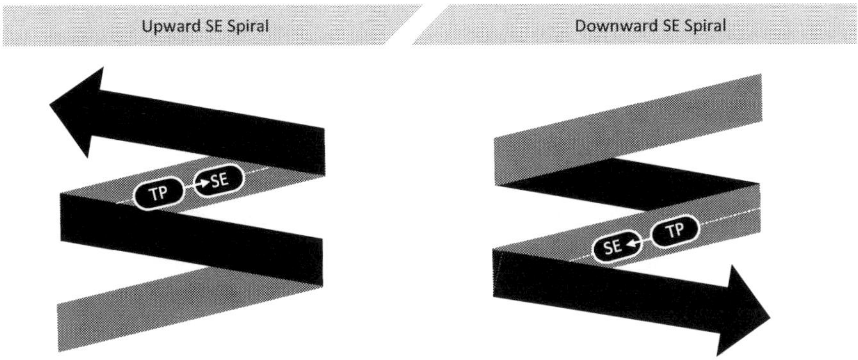

Figure 10.5 Self-efficacy spirals

contribute to increases in the other and vice versa. Put these two things together and we see the creation of upward and downward spirals of confidence that leaders, team members and everyone else are constantly riding.

The impact of these spirals is fairly clear in that upward spirals provide more of all of the positive outputs of optimal confidence that we have spoken about, and downward spirals do the opposite. When we are in an upward spiral, we feel more motivated, we put more effort into tasks, we are more resilient when things go wrong, and we attribute success more internally. These actions typically produce greater levels of performance which result in more success which then triggers further increases in confidence and the spiral continues. When we are spiralling downwards, our low confidence leads to reduced effort and resilience which can lead to sub-optimal performance and unmet goals which dents confidence and starts the next loop down.

Triggers

The fact that spirals occur over longer periods of time than dips and are developed cumulatively by positive or negative influences means that there is no single trigger for them. The basic premise as explained earlier is that being successful typically builds confidence which then improves future performance which further increases confidence, and the spiral is born. The same of course is true for downward spirals but in order to explore this in more detail we need to revisit our previous discussion around self-efficacy amplitude, wavelength and interference. In the last section we used the analogy of a sine wave to explain how multiple events or outcomes can come together to create constructive or destructive interference, and this is what essentially happens in efficacy spirals. Successfully completing a presentation to your team on Monday, followed by successfully chairing two workshops and meetings on Wednesday all come together to create an upward spiral which then fuels confidence for another big presentation to the whole company on Friday. Each successively positive outcome overlaps the other and creates constructive interference, amplifying the increases in self-efficacy and causing an upward spiral.

Downward spirals work in the same way but are also affected by the amount of time between task performances and so to borrow again from our analogy, the wavelength of their self-efficacy curve. Task-specific confidence gradually decreases the longer we don't perform the task as we have less and less recent, and therefore credible efficacy information, to draw on for our appraisals. In this sense, much like the Ebbinghaus forgetting curve suggests that forgetting starts almost immediately after learning, we could suggest that we start losing confidence immediately after being successful. The trick for all of us is to experience task-specific success so often that we are never allowing it to significantly decline.

A final consideration when we talk about triggers for self-efficacy spirals is how frequently their speed and direction can change and for many people it really does feel like they are on a roller coaster of daily confidence peaks and troughs. The amount of efficacy information that we receive during a day or week and the interplay between the positive and negative aspects of that information means that spirals are fragile and sensitive to rapid change. The confidence kick we get by successfully completing a task in the morning may be softened by some negative feedback by lunchtime and then re-ignited in the afternoon by an observation of a peer or a conversation with our coach. It is therefore important to recognise the triggering effect of every thought, feeling and action and to find ways to manage their impact on the direction of our self-efficacy spirals.

Management

Spiral management is the biggest issue for those who are unconsciously and passively approaching confidence creation. Many people have been spiralling downwards for a very long time without any recognition of how it's happening or how to stop it, and so in this section we will predominantly focus on how to manage negative self-efficacy spirals.

The first priority is to slow down or stop if possible the downward trajectory of the spiral and to reduce or remove the negativity that is fuelling it. This may mean making changes to relationships, social groups or management structures that are providing unhelpful feedback as well as quieting your negative inner voice. The most effective way to manage a downward spiral is to create some destructive interference by counteracting the negativity with positivity. We can initially do this ourselves by locating more positive efficacy information in our minds like past successes, positive feedback, encouraging observations and constructive mental visualisations. The presence of positive information linked to the same task challenges the negativity by providing a different perspective and a counterargument to any destructive thoughts or affirmations. We are typically slow to trust ourselves and so the slowing or stopping of negative spirals can be supercharged by working with a trusted peer, partner, parent or a coach or mentor.

Cognitive reframing is a great tool for slowing and redirecting downward spirals as it supports others to view their thoughts, feelings and actions from a different perspective. The process essentially involves the guided identification, exploration and rationalisation of beliefs. In terms of downward spirals we would be challenging the reasons for continued low self-efficacy and providing a positive viewpoint that aims to counteract the negativity. Shifting the individual's viewpoint away from standalone moments of failure or a lack of success and more towards the progress they have made can also be helpful. Recognising that although the immediate feeling is one of failure, the overall picture is one of success and development from a much earlier starting point. Catastrophising is a term used by psychologists and mental health professionals to describe a cognitive distortion where people fixate on the worst possible outcome and experience exaggerated levels of uncertainty, anxiety or stress. Catastrophising can be a major contributor to downward spirals and so needs to be managed again by challenging it. It is often useful to help people moderate the magnitude of the failures they feel they are experiencing and imagining alternative, more likely scenarios.

Zooming out to see the bigger picture is another common technique and links to the previous focus on long-term progress where failures sit amongst other successes. A range of strategies that bridge the gap between stopping the spiral and changing its direction are grouped together under the label of 'self-care' and involve deliberately taking action to preserve and improve physical, mental and emotional well-being. The benefits of self-care for self-efficacy spirals come largely from the associated reductions in stress and tension, the improvements to mood and energy levels, the strengthening of relationships and the boosts to self-esteem. The practice of self-care is a holistic, personalised one with different elements suiting different people

Table 10.1 Self-care strategies

Physical Self-Care	Getting enough sleep
	Exercising regularly
	Maintaining good hygiene
	Eating nutritious food
	Getting regular health checkups
Mental Self-Care	Practicing mindfulness or meditation
	Spending time in nature
	Setting boundaries
	Engaging in hobbies
	Learning new skills
Emotional Self-Care	Expressing your emotions in healthy ways
	Spending time with loved ones
	Practicing gratitude
	Seeking professional help when needed
Social Self-Care	Nurturing healthy relationships
	Saying no to excessive commitments
	Setting boundaries in relationships
Spiritual Self-Care	Finding meaning and purpose in life
	Connecting with like-minded people
	Connecting to something larger than yourself
	Connecting with your inner self

but at its core it should be regular, flexible and not be driven by indulgence in luxury or the abdication of responsibility.

Now that we have stopped and started to re-direct our downward spiral, it is time to look at ways to ensure it continues to move upwards. As we now know, momentum is both a friend and an enemy of self-efficacy spirals, but for now we are going to look at its positive side. Our first priority is to add some positive efficacy information back into the system so that we can make our most recent experiences positive ones. In chapter 6 we spoke about something called our 'locus of control' and how it describes where an individual believes the control of their lives lies and whether that is internal and external. A closely related concept is something called our 'circle of concern' which was popularised by Stephen Covey in his book *The 7 Habits of Highly Effective People* (Covey, 2013) and aligns strongly with the words of the serenity prayer and the Stoic philosophy. In the book Covey describes the presence of two circles but this has been extended by others to include a third and so we will explore all three. Essentially the idea is that we are immediately surrounded by our 'circle of control' which encompasses all of the things we have direct control over. This is sadly not much but does typically include our thoughts, beliefs, emotions, interpretations and judgements. Outside of this we have our 'circle of influence' which contains the elements of our lives which we have a degree of control over but usually indirectly. What goes in this circle largely depends on how optimistic or pessimistic we are and goes back to the position of our locus of control.

The third and often largest circle is called the 'circle of concern' and includes any situations, events, reactions, outcomes or phenomena that are not in our control. This circle contains everything in the past and everything we did not have a choice in, so includes things like where we were born, the illnesses we had and the heartbreak we endured. It also includes things in the present that we do not have direct control over or at least very little influence like government policy, the media, accidents, redundancies and the traffic on the way into work. In his brilliant book on the stoics, *A Guide to the Good Life,* William B. Irvine (2009), clarifies that it is not that we don't or shouldn't care about the things in our circle of concern, it is just that we need to moderate our belief that we can change them. In terms of self-efficacy spirals we need to refocus our energy and thinking away from our circle of concern and more towards the things we can influence and ideally what we can control. By doing this we can figuratively shrink our

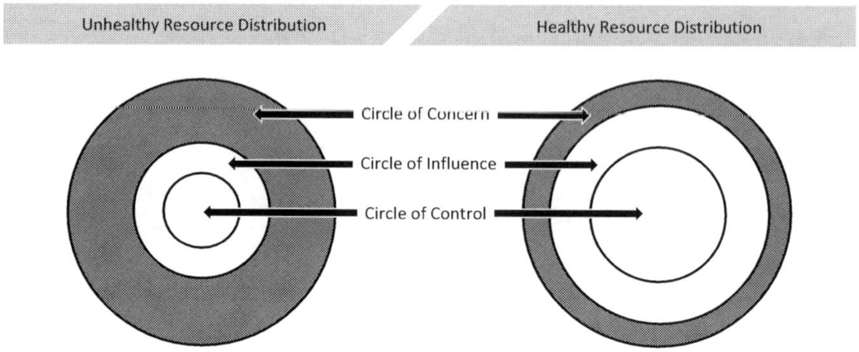

Figure 10.6 Circles of concern, influence, and control

circle of concern and then free up energy to spend more time in our circles of influence and control. This shift can slow and stop downward spirals by minimising anxiety about the uncontrollable and create an upward spiral by refocusing thinking and redirecting actions.

We have spoken about some of the other key strategies for upward self-efficacy spiral creation earlier in the book as they essentially mirror the established ways of creating confidence. Seeking out or providing support such as training, shadowing, secondments, coaching or mentoring can all help to provide the essential pieces of positive efficacy information and nudges in confidence that can stimulate and maintain upward spiral movement. Another strategy that can be really helpful for initiating that upward movement is the reappraisal and re-design of targets and goals. Overly ambitious or unrealistic goals can often be at the root of stalled spirals, as the expected outcome can feel out of reach and then causes a paralysis which stops any upward movement. For this reason, one goal-related strategy is to reduce the size and/or the complexity of any goals or targets that you are set or that you set for others. In an earlier chapter we spoke about the importance of goals being within the Goldilocks zone of difficulty and the difference between outcome goals that emphasise the final result of a task and performance goals that focus more on the ways to achieve the outcome. A shift to more performance related goals that include things like effort, resilience and more controllable elements can help with upward spiral movement because of the growth mindset they foster and the way they shift a person's perceptions of setbacks.

As we reach the end of this chapter, I want you to take a minute to think about your last confidence dip and whether you have any on the horizon because of upcoming change. Do you anticipate your staff having any dips in the next week or two, and what could you do to prepare them for that? Do you have systems in place to anticipate and take care of dips automatically? How good is the support and professional development on offer for people once they get promoted or join your team or organisation? How much of a rollercoaster of confidence peaks and troughs does the current way you do things create for yourself and other people, and how can you create constructive interference? How well do you know your staff and which ones are in upward or downward efficacy spirals? Finally, how can you find ways to re-direct your own and the resources of others away from the circle of concern and more within what can be influenced and controlled?

Nuggets

- Dips in confidence are an inevitable part of life.
- These dips typically occur because of change, novelty and resistance.
- Experts can feel like novices again because of changes to role and responsibilities.
- Over a career we can expect to experience a rollercoaster of self-efficacy changes.
- People need help to recover from a dip in their self-efficacy.
- Using our self-efficacy information can help reaffirm our previously high levels.
- Professional development in the form of coaching, mentoring and training can help.
- The redesign of goals, tasks or systems can also help us and others escape dips.
- Self-efficacy and performance are reciprocal in that they affect each other.
- Increases in confidence typically lead to increases in performance and so on.
- This creates upward and downward confidence spirals which amplify themselves.
- People need help escaping from downward spirals.
- The first step in spiral management is being aware that you are in one.
- Helping others to de-catastrophise their low self-efficacy can help re-direct spirals.

- The redesign of goals, tasks or systems can also help re-direct spirals.
- Increasing levels of support so success is more likely is a key action for leaders.

Next Steps

✓ Reflect on whether you are currently in a self-efficacy dip and why?
✓ Identify any potential dips that may occur within the next year.
✓ Reflect on whether you are currently spiralling up or down and to what extent.
✓ Complete a self-efficacy spiral and dip tracker for your team.

SE SPIRAL AND DIP TRACKER

WHAT

A self-efficacy spiral and dip tracker is a reflective activity for leaders who want to proactively support the self-efficacy development of their team members and peers. The activity enables leaders to identify those individuals who are showcasing symptoms of downward spirals and those who have upcoming changes that may trigger a confidence dip.

WHY

The busyness of the work environment, varying levels of psychological safety and support structures mean that some self-efficacy spirals, especially downward ones are hard to spot. Early identification of these is the key to exploring their origin, halting their decline and re-directing their movement. In a similar pre-emptive way, identifying possible dips due to changes in roles, responsibilities and team dynamics can soften their impact or avoid them altogether. Reducing the prevalence of both of these phenomena can help leaders become and remain confident by design.

HOW

Step 1 – Identify which members of your team are in upward or downward SE spirals and rank their initials from extreme upward spiral to extreme downward spiral.

Step 2 – Identify which members of your team are likely to experience a future SE dip because of planned change, promotion, challenge, etc.

Step 3 – Rank the team members' initials from top (soonest) to bottom based on how soon it is likely to occur and add a label to describe the reason.

References

Covey, S. R., & Collins, J. C. (2013). *The 7 habits of highly effective people: Powerful lessons in personal change*. New York, NY: Simon & Schuster.

Duhigg, C. (2012). *The power of habit: Why we do what we do in life and business*. New York: Random House.

Ferrari, J. (2010). *Still procrastinating: The no-regrets guide to getting it done*. Hoboken, NJ: John Wiley & Sons.

Harari, Y. N. (2014). *Sapiens: A brief history of humankind*. London: Harvill Secker.

Irvine, W. B. (2009). *A guide to the good life: The ancient art of stoic joy*. Oxford: Oxford University Press.

11

THE SWEET SPOT

Earlier in the book we established the positive impacts of self-efficacy, but it would be a mistake to assume the relationship is simple or linear and that more confidence equals more success. The concept of overconfidence is not new, and the term 'hubris' or excessive self-confidence is common in leadership studies and tales of fallen organisations. We probably all know individuals who present such a high level of confidence that they seem to have crossed the line into arrogance and all the negative trappings that come with it.

As we will see in this chapter, there is a fine line between optimal self-efficacy and what we will call 'hyper self-efficacy', and the real power belongs to those who can recognise their position on the confidence curve and manage it to maximise their effectiveness. Before we unpack what hyper self-efficacy is and how it affects us and those around us, let's look a bit deeper into the concept of moderation and sweet spots. History is littered with references to the dangers of overabundance, from the

DOI: 10.4324/9781003558934-12

inscription of 'nothing in excess' found in the temple of Apollo in Greece to the modern-day phrase "everything in moderation". In nature we see the pursuit of balance in things like ecosystems, life cycles and our own body's desire to maintain homeostasis of temperature, blood sugar and pH to create a stable internal environment. Within research circles there are a wide range of studies and findings that will be useful to explore and integrate into our plans for confidence creation.

In 1908, psychologists Robert Yerkes and John Dodson strangely found that rats responded best to a moderate level of electric shock when solving mazes and they created what we now know as the 'inverted U theory'. The theory suggests that arousal or excitement has an initially beneficial impact on performance, but as arousal increases it reaches an optimal band after which further increases actually decrease performance. A key takeaway from the theory is that much like self-efficacy, arousal theory is deeply personalised and dynamic. It can be affected by an individual's skill level with highly skilled performers typically requiring less arousal to reach peak performance and them having a wider range of optimal arousal. Personality has also been shown to have an impact with higher levels of introversion leading to lower optimal arousal levels and the desire for less stimulating environments. Trait anxiety as we have spoken about before is a stable tendency to experience worry and individuals with this type of personality typically perform better in a lower arousal zone. Finally, the task complexity also plays a part in where the sweet spot is with complex tasks requiring a lower arousal level because of the need to maintain focus and attention. The key takeaways from the inverted U theory which will help us with confidence creation are that the optimal arousal zone is different for each individual and situation, balance is key as both extremes hinder performance and arousal is something we need to find ways to manage if we want to maximise our effectiveness. Since being published the inverted U theory has been utilised in a variety of domains and linked to a wide range of sweet spot analogies.

Two key pieces of research into sweet spots that deserve additional attention and are now part of most personal, professional and organisational learning and development programmes are Csikszentmihalyi's 'Flow Theory' and Vygotsky's 'Zone of Proximal Development'.

Table 11.1 Common uses of the 'sweet spot' analogy

Domain	*Description*
Exercise	Excessive exercise can lead to injuries and burnout. A 2018 meta-analysis by Wen et al. found a U-shaped curve between physical activity and mortality, with moderate levels being most beneficial.
Freedom	Excessive freedom can lead to chaos and disregard for others' rights. A 2020 study by Diener et al. found a curvilinear relationship between freedom and well-being, suggesting that too much freedom can be overwhelming.
Challenge	Excessive challenge can lead to stress and self-doubt. A 2017 study by Csikszentmihalyi proposed the flow theory, where moderate challenges matched to skills create the most enjoyable and engaging experiences.
Support	Excessive support can limit our levels of learning. Lev Vygotsky proposed the 'Zone of Proximal Development' which highlighted the sweet spot where support is just right, and learning is maximised.
Information	Excessive information can lead to confusion and decision paralysis. A 2010 study by Kaplan and Simon highlighted the negative effects of information overload, emphasizing the need for curation and selective consumption.
Team size	Excessively large teams face co-ordination and communication issues. A 2016 study by McGrath suggested that a team size of 5–9 members is optimal for maximizing performance and satisfaction.
Innovation	Excessive innovation can lead to change without proper evaluation or implementation. A 2018 study by *MIT Sloan Management Review* found that companies with balanced innovation outperformed those focusing solely on radical innovation.

The Flow State

Mihaly Csikszentmihalyi was a Hungarian psychologist who became fascinated in the 1960s by artists who seemed to reach a dream-like state of extreme focus when they worked. His subsequent research focused on the balance of skill and challenge and how there was potentially a sweet spot between the two where focus, motivation and efficacy were at their maximum. His early work suggested that there were three key states people find themselves in during tasks; anxiety when challenge is higher than skill, boredom when skill is higher than challenge and the flow channel where skill and challenge increase at the same rate. Csikszentmihalyi noticed that people who seemed to be in the flow state experienced the following:

- An intense and focused level of concentration.
- The merging of action and awareness.
- A loss of reflective self-consciousness.
- A sense of personal control.
- A loss of time awareness.
- Increased intrinsic reward.

Figure 11.1 highlights how during his later work he recognised the complexity of the relationship between skill and challenge which resulted in collaboration with other researchers and the identification of various additional states that a person moves between as levels of challenge and skill fluctuate.

The relationship between flow state and self-efficacy is another example of a reciprocal relationship where one element directly impacts on the other. Typically, success is more likely within the flow state and so those who can enter it often, magnify their confidence through the accumulation of successful experiences. The other side of the relationship is little more complex as high self-efficacy levels can lead to the acceptance of higher levels of challenge, which for those experiencing boredom or apathy can help

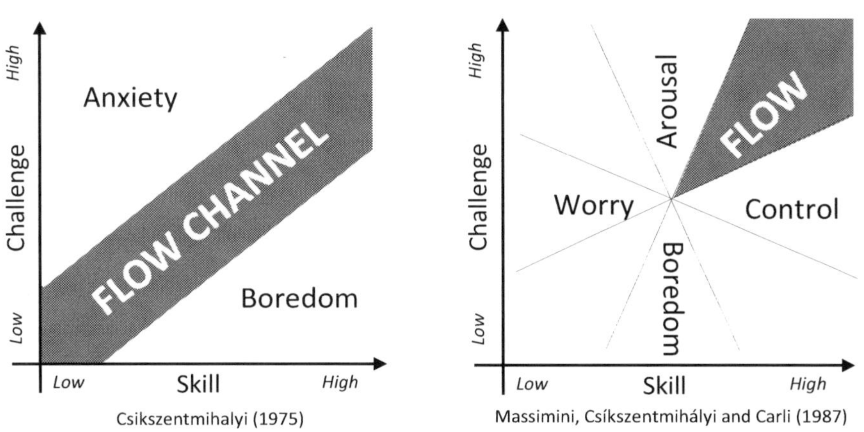

Figure 11.1 The flow state

them into the flow state and be beneficial. As we are starting to understand though, extreme levels of confidence may mean that the levels of accepted challenge outweigh actual skill and put people out of their depth and out of the flow state into anxiety and worry leading to reduced confidence.

The Zone of Proximal Development

Lev Vygotsky was another psychologist who made significant contributions to our understanding of cognitive functioning and development. Vygotsky was Russian and during the early 1900s became dissatisfied with the existing theories of learning which seemed to him to not adequately explain the impact of social interaction and culture on learning. He believed deeply that social interaction was central to learning and that we learn best through interaction with others and in particular those with more expertise. In terms of a sweet spot for learning and development, he suggested that the degree to which someone had external support affected how much progress they made. Activities that people can do on their own without any need for assistance sit at the bottom and provide limited development. At the other end of the scale, we find activities that are so difficult that people cannot complete them independently and so also lack opportunities for development.

In the middle we find a zone of difficulty where people can complete tasks with varying levels of support from external expertise. This is what he called the 'Zone of Proximal Development (ZPD)' and suggested it was the sweet spot of cognitive development. The model suggests that when we are close to the edge of our current abilities, we make the most progress which has clear links to confidence development, and something we will look at in the next chapter through what we will call self-efficacy circles. When we accomplish something that we thought was out of reach, we make strides in our confidence development which then fuels a further stretching of our ZPD and the cycle continues. As with the flow state, it is worth recognising the complexities of the ZPD and how it varies between people, the quality of support and its fluctuations over time.

Hyper Self-Efficacy

Let's switch our focus back to confidence creation and examine the concept of hyper self-efficacy in greater detail. Figure 11.2 shows a very similar

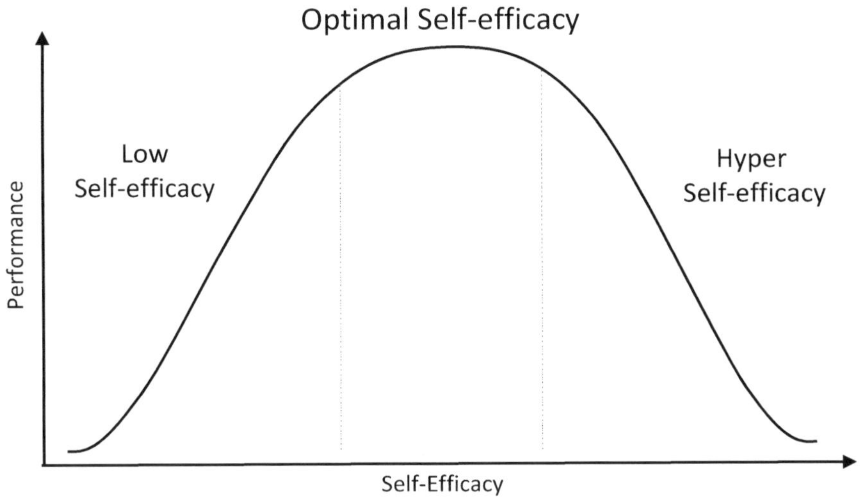

Figure 11.2 Hyper self-efficacy graph

cure to that of Yerkes and Dobson's 'inverted U' and highlights the personalised nature of the sweet spot. As with arousal, the suggestion is that the optimal level of self-efficacy is different in different people and situations, it is affected by a range of internal and external factors, and it is something worth managing. As we have covered that area in the earlier chapters, we are going to focus on the impact that hyper self-efficacy can have on planning and preparation, information processing, collaboration, workload management, relationships and psychological safety.

Planning and preparation

One of the first effects we see in leaders who are overconfident is a change to the way that they plan and prepare. In chapter 3 we saw that self-efficacy beliefs are closely linked to resource allocation and the level of effort and time people attach to tasks. Hyper self-efficacy often leads to a similar drop in effort during the preparation phase because of an overinflated likelihood of success and a belief that "it will all be fine" or that we can "wing it". This lack of preparation often leads to leaders failing to conduct thorough research about task demands, possible risks and suitable solutions and subsequently leads to blind spots and avoidable mistakes. A lack of preparation can also have a negative impact on the external resourcing decisions that leaders make in terms of the people, time and finance required to successfully complete a task, and we will see how that ripples out as we move through this chapter. Another element of the planning and preparation phase of a task which is negatively affected by hyper self-efficacy is risk management and was highlighted in chapter 6 when we explored the concept of a 'pre-mortem'. Extreme levels of confidence can lead to the often-unconscious ignorance of potential problems and an underestimation of the complexity involved in tasks. Overconfident leaders are less likely to develop contingency or backup plans as they dismiss the need for them, which then of course leaves them vulnerable if problems do arise and subject to reduced effectiveness and impact.

Information processing

Earlier in the book we made reference to something called the confirmation bias which describes our inclination to seek out and interpret information in a way that supports our existing beliefs. Hyper self-efficacy can have a negative impact on our information processing and send this bias into overdrive. When we are in a hyper confident state, we tend to selectively attend to information that confirms our thoughts and ignore anything that contradicts them, leading to faulty conclusions and poor diagnosis. We can also suffer from something called memory distortion when confidence is high which leads to us embellishing past successes, downplaying previous failures and twisting task and situation details to fit our perspective. Other issues linked to information processing include interpretation bias where we make sense of things through a pre-convinced lens and source credibility bias where we preference information if that matches our beliefs even if it is from unreliable sources. As we will see later in the chapter, an awareness of the cognitive traps associated with hyper self-efficacy is the first step in managing them.

Collaboration

Collaboration is key to most organisational and even individual effectiveness due to the inherent levels of interdependence within most tasks. It is rare that working with others does not make things easier or more successful and yet hyper self-efficacy often leads to a reduction in collaboration. Overconfident leaders often believe that they have the resources and expertise to carry the success of tasks on their own and that to accept support from others is a sign of weakness. They tend to resist inviting others into projects or delegating responsibility and can even be dismissive of suggestions and constructive criticism from others. If leaders are involved in shared tasks, overconfidence can mean that they also demonstrate a lack of collaboration through their dominance of discussions and their tendency to make decisions unilaterally. Leaders or followers that are part of teams but not in overall responsibility can find that their overconfidence negatively narrows their focus onto their contribution, and they lose sight of shared goals and objectives. This narrowing and lack of alignment can lead to miscommunication, missed deadlines and a lack of team cohesiveness.

Workload management

Doing it alone is not only inefficient and isolating but it also adds a great deal of additional work and pressure to individuals. Leaders and team members who have extreme levels of confidence also often suffer from workload management issues. In the first instance, unrealistic expectations about our capacity for workload can lead to an overcommitment to the number of tasks that we accept and the deadlines that we agree to. This often leads to an overallocation of personal resources which creates a false economy and leads to increases in stress and illness and decreased effectiveness and our ability to maintain deadlines. Two other lenses for workload management are how overconfidence affects our work as a team member and how our overconfidence of others can have negative consequences. As we highlighted above, hyper self-efficacy is not just a problem when we are leading tasks but also when we are working interdependently, and overconfident people often absorb responsibilities from others, blurring the lines of accountability because they feel that progress is too slow or that they could do a better job. This conflation of tasks naturally has a negative impact on their own workload and either means that all tasks get done to a mediocre standard or some tasks take priority and deadlines get missed. A lack of belief in others or at least a perception of superiority is a common element of overconfidence and can affect levels of trust, delegation and collaboration. This as we will see in this next section can have a significantly detrimental impact on a leader or follower's relationships within their teams and organisation.

Relationships

So far, we have mainly spoken about the organisational effects of hyper self-efficacy, but potential a more invisible and destructive impact is the interpersonal one. The differences in preparation, information processing, collaboration and time management all at some point affect other people, and when they result in negative consequences, they subsequently have a negative impact on relationships. Relationships are often like organisational culture in that every action has an impact and therefore subtle changes are often happening at all times in every interaction. In his book *The 7 Habits of Highly Effective People* (Covey, 2013), Stephen Covey uses the metaphor of an emotional bank account to explain how relationships are built and eroded. He suggests that we have an account for every relationship in our lives and set these up the instant that we meet someone new. From that point on, every interaction is a mixture of deposits and withdrawals affecting the overall level of credit in the account. Deposits can be as small as a smile or remembering someone's name or more substantial like keeping a commitment, being empathetic or helping someone reach a goal. Withdrawals of course are the opposite and include things like being dishonest or deceitful, criticism, negativity or controlling behaviour. The goal is therefore to make regular, sincere deposits and to repair any withdrawals as quickly as possible if we want to build strong relationships. Many of the negative outputs of hyper self-efficacy, especially the interpersonal ones, could be seen as withdrawals from our emotional bank accounts and so it is definitely something for members of teams to be aware of and actively manage.

Psychological safety

Another interpersonal impact of overconfidence and one that we spoke about in chapter 4 is the level of psychological safety within relationships and groups, and describes how safe people feel being vulnerable. Overconfident people by design believe strongly in their knowledge, abilities and probably most fundamentally, the strength of their beliefs. When they are asked for their opinion they give it with gusto, and when required to present an idea or proposal they do it without hesitation. This level of assurance can have the opposite impact on the contributions of others and especially if they are further back on the hyper self-efficacy graph. Extreme confidence from others often causes us to doubt our own thoughts and feelings and question the validity of our beliefs. This is further magnified when the overconfident person is a superior for whom challenging would be uncomfortable and brave with a normal level of confidence let alone when it is hyper. This is why researchers of psychological safety like Amy Edmondson recommend leaders model vulnerability and include a level of tentativeness when presenting their ideas so that there is space for others to contribute. Simon Sinek, the author of *Leaders Eat Last*, talks about leaders being the last to speak so that others can feel heard and valued, in turn fostering a more collaborative and engaged working environment.

Before we move onto strategies for hyper self-efficacy management, it is worth continuing to return to the delicate and personalised nature of task specific confidence. Although the previous sections have espoused the negative sides of extreme confidence, we must remember that the sweet spot of confidence sits within a zone which is different between people, different for the same person between tasks, and also changes over time as self-efficacy develops. For most of the time, high levels of confidence are positive and even levels just beyond the sweet spot are not significantly destructive. As we said at the start of the chapter, 'moderation is key' and as leaders it's our responsibility to manage how close we and others are to that confidence sweet spot.

Hyper Self-Efficacy Management

So, now that we have established the dangers of hyper self-efficacy, let's look at what strategies we can use to find both our own confidence sweet spot and help others find theirs. Private victories should precede public ones and so firstly we will explore how we can stop ourselves slipping into overconfidence. If we think back to chapter 3 and the introduction of cognitive appraisals where we consciously and sometimes unconsciously use stored information to make predictions about our chances of success, we find our first strategy.

Rational tempering

Rational tempering is a collection of practices that can be used to tame overconfidence by acknowledging and adjusting potentially inflated beliefs based on a sober and objective assessment of evidence and facts. It has its roots in the avoidance of cognitive bias and so flows from work as far back as Plato and his emphasis on critical thinking through to Karl Popper's exploration of 'falsifiability' and Daniel Kahneman's 'prospect theory'. In practice, leaders can use rational tempering to moderate the information that they are using during their self-efficacy appraisals to ensure that they don't start with inflated perspectives and overconfidence. Popper was a prominent philosopher in the 1930s and challenged the traditional view of science as a process of verification through repeated confirmation. He suggested instead that the focus should be on disproving things if we want to strengthen our belief in them and not by trying to relentlessly prove them. For us this would involve an individual seeking out evidence to disprove their self-efficacy beliefs rather than finding information to support them. If someone believes strongly that they will succeed and there is no or little evidence to falsify that claim, then the belief can stand. If they can find past experiences, observations or feedback that challenges their view, then they may need to lower their self-efficacy appraisal which may then pull them back from a state of hyper self-efficacy.

Daniel Kahneman's work on prospect theory (1979) may also provide a useful strategy for tempering our self-efficacy beliefs but in the other direction. As we spoke about at the start of the chapter, there is a zone of optimal self-efficacy (ZOSE) which people need to manoeuvre themselves into if they want to maximise their effectiveness. Self-efficacy levels below that sweet spot also have negative effects on performance and therefore require management. One of the key features of prospect theory is loss aversion and the idea that people are typically more sensitive to losses than gains of the same magnitude. This would suggest that we are more likely to recall unsuccessful past experiences and negative feedback during confidence appraisals which would then bias the resulting self-efficacy level. The aversion to loss may lead individuals to undervalue their confidence in order to protect themselves and thus stop them from reaching their self-efficacy sweet spot. Prospect theory also highlights the influence of the 'framing effect' where we are subject to a cognitive bias in the way that we present information to ourselves and others. Subtle changes to the way that we perceive or remember information can affect the choices we make and the way we feel about things. In our example an individual suffering from the framing effect may have low or hyper self-efficacy because of the way that they are remembering past experiences, observations or feedback. They might temper past losses by framing them as unjust or due to external forces or temper positive feedback because of their relationship with the sender or their general positivity.

Interrogative self-talk

Another key strategy for moderating confidence during efficacy appraisals is interrogative self-talk which we spoke about in chapter 5. As you will remember interrogative self-talk requires the individual to ask questions about whether they can complete a task successfully or not, and is in contrast to declarative self-talk where statements of potential are made. Interrogative self-talk is useful for managing hyper self-efficacy because it forces the user to pause and think about what corroborating or conflicting information they have that can support or challenge their initial confidence projections. As with rational tempering, it offers an opportunity to fine tune our confidence levels ahead of an activity so that we don't start off in an overconfident state.

Reflective practice

If rational tempering is a strategy to use during confidence appraisals and typically prior to task acceptance, then we also need to think about ways in which we can tweak our efficacy levels during and after tasks in order to remain in the ZOSE. A key process that most of us do without conscious thought but would be significantly improved by systematically approaching it is personal reflection. Reflection is defined as serious thought or consideration, and when used systematically for personal or professional development is often called reflective learning or reflective practice. Reflective practice has gained its popularity amongst individuals and professional development providers due to the significant part it plays in the learning process and the range of benefits it provides. Reflecting on one's own practice provides an immediate impact during learning or performance and longer term on things such as responding to challenges, decision making, managing emotions, conducting productive relationships and coping with stress (CIPD, 2016). Reflective practice is important to personal and professional development as it deepens understanding by enabling individuals to make more sense of their experiences, what they learned, why they learnt it and how that learning took place. Through reflection, individuals can integrate, internalise and personalise their learning as well as use alternative perspectives to challenge established assumptions and patterns of behaviour. Reflective practice is also seen as an important component of double loop learning which is particularly effective in situations requiring creative thinking and innovation.

A key voice in this space was American philosopher and professor Donald Schön who in his book *The Reflective Practitioner: How Professionals Think in Action* (Schön, 1983) laid the foundations for what would become the Schön model of reflective practice. In the model he suggested that to maximise the impact of reflection we need to do it both 'in action' and 'on action'. In-action reflection, as the name suggests, happens during tasks and requires the individual to make sense of a situation as it unfolds, drawing on tacit knowledge and past experiences to improvise and adapt. Schön felt that people should have a 'dialogue' with the situation by experimenting with different actions, observing and evaluating their outcome and then making micro-adjustments to improve performance. In our example of hyper self-efficacy, this would involve the individual constantly taking the temperature of how their current confidence level is affecting their performance and adjusting it accordingly to stay within the optimal zone.

The second part of Schön's model, on-action reflection, describes the reflection that takes place after an event which is often more deliberate, retrospective and recorded. In practice it firstly involves the individual recalling the experience and focusing specifically on key moments and decisions. Then they critically examine their choices and actions to find causal links and uncover alternative approaches. The final step is to formulate new levels of understanding by identifying what learning has occurred and how future practice can be improved. In our example it would involve reflecting on our proximity to the confidence sweet spot and how that affected our choices and actions. We would then examine the reasons for that self-efficacy level and what changes could be made in the future to nudge us closer to optimal self-efficacy.

Goal setting

Now that we have saved ourselves from the abyss of hyper self-efficacy, let's look at some strategies we can use with those that we lead and the others around us. If we again return to the pre-acceptance phase of a task where confidence appraisals must deliberately take place, we find ourselves supporting others to set effective goals. Choosing the wrong destination in the form of an overly ambitious and unachievable goal is often the first sign of overconfidence and the first step to a series of negative consequences. In chapter 7 we spoke about the distinction between outcome and performance goals and how confidence is more protected and developed through performance goals because of their increased controllability. When we look at strategies for effective goal setting, we find two prominent approaches that also emphasise different elements of performance.

Edwin Locke, an organisational psychologist, and Gary Latham, a professor of management, are seen as two of the most influential figures in the field of goal setting. In their 1990 book *A Theory of Goal Setting and Task Performance*, they laid the groundwork for what we know today as goal setting theory. They outlined five principles of effective goals and later went on to introduce the well-known SMART acronym for goal setting which we will unpack later. Locke and Latham suggested that first of all, effective goals need to have direction and focus, and clearly define what it is that the individual wants to achieve. Like a map with no destination, vague goals leave us unsure about where to direct our efforts and whether we are on the right track. The second principle was to be challenging, as goals that are too easy often lead to complacency and a lack of motivation, and effective goals should stretch us beyond our comfort zone. They suggested that goal complexity should be matched to the task complexity with a focus on reducing confusion and increasing engagement by keeping goals as simple as possible. Locke and Latham highlighted commitment as the fourth principle by highlighting the need to personally invest in and be accountable for our goals if we want to succeed in them and how individuals should be actively involved in setting them. The final principle of goal theory was feedback with the idea that for goals to be accomplished, there needs to be regular tracking of progress and ongoing dialogue around effectiveness and possible improvements.

So now, let's look at two specific models of effective goal setting and the characteristics that they share and those that set them apart from each other. Locke and Latham's SMART acronym (Specific, Measurable, Achievable, Relevant, Time-bound) is probably one of the most well recognised and applied formats and has been adapted over time to incorporate different and additional elements. In its original form, the S stands for 'specific' as it is important that individuals clearly define what it is they want to achieve. This means going deeper than goals like "get better at delegation" into more detailed goals where the parameters are more explicit like "improve the frequency of delegation to middle managers" or "increase the delegation of administration tasks". The M stands for 'measurable' as we need to objectively know when we have achieved the goal. This means including a metric in its description and is often linked to things like volume, time and percentages. Tweaking our previous goals, we would end up with something like "delegate all tier three tasks to middle managers" or "increase the delegation of administration tasks by 50%". The A in the acronym stands for 'achievable' as we need to ensure that if we want to secure success and protect confidence then goals must be challenging but realistic. This means being honest with ourselves and others about their capabilities and the resources available. In our examples we may need to soften the level of challenge in our goals to change to "delegate all tier two tasks to middle managers" and "increase the delegation of administration tasks by 30%". Now we move onto the R and how effective goals must be 'relevant' and align to the larger vision, values and goals of the individuals, group or organisation. Highly relevant goals are more likely to motivate, attract others for collaboration and secure resources like time and finance. In our example it turns out that the organisation is currently focusing on the development of middle managers and so there is particular relevance to our "delegate all tier two tasks to middle managers" goal. The final piece of the puzzle is the T which stands for 'time-bound' and signifies the importance of including deadlines within goals. Adding a time element can help create a sense of urgency, enable progress tracking and help individuals stay focused. Our complete SMART goal would then look something like "delegate all tier two tasks to middle managers by the end of project cycle 1".

Another goal setting format which has gained popularity because of its focus on continuous action and progress rather than just the destination is called PACT (Purpose, Actions, Continuous, Trackable). PACT is largely attributed to the entrepreneur and cognitive neuroscientist, Anne-Laure Le Cunff. Users of the technique praise its flexibility and adaptability, its focus on effort and progress rather than outcomes, and its encouragement of experimentation and creativity. In terms of self-efficacy, it seems like a great option as it may generate more sustained success than the traditional SMART system. Let's take a closer look.

Making a PACT with yourself starts with selecting something that is deeply meaningful to you and so has a strong 'purpose'. Purposeful PACT goals are typically longer-term aspirations, and their personal relevance is the source of their motivational power. One of my PACT goals is to become fluent in Spanish and we will unpack its components as we go. PACT goals must be 'actionable' in that they contain easily definable and ideally controllable outputs. The aim is that these actions are reachable and continuously achievable so that momentum can be maintained and confidence protected. This is the first difference from the SMART system, and the creation of these micro-actions may be one of its core benefits. The key action for my Spanish goal is to complete 20 minutes of online practice every day. PACT goals need to be stretched over enough time that they are flexible and can be 'continuously' reviewed and refined. The aim is to avoid the paralysis that often comes with poorly designed or overly ambitious goals and to just get started, knowing that tweaks can be made along the way. In my example, I have no idea how long it is going to take me to become fluent and so putting a timeline on it would probably be de-motivating. When we make a PACT with ourselves, we need to make sure that we feel a deep sense of responsibility and accountability if we are going to be successful. The 'T' in PACT stands for 'trackable' and points to the need to be able to objectively track the progress of the goal at any time. Typically, PACT goals have actions built into them that are either done or not done, and so monitoring is reliable and regular and any course corrections that are needed can be implemented as soon as possible. My goal makes this simple because there is no hiding or ambiguity with my 20 minutes of practice every day, it has either been done or not done and "no te preocupes, hice mi práctica esta mañana".

Decision-making frameworks

A common thread of strategies for managing overconfidence in others is the presence of a challenging voice or a method for facilitating further appraisal and even justification of self-efficacy levels. The use of what we call decision-making frameworks can be traced back to the early Greek thinkers like Socrates and Aristotle who championed critical thinking, and through military leaders in the great wars. Fast forward to more modern times and although we still value our gut instinct, more and more organisations, teams and individuals are using systematic processes and tools to strengthen their decision making and moderate their confidence. One of those key strategies is called a 'theory of change' and its origin can be traced back to a series of meetings organised by the social psychologist Carol Weiss called the Aspen Institute Roundtable. The meetings brought together a diverse set of stakeholders with interest in community change and aimed to explore ways to improve the evaluative practices of large-scale community initiatives. Weiss and the group developed the 'Aspen principles' which suggested that effective change must focus on understanding underlying theories of change, use multiple methods for data collection and analysis, build partnerships with communities and stakeholders, and promote learning and knowledge sharing.

The popularity of that early work and Weiss's article "Nothing as practical as good theory" (1995) have led to a proliferation in the use and modification of the process and resulted a variety of different approaches and some misunderstood interplay with change management theory. So, what is a theory of change? A theory of change (TOC) is essentially a comprehensive description and/or illustration of how and why a desired change is expected to happen. It focuses particularly on describing what a program or change initiative does (its activities or interventions) and how these lead to desired goals being achieved. Theories of change are often in the form of a descriptive paragraph and/or a visual diagram, and a typical conversation focusing on a TOC may sound like…

(Staff Member 1) "I want to improve A and so I think we need to do B and C."

(Staff Member 2) "That sounds exciting. Talk me through your theory of change?"

The process of creating a theory of change is as beneficial as the product itself as it enables the creators to:

- Locate the different stages of the change process.
- Ensure that they logically fit and flow together.
- Highlight possible roadblocks.
- Anticipate what support will be required.
- Identify key evaluation milestones.

and creates:

- A clear and testable hypothesis about how change will occur.
- A visual representation of the change how it is expected to come about.
- A blueprint for evaluation with measurable indicators of success.
- An agreement among stakeholders about what defines success and how to get there.
- A powerful communication tool to capture the complexity of an initiative.

The first step in creating a TOC is to identify the outcomes of the change process and what exactly are the A+B+C+D =. These are sometimes called results or outputs but essentially ask the question; what are you trying to achieve and what are the steps in getting there? Outcomes should be well defined, measurable and plausible. The next step in this stage is to draw the links between the outcomes, highlighting the causal or impact pathways. These will not always create a linear image as some outcomes will create multiple pathways to multiple outcomes. It is also important to critically reflect on the evidence linking two outcomes. How likely is it that A will lead to B? The final step in this stage is to take a step back and ensure that the outcomes are in the right order, that none are missing and that the pathways create the correct links.

The second stage in the process is to identify the interventions that will be put in place to successfully link outcomes together. These are also called activities and essentially ask the question; what is going to happen in order to move the change from A to B to C, etc. Interventions should

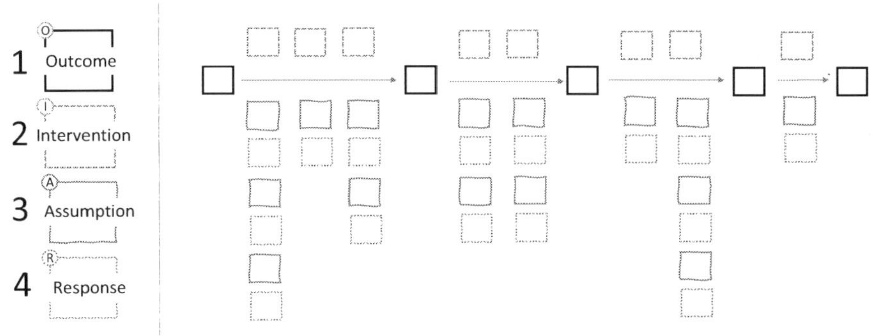

Figure 11.3 Theory of change components and diagram

be realistic, credible and sustainable and it is important to recognise that outcomes may require multiple interventions. Stage three of the TOC design is often the most overlooked during conversations about change. This stage requires the creator to reflect on what assumptions they have made between outcomes and attached to interventions. A common set of assumptions within professional development would be that the creation of an event will ensure attendance (assumption), that attendees will engage once they attend (assumption) and finally that learners will apply their new knowledge and skills after training (assumption). This stage essentially tries to seek out what might hinder movement between TOC outcomes. The assumption stage is the most important stage for confidence moderation as it is where the highest levels of challenge are and where overconfidence is most likely to hide. Hyper self-efficacy can easily lead to unconscious assumptions about our own ability and that of others as well as the availability of resources leading to unrealistic levels of assurance.

The fourth stage is to identify the set of possible responses that you could use to address each assumption and increase the likelihood of A leading to B. Using the previous professional development example, we would need strategies for ensuring attendance at the event, maximising learner engagement and systems to ensure that the learning made it back to the workplace. As with interventions, responses need to be realistic, credible and sustainable. At this point the initial theory of change is in place and described through a descriptive paragraph and often a visual diagram as we spoke about earlier. The final stage is to briefly evaluate the strength of the theory by asking the following questions:

- Are all the elements present and in the right place?
- Are the causal links, accurate?
- Have all the assumptions been identified?
- Have possible responses been thoroughly explored?

Further analysis of the theory of change can be completed by additional stakeholders and use a more robust set of questions as can be seen in the TOC activity sheet.

A more simple but equally impactful decision-making framework has its roots in Japanese car manufacturing and the work of Sakichi Toyoda and Taiichi Ohno of Toyota. What we now know as the 'five whys' technique has a probable origin in Toyota's core principle of asking 'why' to get to the root cause of a problem, situation or inefficiency. Toyoda and his team found that repeatedly asking 'why' helped identify and resolve quality issues on the manufacturing floor and drove continuous improvement. Ohno helped ingrain the practice into the organisation by also using it as a training tool to develop critical thinking and problem-solving skills in its employees. Beyond Toyota the technique continues to be used in quality management frameworks like 'Six Sigma', project management, product development, healthcare and education.

The technique is simple in design and only slightly more complicated in practice. It consists of a number, typically five or above, iterative why questions asked repeatedly to better understand cause and effect relationships. The first step is to clearly identify the problem that requires exploration and then ask the first why: "Why is this problem happening?" The answer to this question should be written down and then followed by another related why question. This process repeats itself until an agreed level of understanding about the root cause of the problem has been reached and the answers are no longer additional symptoms.

Despite its apparent simplicity, users of the five whys techniques are keen to highlight the skill involved in asking good questions, the need to be patient about finding the cause and the comfort with complexity that is required on both parties. Those wishing to utilise the technique should ensure that the process remains focused on facts and evidence rather than assumptions and opinions, that people don't get drawn away from why and into 'what' questions and to not see the number five as a fixed end point. Those wishing to supercharge their five whys can extend it to include 'how' questions and use visual frameworks such as the Ishikawa fishbone diagram, the CT tree, and the Pareto chart.

Rumbling

All the above techniques involve the guided reframing of confidence levels and require a great deal of psychological safety and radical or compassionate candour which we spoke about in chapter 7. Another key contributor to this space is Brené Brown whose "Be clear to be kind" mantra is central to her suggestion that we need braver leaders and more courageous cultures. Like Kim Scott, Brown believes that leaders often avoid tough conversations

Table 11.2 Five whys example

Problem	*Customer satisfaction scores are consistently below target*
Why?	We are receiving complaints about long wait times for customer service.
Why?	We don't have enough customer service staff.
Why?	We are experiencing high staff turnover and difficulty recruiting.
Why?	Our salary and benefits packages are not competitive.
Why?	We are trying to save costs.
Root Cause	A focus on saving costs has led to low staff recruitment and retention.

and uncomfortable feedback because of fear or a lack of skill or courage. In our situation this plays out in leaders allowing others to continue with overinflated and unevidenced hyper self-efficacy for fear of upsetting them. What we need to do is use a technique which Brown calls a 'rumble' where both parties show up for a hard conversation and work with each other to make progress. The success of this techniques lies partly in the shared understanding about the word 'rumble' and its associated characteristics.

To rumble effectively, people need to remove their armour and be open to being vulnerable. They need to put aside any perfectionism, forget about being right, stop hustling for their own worth and avoid using any inherent power dynamics. There should be an atmosphere of curiosity where all participants are committed to understanding first before being understood. Rumbles are most successful when people are genuinely curious about the current state of the situation, other people's perceptions and the wealth of creative solutions available. Rumbles rarely end in solutions, so it is important to get comfortable with complexity and enter into them with that mindset. Most problems are complicated and multi-causal so the best we can hope for is forward motion towards a solution. Finally, people need to be brave during confidence curation conversations, rumbles are characterised by the wealth of voices in the conversation and the vulnerability that those people show during their contributions. Leaders need to create the safe space for people to be brave about their ideas and points of view if they are going to reach useful insights into the source and impact of hyper self-efficacy.

As we reach the end of this chapter, I want you to take a minute to think about your own levels of confidence and how close you are to optimal self-efficacy. Do you recognise any of the symptoms of hyper self-efficacy and would others describe you as overconfident in some areas? Have you got any team members who need to pull back a bit in order to reach their optimal level and how can you help them do that? How can you use the goal setting and decision-making processes to moderate confidence and ensure that it remains a positive force in the workplace? Finally, how can you create enough psychological safety in your relationships, teams and organisation to be able to tell people that they need to reign it in, and who would you tell first?

Nuggets

- More self-efficacy is not always better.
- Extreme or hyper self-efficacy can cause a range of negative consequences.
- Overconfident people tend to reduce their levels of planning and preparation.
- They tend to collaborate less when they have high levels of confidence.
- They tend to reduce or do less effective risk management.
- People with hyper self-efficacy tend to make quicker decisions.
- They tend to take on more and more and their workload management suffers.
- This typically leads to decreases in the quality of their time management.
- A combination of these effects can cause damage to relationships.
- It can reduce psychological safety as others are then afraid to show weakness.
- We should all be conscious of and actively manage our self-efficacy levels.
- Being objective about appraisals and seeking honesty feedback can help.
- Challenging and replacing negative thinking can improve self-efficacy balance.

Next Steps

✓ Reflect on your levels of hyper self-efficacy by completing an HSE (hyper self-efficacy) graph.

✓ Get your colleagues to also complete an HSE graph and compare the results.

HYPER SELF-EFFICACY GRAPH

WHAT

Completing a hyper self-efficacy graph is an activity which enables leaders to reflect on the possible presence of under and overconfidence within their performance and specifically which tasks this relates to.

WHY

Hyper self-efficacy is often more hidden and unconscious than low confidence and because of this requires a deeper level of reflection and purposeful exploration. Once uncovered and acknowledged, leaders can take steps to moderate self-efficacy levels and avoid the possible reductions in planning, collaboration, workload management, relationships and psychological safety. Continuously moderating SE levels so that they remain optimal is one of the keys to being confidence by design.

HOW

Step 1 – Identify the elements of your role which have lower than optimal levels of self-efficacy and add them to the left section of the graph.

Step 2 – Identify the elements of your role which have optimal levels of self-efficacy and add them to the middle section of the graph.

Step 3 – Identify the elements of your role which may be overconfident in and add them to the right section of the graph.

References

Covey, S. R., & Collins, J. C. (2013). *The 7 habits of highly effective people: Powerful lessons in personal change*. 25th anniversary edition. New York, NY: Simon & Schuster.

Csikszentmihalyi, M. (2017). *Flow: The psychology of optimal experience*. London: Hachette UK.

Diener, E., Helliwell, J. F., & Lucas, R. E. (2020). Freedom and subjective well-being: International evidence. *International Journal of Wellbeing*, 10(2), 339–360. doi: 10.1080/17439749.2018.1495892

Kahneman, D., & Tversky, A. (1979). Prospect theory: An analysis of decision under risk. *Econometrica*, 47(2), 263–292.

Kaplan, S. N., & Simon, H. A. (2010). *News overload: The paradox of choice for a democratic culture*. Oxford: Oxford University Press.

Locke, E. A., & Latham, G. P. (1990). *A theory of goal setting & task performance*. Englewood Cliffs, NJ: Prentice Hall.

McGrath, J. E. (2016). *Groups: Interaction process and performance*. Hove, East Sussex: Psychology Press.

Schön, D. A. (1983). *The reflective practitioner: How professionals think in action*. New York: Basic Books.

Weiss, C. H., & Connell, J. P. (1995). Nothing as practical as good theory: Exploring theory-based evaluation for comprehensive community initiatives for children and families. In *New approaches to evaluating community initiatives* (pp. 63–92). Washington, DC: Aspen Institute.

Yerkes, R. M., & Dodson, J. D. (1908). The relation of strength of stimulus to rapidity of habit formation. *Journal of Comparative Neurology & Psychology*, 18(4), 459–482. doi: 10.1002/cne.920180503

12

THE CONFIDENCE CODE

So, we now understand how our self-efficacy levels have developed, how they impact on our lives and some techniques for improving them, but if we are going to create sustainable change then we are going to need to approach it systematically. Much like any professional development, the first step is going to be moving the process into our consciousness and making it deliberate, and I feel like that process is best represented by Figure 12.1 and the four sequential stages of Pinpoint, Prepare, Perform and Process.

Pinpoint

The first thing we need to do is to locate the area of our personal or professional lives that we want to be more confident in. This could be a role specific task that has just been given to us or one that has for a long time been something we feel like we are underperforming in because of low confidence. It could also be a more foundational attribute of our personality or performance like assertiveness, communication or goal setting. To explore the process of selecting this focus area in more detail, we are going

DOI: 10.4324/9781003558934-13

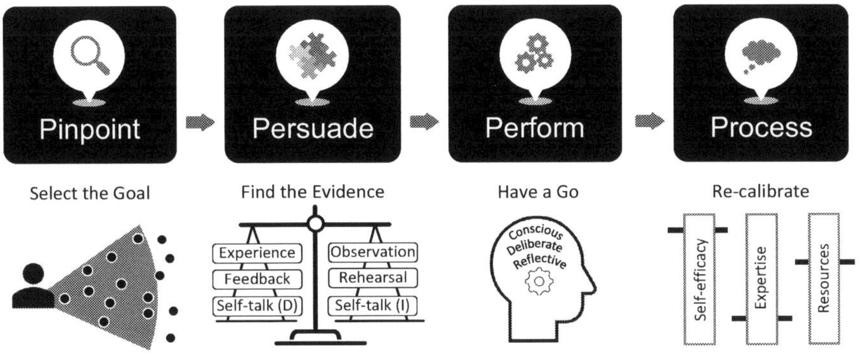

Figure 12.1 The confidence code

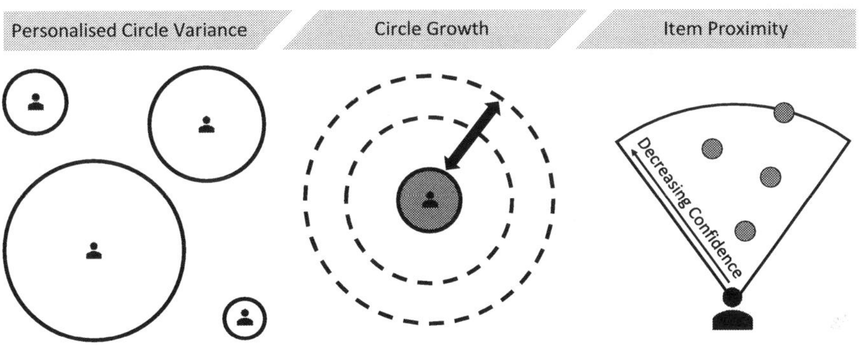

Figure 12.2 Self-efficacy circles

to introduce the concept of a self-efficacy circle. I want you to imagine that you and everyone else is surrounded by an imaginary circle or boundary. This circle is a different diameter for every individual and has dynamically changed throughout their lives and continues to do so. Within the circle are things that they would feel confident to successfully achieve at any particular moment. Outside of the circle are the things that they would feel unconfident about completing successfully. Figure 12.2 shows how this might look in our minds and how our levels of self-efficacy increasingly decline the further out from the centre an item is.

Before we start thinking about assigning specific items to positions, we need to explore some of the intricacies of self-efficacy circles.

If we visualise our circle completely surrounding us, then it might be helpful to place our items purposefully and think about their **location**. The first consideration is the focus of the circle itself as much like with the wheel of life or wheel of work, we can have multiple circles for the different aspects of our personal and professional lives. We can also divide a single self-efficacy circle into different segments, each having a specific focus. In a leadership focused self-efficacy circle, we may decide to assign segments into items like setting direction, creating engagement, building relationships, developing others and delivering impact. The organisation of our circle and level of granularity is a personal preference and should be chosen to meet the goals of the reflective exercise. The individual location of items within those segments should be another conscious decision as it has a significant impact on confidence creation. Items that have similar characteristics should be grouped closer together laterally and increasingly separate as their differences increase. An example would be if we had created a segment for communication, then items that require verbal communication would be closer together than a verbal and a written communication goal or if the segment was on developing others, then individual support like mentoring or coaching would be further away from group support like workshops or asynchronous input like online training design.

The next and most importance consideration is the item's **distance** from the centre of the circle. As we mentioned earlier, items closest to the centre are those that we are most confident about and would therefore have the highest levels of self-efficacy for. The positioning of items should not however be a loosely guided decision as there are a range of considerations that need to be made.

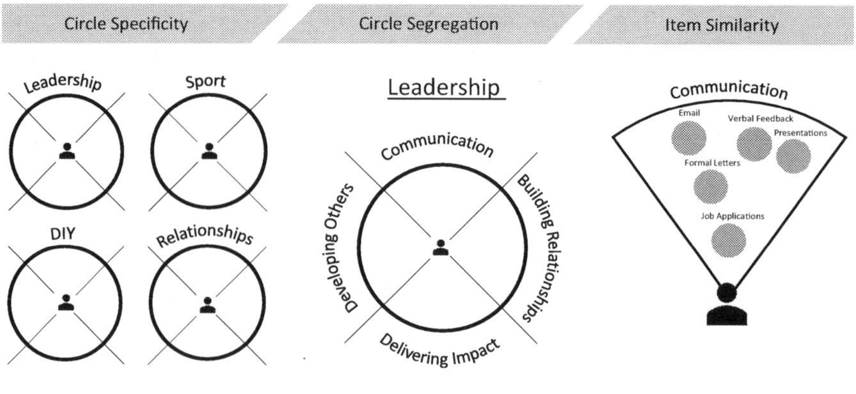

Figure 12.3 Self-efficacy goal organisation

Familiar tasks

The first items we are going to place inside the circle are those that we have already completed in the past. The most obvious indicator of location is of course the degree of success we achieved in those previous attempts. We can broadly say that the more complete the success, the closer the item is to the centre, with moderate or minimal success progressively moving further towards the circle boundary. As we saw in chapter 3, we also need to consider the time since the last successful completion as items with the most recent success have the strongest impact on our task-specific confidence. For our circle this means that although the item would be inside the circle because of past success, it may be further towards the edge if that success was a long time ago. The next consideration is the level of support we had during those previous successes. If we were successful but we had a high degree of support and assistance, then again this would move that item closer to the boundary of our circle. The final consideration is the level of effort that the past attempts and successes required. Items that required a great deal of physical and or mental effort are positioned further towards the boundary as opposed to those where success was achieved easily. To summarise those last three points, items that were completed recently with no support and limited effort would be closest to the centre of our circle as they represent items for which we have the highest levels of self-efficacy.

Novel tasks

The dynamic nature of life and professional working means that there is no guarantee that we will have experience of tasks with which to base our self-efficacy levels on, so we will need to include additional considerations for locating those items. The changing of roles and responsibilities mean that we often need to place items in our circle based on factors other than experience. In chapter 3 we saw how observation and persuasion were key drivers of self-efficacy, and so in this situation these can provide a useful guide for item location. Typically, things that we have seen others successfully complete are positioned closer to the centre than those for which we are not even sure are possible. The complexity with using observational information comes through the alignment between us and the model in terms of demographic and expertise differences. When we see other people like us complete tasks, our confidence is inflated and items are located closer to the centre than when we see people who are different from us complete them. Although watching Roger Federer play tennis or Tony Robbins present to 10,000 people gives me confidence it can be done, my lack of 'federerness' means that those feelings are quickly moderated down.

We can also use our stores of persuasive information and the feedback we have received to locate items within our efficacy circle. Items that we have been told we are good at are naturally located closer to the centre than those which we have negative feedback attached to. This works for our self-talk as well and if we have in the past or presently told ourselves that we can or can't be successful at something, then it affects where we locate the task. A key consideration when it comes to persuasive information is its credibility. Feedback from credible sources has a greater impact on our self-efficacy than when we doubt the sincerity or expertise of the information provider and so also affect where we place items on our circle.

Challenging tasks

The final set of items that we need to add to our circle are those that we do not currently feel confident to complete successfully, and for me are the most exciting ones. It is in these tasks where we find our self-efficacy growth, and the amplitude of this growth is directly linked to how far outside our circle they are located. Although all items that we don't feel confident about need to live outside of our current circle there is an additional set of considerations which affect their proximity. The major factor in determining how far outside our circle an item is located is typically the perceived level of difficulty that we attach to it but within this there are some interesting nuances. Our levels of familiarity with things make a difference to our perceived levels of confidence with items where we have no prior knowledge or comparable experience, causing us the most hesitancy and thus being located the furthest outside of our circle. Items get closer to the circle boundary if we can locate similar past experiences or at least understand what success looks like or how the task is constructed. We spoke earlier in the book about the differences between complicatedness and complexity and both play a part in item location outside of our circle. The number of moving parts within a task and the strength of the logical chain between them broadly dictates how complicated it is, and items that are not complicated are placed closer to the centre than those deemed more complicated. We use complexity to describe the unpredictability of a

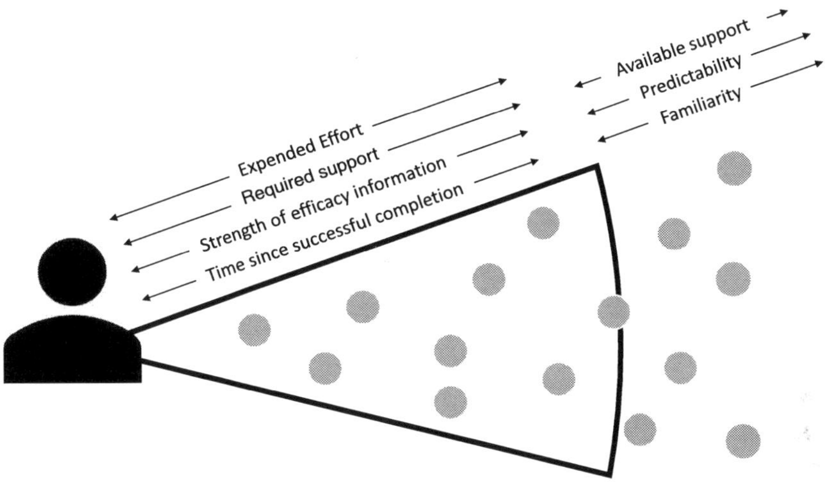

Figure 12.4 Self-efficacy goal distance

task, and so naturally the more complex something is, the further outside the circle it will be located. Items which are more within our control and predictable are located closer to our circle boundary even if we still don't feel confident to complete them successfully.

And so, we return to the name of the first stage 'Pinpoint' and the need to pinpoint exactly what it is that you are going to try to improve your confidence in. The selection of this as we now know needs to come from the items outside of your current self-efficacy circle, and ideally if we are being sensible, we choose something that is just outside our current confidence boundary and high in familiarity, predictability and available support. Now, if you want to really supercharge your confidence in a specific area, you reach even further outside of your circle and take on something really challenging. The risk of course is that the goal may be too ambitious and actually lead to failure and a dent in your confidence, but the rewards are substantial as we will see later.

Persuade

The next stage of the confidence code is called 'persuade' and closely links to the interrogative self-talk technique we spoke about in chapter 6. If you remember, this type of internal dialogue is often superior to the empty "you can do it" declarations that many of the vanilla-flavoured self-help books promote. Asking yourself whether you can do something rather than just telling yourself that you can or can't opens up the need for evidence-based validation. It is the examination of this evidence that creates a genuine feeling of confidence or provides a realistic view of under confidence. So, once we have pinpointed what we want to become confident in, we now need to find some efficacy information we can use to persuade ourselves to give it a try. The persuasion stage of the code is essentially a consciously controlled self-efficacy appraisal, like we spoke about in chapter 3, where we evaluate stored efficacy information and consider associated antecedents in order to arrive at a perceived level of confidence.

Experience

In chapter 3 we saw that Albert Bandura, the godfather of self-efficacy, highlighted our past experiences as the most impactful influence on our confidence levels. Put simply, if we have done something successfully before, then we are more confident about doing it again. The first goal then, during the persuade stage is to look into our mind to find any successful experiences that we could draw on to boost our task-specific confidence. Ideally these are exact copies of the current task in terms of their difficulty, levels of support and resource allocation, and were completed recently so that our use of the information is not affected by any hesitation or rejection. Successful past experiences that are similar but lower in the above characteristics can still provide a confidence boost, but this is moderated down in relation to their similarity and recency. Having access to past experiences that were more recent, more difficult and completed with little support or effort is the best situation as these often result in self-talk declarations like "If I did that, then I can definitely do this".

Observation

We can further persuade ourselves by reflecting on any observations that we may have made that showcased successful completion of the task. This may be of a colleague within our organisation or someone external via recorded media like video. It is worth noting that observational persuasion does not need to come from visual demonstrations and many people fail to differentiate between models and modelling. We can gain a great deal of learning and confidence from static models like diagrams and descriptions, as these can also effectively describe success and break down the steps required to achieve it. If we don't have any stored memories of models or modelling associated with the task, then we need to be proactive and go and get some. If we have the luxury or time between our cognitive appraisal and the start of the task, then we can use this to seek out opportunities to observe excellence. This might include locating video footage or explanations online which we can use asynchronously to observe and re-observe to persuade us. It might also include arranging the observation or shadowing of internal colleagues or external peers in order to persuade ourselves that we have what it takes to also be successful. It is important that if we want to maximise the impact of observational persuasion that we ensure that models are as close to us demographically and contextually as possible as any incongruence will lessen its impact.

Feedback and self-talk

Feedback from past experiences can also have a significant impact both positively and negatively on the persuasion stage of the confidence code. Positive comments from others either written or verbal typically serve to increase confidence, and the opposite is true for negative feedback. The complexity of feedback's role is tied up as we spoke about before in the credibility of its source, the validity and reliability of the information and the time since the feedback was received. Ideally, we can locate some recent feedback from a trusted superior who is an expert in the task we are trying to achieve and has a deep knowledge of our ability and potential. Much like observational information, we may need to seek out feedback if we don't have access to any stored information, and again it is important who we get this from. If we do need to collect additional feedback, then it is important that we find multiple sources so that we can triangulate comments and increase its trustworthiness. Positive affirmations from a friend or direct report may be nice to hear but the presence of the social desirability bias may mean that the feedback is less useful. This cognitive bias drives people to respond in ways which they feel are what the listener wants to hear and is very common in feedback between people who know each other. The solution is to create an environment of psychological safety as we spoke about in chapter 5 so that people feel comfortable being vulnerable and speaking clearly and honestly. Another element of the persuasion stage that we can take advantage of is self-talk and the feedback we give ourselves. In chapter 5 we acknowledged the difference and benefits of both declarative self-talk, where we persuade ourselves through statements and affirmations, and interrogative self-talk, where the use of questions can also build or erode confidence. A balance of both is the ideal situation with a slight leaning towards questions, so that we are required to pause and justify any self-efficacy judgements with corroborating evidence.

Rehearsal

The persuade stage can also involve rehearsal of the task we are trying to be more confident in. Rehearsal involves us purposefully practicing and is different from performance because it is typically done in a safe environment void of the real-life pressures of the task itself. Rehearsal can be done individually or with the support of a coach, mentor or peer and completed physically or in our minds. Mental rehearsal as we saw in chapter 5 involves running through the task in our heads, visualising both the outcome and rehearsing the steps required to achieve it. If the detail is rich enough, the process can both increase confidence and help to uncover possible issues, misconceptions and to hypothesise mitigation strategies. To maximise the impact of rehearsal it is often wise to gradually increase its intensity by starting with private mental practice, moving to private live rehearsal and finishing with guided rehearsal with another person. This final stage adds the possibility for feedback during the rehearsal process which significantly improves the impact of the rehearsal and is something we will discuss in more detail when we talk about deliberate practice in the next section.

Perform

So, the pinpointing and persuasion are done, we have looked back into our stored efficacy information, found the positive stuff and proactively filled any gaps by seeking out additional observation and feedback, now it's time to perform. This 'knowing-doing' gap is a persistent problem in professional development, performance management and just generally in life, and results in people knowing what needs to be done and how to do it but resisting taking action. For me this gap is a big part of the reason for writing the book and the cause of my delayed confidence creation. Of course, I only recently recognised that I was underconfident for all that time, and it took the completion of a doctorate and the writing of this book to know how to develop confidence, so you are already much further down the road.

Conscious

The first challenge in the perform stage of the confidence code is to ensure that we have a level of consciousness that produces fluidity and protects cognitive capacity but still allows us to reflect on the performance and intentionally select and perform actions. If we think back to chapter 7 when we introduced the ladder of consciousness, we see that unconscious competence is not where we need to be and that we must climb back down to conscious competence if we want to reap the most improvement. Conscious competence allows us to be deliberate about our awareness, attention, resource allocation, strategy selection and actions. We will talk more about this deliberate self-control in the final chapter of the book when we explore the development of influencing efficacy and the work that Albert Bandura did on agency and more specifically self-reactiveness.

Deliberate

Our next challenge during the perform stage is being as purposeful and efficient as possible with our actions. Ensuring that we begin with the end in mind at all times and that every action contributes to the success of the end goal is important if we are to be effective and build confidence. This purposeful selection of behaviours will also support the sustainability of our successes by improving our ability to recall what we did to succeed. This reflection on what worked well and what should be repeated in the future is a big part of the process stage of the confidence code which we will speak about later. Improving our efficiency during the perform stage has obvious pay offs to things like energy, motivation and our cognitive capacity but how do we achieve it? Being deliberate during performance means directing our resources in the right direction, and something which may help here is the idea of active ingredients that we spoke about in chapter 8. The term active ingredient is used to describe the elements of something that cannot be damaged or removed if we want the thing to maintain its effectiveness. If we take toothpaste as an example, the active ingredient is fluoride and is essentially what makes it work. The rest of the ingredients and characteristics like colour, consistency, flavour or smell are not active ingredients or crucial to its effectiveness. Knowing which parts of a technique or process actually decide its effectiveness may help us direct our energies in that direction, avoid chasing poor proxies and allow us to be much more successful.

Reflective

An important part of effective performance is being reflective and as we saw in chapter 5 when we looked at the work of Donald Schön, we can both reflect during action and after action. The final stage of the confidence code is devoted almost entirely to reflection on action, and so here we will focus on what to do during our performances.

We need to reflect during the perform stage so that we can make tweaks to our thoughts, emotions and behaviours and increase our chances of success. With practice this will become easier and easier but if in-action reflection is something new to you then you may need to plan in or at least take advantage of what we call reflection points. These points in time are natural breaks in performance that allow conscious reflection and evaluation. These may seem really rare, but if you look closely there are small pockets of time during meetings when you are not speaking or leading, during presentations where delegates are discussing or completing activities and during coaching, mentoring and line management where the other person is themselves reflecting.

The focus of our reflections will differ between performances, but at a basic level we are striving to continually monitor the links between stimuli, our response and the outcome. These SRO chains hold within them the reasons for success and the clues to dips in performance. SRO reflections in action are typically shallower than the more in-depth exploration that happens after an event and are largely driven by questions like, "what happened?", "what did I do?" and "how well did it work?". This simple chain of reflective questioning can allow us to not only make adjustments during the perform stage but also provide important information for the next stage of the confidence code, process.

Process

And so, we reach the final part of the confidence code. The one that is often overlooked and is sadly the reason why for many people, confidence creation happens passively and not by design. Prior to reading this book, you may have had a superficial awareness of the outcomes of tasks and challenges which probably stopped at whether they were successful or not. This stage of the code suggests that in order to make the biggest jumps in our confidence, we need to treat this element more seriously and devote more time to it. When we say process, we mean that the information gained during and at the end of a task or challenge needs to be purposefully processed and integrated into our efficacy information store.

Analysis

The first step in the process is to analyse the performance in terms of the level of success, the level of support used and the level of resource allocation that were required. When we analyse the success level, we are placing it on a continuum somewhere between the extremes of complete failure to complete success. The analysis aspect of these means that we need to take into consideration how closely the outcome matched our pre-task goals and expectations and its comparison to previous attempts. Once we have completed this blunt initial evaluation, we need to delve deeper into which specific elements were successful and which of them was less so or an obvious failure. This level of granularity will be helpful in the next part of the processing where we identify possible adaptations. Once we have broken our performance down into its constituent parts and separated them by their level of success, it is time to prioritise them. Ranking them from most impactful to least impactful on task success helps to moderate their impact on our current self-efficacy and identify where we are best place to spend our adaptation attention.

As an example, let's imagine you have just given a new product proposal presentation to your senior leadership team. Your initial reflective analysis may place it towards the failure end of the continuum because of a lower-than-expected level of engagement from the audience and your awareness of your nerves and stuttered speech at the beginning. Further analysis though may allow you to identify the strength of your responses to the financial questions, the usefulness of the physical demonstration and some smaller areas like voice projection that you thought could have been better. The prioritisation process may then put the successful areas, such as successful question response, higher in the order of importance than the voice projection and thus actually soften the initial dent to self-efficacy. Stuttering at the start may also have a high level of importance and so would then be placed as a developmental priority ahead of the next presentation further strengthening the usefulness of the analysis process.

Adaptation

The next part of the process stage is where we focus on the adaptations that we will make to any future attempts at the same or similar tasks. The famous quote, "Insanity is doing the same thing but expecting a different result" is relevant here. If we want to be more successful in the future and build confidence, we need to gradual weed out any ineffective practices. When we reflect on possible adaptations, we need to zoom in on what changes we feel we need to make to our thoughts, emotions and actions. Table 12.1 highlights some possible reasons for variation in success and some possible adaptations.

Recalibration

The last part of the confidence code is essentially a self-efficacy re-calibration exercise where we consider the resulting changes to our self-efficacy levels, our current level of expertise and any additional resources we will need to be more successful in the future.

As we learnt in chapter 4, our self-efficacy levels are incredibly dynamic and changeable, and so we are regularly conducting cognitive appraisals to review them and arrive at a current confidence level. Post-performance reflections of self-efficacy broadly result in either a perceived increase or decrease in confidence, with a magnitude related to some of the characteristics like level of effort, support required and task demands that we explored earlier in the book. One way of viewing this recalibration is through the lens of the self-efficacy circle analogy that we introduced earlier in this chapter. The dynamic nature of self-efficacy means that it is important to see the layout of those self-efficacy circles as temporary

Table 12.1 Possible internal causes of task success and failure

Limiting Factor	*Possible Adaptations*
Lack of expertise	Seek out further training and professional development opportunities to improve knowledge, skills or experience.
Lack of motivation	Adjust our level of engagement to improve intrinsic motivation or create/request some extrinsic rewards that we could strive for.
Negative self-talk	Rationalise any negative declarations and foreground positive efficacy information. Seek out the support of a mentor or coaching who can help with cognitive reframing.
Poor decision-making	Increase time in the exploration phase to ensure understanding before action and utilise a systematic decision-making process.
Interpersonal issues	Explore emotional intelligence strengths and weaknesses, and create and complete an action plan for improvement.
Poor self-management	Utilise tools like the Johari window to increase self-awareness and the Eisenhower matrix to improve time management.

and only representative of the exact moment in which they are created. The ongoing collection of efficacy information related to specific tasks and attributes will undoubtedly mean that items move into and out of our circle and create smaller adjustments along the continuum of very confident to very unconfident. The discussion of movement works best as a mental visualisation, so I want you to close your eyes and imagine your current circle. Look around it at the different segments and where you have placed the different items in terms of your current confidence levels. Try to focus in on where the boundary is between those you are barely confident in and those that just creep over into a lack of confidence. If you were to pinpoint one of those items just outside your circle and use the confidence code to successfully complete it, then it will move towards the centre and thus enter your circle. To finish your visualisation, I want you to imagine yourself repeatedly reaching out into different segments of your self-efficacy

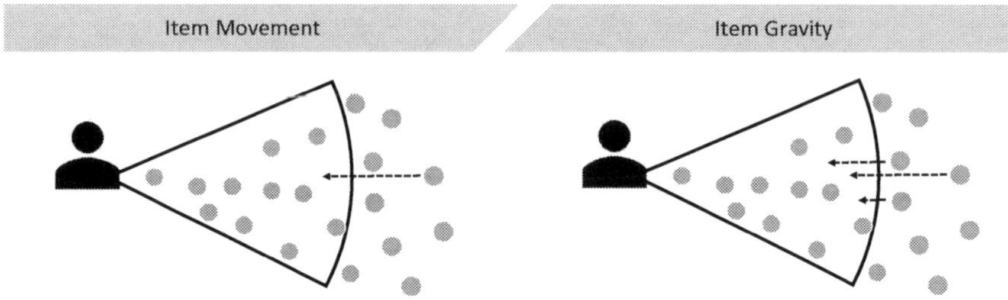

Figure 12.5 Self-efficacy goal movement and gravity

circle and dragging items towards its core and effectively building your confidence by design. This process of moving items into our circle gets really exciting when we consider the idea that each item or task has its own gravity and affects the movements of the other items that are close to it. Conceptually the successful completion of any task then also moves any similar tasks that are lower in difficulty as it travels. To use a sporting example, successfully completing a marathon moves that distance into your circle but also drags with it the 10KM and 5KM distances because they are lower on the perceived scale of difficulty. At work the successful completion of a keynote presentation at the annual conference also pulls small regional and local presentations into our circle.

The next item to be recalibrated during the process stage of the confidence code is our perceived levels of expertise. In chapter 9 we saw that an individual's expertise can be seen as the combination of their knowledge, skills and experience, and the good news for us is that these too are developable. Post-performance reflections of expertise typically centre around whether our levels of each element were sufficient and how they contributed to either our success or failure. These reflections and those about resourcing, which we will speak about next, are a vital element of systematic confidence creation as they provide the stimulus for the proactive action that fuels future success and growth. An example of this expertise recalibration could be a leader whose reflections on the success of a recent sales presentation highlight a weakness during the Q&A section and their inability to confidently answer some of the questions pitched at them. These reflections could then drill down to identify a lack of knowledge as the main reason why their responses were not as accurate as they could have been or a lack of experience with strategic thinking. These reflections could then trigger the proactive acquisition of that knowledge and the identification of opportunities to gain more strategic thinking experience.

The final part of the recalibration process is the evaluation of resourcing, and again this initially focuses on whether it was sufficient and what changes need to be made to improve success in the future. When we talk about resourcing, we need to widen our perspective by not only considering the obvious external resources such as time, finance and staffing but also our internal resources like effort, motivation and resilience. Examples of post-performance reflections may include a leader who attributes a lack of success to insufficient time, a leader who feels that they achieved success because of the number of team members they had or even more simply that they had the right level of financing. These reflections as with those linked to expertise can then drive either the maintenance of those attributes to maximise future success or the proactive acquisition of additional resourcing. The internal resourcing reflections are often more difficult to complete but also hold the most potential for change as they sit more within the control of the leader. In chapter 6 we spoke about something called our 'locus of control' and how it describes where an individual believes the control of their lives lies and whether that is internal and external. Attributing failure or poor performance to external sources is common for leaders with low levels of self-efficacy as they strive to protect what confidence they have and their self-esteem. Although comforting, this abdication of responsibility robs us of our power to change, and so if we want to create confidence by design, we need to look in the mirror and accept the power of our internal resourcing. A good example of this resource recalibration would be the leader who attributes their poor performance in running a team meeting to a lack of effort during the planning stage or a lack of sustained motivation to see a project all the way to completion. Internal resources like effort and motivation are much more in a leader's control, and if we can combine those reflections with the honest recalibration of self-efficacy and levels of expertise, then we are on the path to sustainable confidence growth.

As we reach the end of this chapter, I want you to take a minute to think about how you could implement the confidence code tomorrow in your life and the lives of the people in your team and organisation. What does your self-efficacy circle look like? What items are placed where, and which ones are just on the edge of possible success? Which one will you pinpoint first, and how could you maximise impact by choosing ones with a large gravitational pull? How will you prepare for success? What do you need to learn? Who do you need to see and what will you tell or ask yourself to maximise your confidence? How will you make sure you are conscious, purposeful and reflective during your performance, and what techniques will you use to process the outcome? Finally, how can you make the confidence code a key part of your team's and organisation's professional development plan and so build confidence by design?

Nuggets

- If we want sustainable self-efficacy improvements, then we need a system.
- The first step is to PINPOINT what we want to be more confident in.
- What we choose must be ambitious and beyond our current confidence boundary.
- What we choose must also be specific, measurable and realistic.
- The next step is to PERSUADE ourselves that success is possible.
- We need to draw on successful past experiences and observations.
- We need to draw on any positive feedback we have had in the past.
- We can also use mental rehearsal and visualisation to strengthen the persuasion.
- We need to proactively seek out any additional information that might help us persuade us of our potential success.
- The third step is to PERFORM the task.
- We need to perform consciously and deliberately to improve the chance of success.
- We need to proactively alter our thoughts, feelings and actions to maximise success.
- We need to reflect during the task so that we can collect appraisal information.
- The last step in the system is to PROCESS the performance information.
- We need to analyse levels of success and the contributing factors.
- We need to then re-calibrate our task-specific self-efficacy levels, our current expertise and the levels of external and internal resourcing.
- This recalibration must then result in the proactive acquisition of additional expertise and resourcing so that future success is more likely.

Next Steps

- ✓ Populate your own self-efficacy circle.
- ✓ Get your team to create their own circles and then explore the item locations.
- ✓ Integrate the self-efficacy circle activity into performance management and goals setting processes.

SELF-EFFICACY CIRCLE

WHAT

Creating a self-efficacy circle is an activity that enables leaders to identify their levels of self-efficacy for specific elements or tasks within their roles. The process requires leaders to locate these tasks closer or further away from the centre of the circle depending on their perceived levels of current confidence. Items can be grouped into categories and multiple circles can be created to enable a wider level of reflection.

WHY

The first step in developing confidence is to identify the thing that we want to be more confident in and this process not only narrows our focus but also serves as a mental commitment to change. Fully populating the circle and its outside boundary also enables leaders to identify patterns within low or high confidence tasks and prioritise development needs. Sharing self-efficacy circle information within groups and line management structures can improve the specificity of professional development the accuracy of support.

HOW

Step 1 – Draw a circle and separate it into segments according to the focus of your SE reflection.

Step 2 – Add labels to each segment of the circle to represent your chosen SE categories.

Step 3 – Place dots within the circle to represent tasks that you have high levels of self-efficacy in and add a label for each.

Step 4 – Place dots outside the circle to represent tasks that you have low levels of self-efficacy in and add a label for each.

13

THE BIG THREE

The specificity that separates self-efficacy from more general confidence can be both a blessing and a source of anxiety. On one hand, it means that people feel safer to admit weakness because of it describing only one element of their performance, but equally it is easy to feel overwhelmed by the scale of different elements of self-efficacy that we all hold and need to develop.

The often volatile and unpredictable world that we live and work in can also add to this anxiety as people naturally slip in and out of self-efficacy dips as they experience change or take on new roles and responsibilities. The solution to the unachievable task of complete self-efficacy mastery may lie in never seeing that as the goal in the first place and by switching our attention to the creation of some foundational types of self-efficacy which we are going to call the big three.

If we look back at the self-efficacy circles we explored in the previous chapter, we see a visual representation of the myriad of things that one individual might have confidence in or want to develop. A useful addition to those images might be three core types of confidence that sit closer to the individual and affect all other confidences.

DOI: 10.4324/9781003558934-14

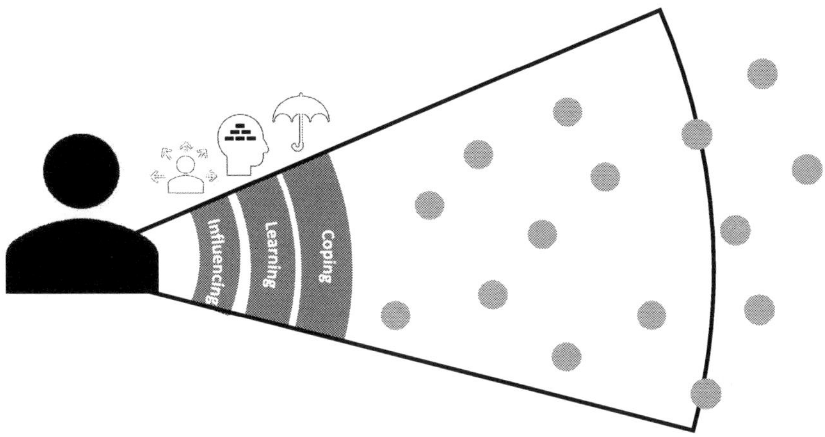

Figure 13.1 Foundational self-efficacies

Influencing Efficacy

As we move into this final chapter, we are actually returning to the beginning of our whole journey and returning to the idea that the future belongs to those who take control of their confidence and build it by design.

Influencing agency means being confident that our actions have impact and that we have the power to influence our own thoughts, feelings and actions and those of the people and environments around us. Unless people believe their actions have impact, they have little incentive to act in the first place or to persevere in the face of difficulties. This core belief often comes before any other forms of intrinsic or extrinsic motivation and acts as the absolute gatekeeper to action. Our confidence in our ability to influence is a core aspect of a more well-known concept called agency. The concept of agency has a story that spans much of history and across various disciplines such as psychology, sociology, philosophy and even anthropology. Aristotle's concept of 'Prohairesis' is often translated as 'deliberate choice' and was an early exploration of reason, deliberation and intentional action. In the 17th century, philosophers like Descartes and Locke actively debated the role of the mind in action and shaped the current and future thinking about self-determination and agency. In the late 19th century, American philosopher William James published the first comprehensive textbook on psychology written in English and challenged the prevailing view of the mind as a passive recorder and emphasised its role in effortful action. Fast forward to the mid-20th century and we find Albert Bandura's work

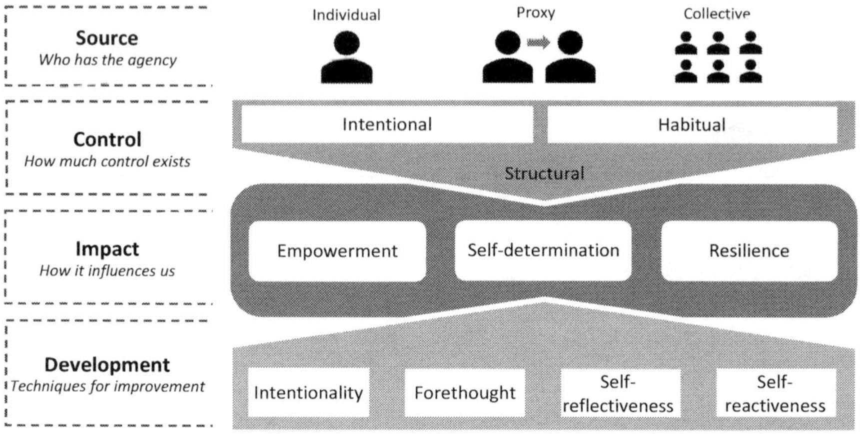

Figure 13.2 A framework for human agency

on agency and his belief in the active role that individuals play in their learning and behaviour.

When we break the concept of agency down, we initially need to consider the source of the agency and therefore whose actions are having the impact. Individual agency is the most active type and describes a person's capacity to act independently and make choices based on their beliefs, values and desires. This is the agency that is required for personal change but also directs our choices of career, hobbies, romantic interests and as we saw in the previous chapter, decides whether we reach out of our self-efficacy circle or not. Proxy agency on the other hand is where individuals rely on other people to act on their behalf to complete tasks and reach goals. As leaders this is an important ability to have as the interpersonal nature of most organisations means that distributed leadership is commonplace, and teamwork is the norm. Examples of this would include hiring external consultants, delegating tasks to direct reports or collaborating with peers on joint projects. The final source of agency is called collective agency and much like collective self-efficacy it describes the power of teams and groups. Collective agency is the belief that collaborative actions have an impact, and we see it strongly through social movements, collective bargaining and community intervention projects.

The next consideration in our study of influencing efficacy is how much control we have over our actions and those of other people. Intentional agency is the type that we are trying to develop and describes the conscious consideration of consequences and decision-making that goes into the planning of actions. This is what allows us to engage in goal setting, action planning and self-directed learning and plays the most central role in our pursuit of confidence by design. The next level is called habitual agency and describes our unconscious impact on ourselves and others, and although the process may be unconscious, the initial decision to develop the habit or first perform the behaviour is often a conscious one. The last level of agency is called structural agency and is less of a type of agency and more like the appreciation that agency is never absolute, and that we all work and live within systems and power dynamics that affect our ability to act. For us this is worth considering as we may have limiting factors within our environments, socioeconomic status and relationships that limit our ability to develop the level of confidence that we want or require.

The pursuit of more agency or control over ourselves and others seems like an obvious thing to crave but it's worth pausing a little longer to explore exactly how increased agency can improve our effectiveness as leaders. Agency is a powerful attribute to develop as it affects the management of some other key performance-related concepts like empowerment, self-determination, resilience and impact.

Empowerment is a word synonymous with agency and whose definition and description often bleed into each other. For us we will see it simply as 'obtaining things in order to increase effectiveness' and therefore position it at the root and the tip of agency. Becoming more empowered often flows from increased agency but paradoxically you typically need agency in order to feel empowered. A closely linked attribute which also emerges from increased influencing efficacy is self-determination and focuses on the internal potential to make choices and is independent of external factors like empowerment. If empowerment is collecting the knowledge, experience and skills to be a leader, then self-determination is the ability to use them. Being less passive and having the confidence to influence the world around us, naturally leads to more personal and professional growth. The pursuit and completion of challenges or goals builds self-efficacy and is not possible without agency. Career progression, notwithstanding the presence of luck, requires agency and the confidence that applying for new roles is worth it, the acquisition of knowledge is possible and our success once in role is somewhat in our control. High levels of influencing efficacy are also linked to high levels of resilience and the ability to cope with resistance and challenge when it appears. The confidence that you can solve problems as they occur and that acting is more beneficial than being passive is an important shift in the minds of agentic people. The final benefit of agency or what we are calling influencing efficacy is the impact that individuals can have on the world around them and the contribution they can make to society. In a world full of challenges, struggles and hardship, we need more people who believe they can make a difference, more people who actively advocate for change and more people who act when they see and feel that they can.

Developing influencing self-efficacy

To explore how to build influencing agency we are going to return to the work of Albert Bandura, but this time focus on his contributions to the concept of agency. Much later than his work on self-efficacy, Bandura published a paper called "Toward a Psychology of Human Agency" (Bandura, 2006), which became foundational in the field of social cognitive theory and emphasised our ability to act on and shape our surroundings, rather than simply being passive recipients of external forces. In the paper he describes four core properties of agency: intentionality, forethought, self-reactiveness and self-reflectiveness, and we will explore these now in more detail with the aim of unlocking some strategies.

Intentionality

Intentionality in the way we will look at it refers to the process of doings things with intention or on purpose. When we are being intentional, we have a specific aim or outcome in mind and we direct out thoughts, feelings and actions towards that purpose. Intention has a cognitive element where we are mentally representing the aim, barriers and possible consequences in our mind, and a behavioural element where we are directing our actions towards the intended goal. If we want to improve our influencing efficacy, then we need to increase our intentionality, and we can do so by improving our ability to develop goals and intentions and also develop greater levels of awareness and objectivity.

Mindfulness is a strategy that has a broad range of benefits to mental and physical health and can be particularly useful in the development of intentionality. Mindfulness is often described as the ability to be fully present in any given moment, aware of where we are and what we are doing. We all have times where this happens naturally, and we zone out for a moment, but the power is in being able to do it on command and do it effectively. The fascinating thing about mindfulness is that it is multidimensional and can be seen as a state of being as well as an act or strategy. Being in a state of mindfulness should not be confused with having an empty mind or escaping reality as it is much more to do with curiosity and an openness to learn. The act and process of mindfulness are similar in that they involve the purposeful use of specific actions which if deliberately practiced can lead to mastery, increases in intentionality and improvements in influencing efficacy. The goal of most mindfulness techniques is to intentionally direct attention and to actively reject distractions. Meditation enables this and so is often closely associated with mindfulness but any activity that enables a focusing of attention and greater self-awareness will also contribute to mindfulness strength. Body scan is a technique that involves lying or sitting comfortably and systematically bringing your attention to different parts of the body and noticing any sensations. Mindful breathing is where intense attention is given to the sensation of air entering and leaving the nostrils and is similar to mindful eating where individual's consciously slow down and pay attention to taste, texture and aroma. Regardless of how you reach a focused, self-aware state, the trick is to keep it short, do it often and be patient as it is a skill that improves with practice.

Forethought

Simply put, forethought is the process of considering the future and is a process we often take part in prior to events and activities. It has a strong influence on motivation and confidence, as it's the process that guides the self-efficacy appraisal process that we have spoken so much about in previous chapters. Those skilled in forethought are able to imagine the future consequences of their actions before they take them, anticipate the success criteria of desired outcomes and use that information to improve their action planning. It differs from mindfulness in that it is future focused, and the thinking is purposeful leading to tangible changes instead of an anchor to the present moment. The benefits of effective forethought and the reason why it contributes to agency development stem from its power to anticipate and mitigate challenges. This awareness of and planned avoidance of roadblocks reduces uncertainty and thus provides a surge in confidence about the completion of tasks and our ability to cope with challenges.

A key technique used in forethought is scenario planning or sometimes known by associated terms like scenario thinking, analysis or prediction. Scenario planning is described as a strategic thinking process that requires its users to envisage and explore possible future situations and is akin to the pre-mortem exercise we spoke about in chapter 7. Although they are similar in that they both help individuals, teams and organisation prepare for the future, the difference is that scenario planning also involves the visualisation of positive outcomes. There are a range of different models and processes for scenario planning, but most share some key characteristics. The first of these is forethought's focus on the plausible not the probable and highlights how the process does not strive to predict an exact future. The power of scenario planning lies in the breadth of plausible futures that are created and the challenge that they provide to assumptions and blind spots. Scenario planning should be a collaborative activity which incorporates different perspectives and divergent thinking so that the breadth is achieved through constructive challenge, compassionate candour and the removal of any professional armour. Scenario planning also needs to be approached systematically through a robust, repeatable process and used both prior to the launch of new initiatives and flexibly during projects to add an element of responsiveness and adaptability.

An example of a systematic approach to scenario planning can be found within the Shell Oil company and was developed in the 1970s to manage the turbulence of the time. The first step of the process is focused on 'identifying driving forces' and involves a robust analysis of the social, political, economic, technological, environmental and legal (SPETEL) trends of the moment. The aim of this step is to identify any high impact, high uncertainty trends that could cause significant issues in the future and yet are hard to predict. This analysis often includes consideration of both quantitative data from reports and more qualitative data from interviews and focus groups. The next step in the process is called 'scenario framing' and involves setting the boundaries of the scenarios that will be generated in step three. Users need to agree on the timescale, the geographical limits and the stakeholders involved, and these boundaries are set to ensure there is consistency across the scenarios and their plausibility is reliably comparable. The third stage, as mentioned above is focused on 'building scenarios' and is where the imaginative storytelling takes place. The scenario planning team uses the driving forces identified in stage one to produce up to four contrasting narratives, each representing a plausible potential future. It's important that each of the scenarios have strong internal consistency in that they follow a logical pathway with a plausible chain of cause and effect. Scenarios need to be entirely believable and include realistic resource demands, be based on known trends and contain recognisable elements. Both the levels of internal consistency and the believability will have an impact on how well members of the team engage with the scenario planning process. During the storytelling process, scenarios need to be told and sold with a clear storyline and an explicit narrative arc. Creating a structured narrative which has a beginning, middle and end further supports engagement and helps team members explore the scenario's implications. The fourth and final step of Shell's scenario planning method involves 'testing and using the scenarios' and is where the team evaluates the potential impacts of each scenario. The insights that come from this evaluation process are then used to challenge any biases or assumptions that may be present, support the strategic decision-making process and help develop contingency plans.

Self-reflectiveness

If agency and influencing efficacy are about believing in the impact of our actions then a key pre-cursor to that is our ability to think deeply about ourselves and be able to evaluate our thoughts, feelings and behaviours. Strangely, even the ability to examine and evaluate these things is an act of agency and control itself, which of course then contributes to a greater sense of the thing that is required. The process of self-reflection is often broken into the two distinct actions of observation and exploration. Self-reflective observation involves focusing our attention on how we think, feel and act and being an observer of those things without judgement. This part of reflection can be done in the moment or more broadly over time with the aim of noticing patterns, defaults or core values. The exploration element of self-reflection is often where the greatest personal growth occurs as it involves trying to understand the root of thoughts and emotions or the rationale behind actions and behaviours. This is the fascinating but fragile process of uncovering underlying motivations, assumptions, beliefs and most dangerously, unconscious cognitive biases.

The study of cognitive biases is growing in popularity as individuals, teams and organisations realise the hidden influence that they have on our personal and professional lives. Awareness is again the first step in addressing them and so a closer inspection of their presence in your own life is another great step towards self-reflectiveness. Table 13.1 highlights some of the more common cognitive biases.

A key technique for those of us who want to improve our self-reflectiveness is journaling and is something that has informally been around since the beginning of written language. The formal or structured use of journalling is more recent and has been popularised through frameworks, pre-formatted journals, writing retreats and the rise in online methods and social networks. The act of writing down our thoughts, feelings, goals and frustrations has a wide range of suggested benefits not restricted to increasing self-awareness. Journalling has been linked to improved emotional regulation through its cathartic release and its ability to challenge us in a sensitive way. It can enhance problem-solving by allowing space to reflect on past experiences and their outcomes as well as consider alternative perspectives. The mindfulness element of journalling also helps with creativity and freedom of expression as there is arguably no greater level of psychological safety than in a private journal. The final benefit of journalling lies in its ability to help encode information into our memory, making it easier to recall and use later as well as spot patterns and trends. For those new to journalling, the recommendations are to start small with just a few minutes at a time, to experiment with online, offline, written and audio formats and most importantly not to worry about grammar, structure or the opinions of an external audience.

Self-reactiveness

And so, we reach the last of Bandura's elements of agency and the end of our exploration of the first of our big three, influencing agency. People with high levels of influencing agency are not just intentional, forward thinking and self-aware, they also have a high degree of control and regulation over themselves. This area sits at the heart of the book's message about not being able to cheat the harvest or take a passive approach to confidence development. You may know that you lack confidence and that you need more but until you actually make the choice to change, develop a plan and then take action then nothing will shift. Self-reactiveness is described as the ability for an individual to regulate their own motivations, emotions and

Table 13.1 Common cognitive biases

Cognitive Bias	*Description*
Anchoring Bias	The tendency to rely too heavily on the first piece of information you learn. The danger is that we interpret newer information from the reference point of our anchor, instead of seeing it objectively.
Attentional Bias	The tendency to pay attention to some things while simultaneously ignoring others. The danger is that our attention is directed towards the wrong information and thus we don't have what we need to make a good decision.
Availability Bias	The tendency to place greater value on information that comes to mind quickly. The danger is that we jump to quick decisions without exploring the evidence or alternatives appropriately.
Confirmation Bias	The tendency to favour information that conforms to your existing beliefs and discount evidence that does not. The danger is that we drive our personal agendas and trust information because of familiarity instead of rationality.
Negativity Bias	The tendency to pay more attention and be affected more by negative events and emotions than positive ones. The danger is that we gain an inaccurate view of situations or lose a sense of perspective.
Projection Bias	The tendency to project our beliefs, values and behaviours onto others or into the future. The danger is that we do not seek alternative views and that we underestimate the need for change.
Sunk-Cost Bias	The tendency to continue a behaviour or endeavour as a result of previously invested resources (time, money or effort). The danger is that we fail to stop or change ineffective actions in time to improve their impact.
Social Desirability Bias	The tendency to answer questions or behave in a manner that will be viewed favourably by others. The danger is that we over-report the good and under report the bad.

actions so that they align with personal goals and standards. It is important to us because it also affects how good we are at monitoring our progress, identifying any deviations from the plan and taking action to correct or modify our behaviours.

The exploration of self-reactiveness can be traced all the way back to philosophers like Immanuel Kant and Wilhelm Wundt who in the 18th and 19th centuries carried out early studies on self-control and through to modern applications within neuroscience and self-determination theory. When we break down the concept of self-reactiveness, we find some discrete elements that all require development and so all deserve some additional attention. 'Self-monitoring' is the first of those elements and describes our ability to pay attention to our thoughts, feelings, and behaviours and acts as a foundational stage of agency. As we have said before, we can't change what we don't acknowledge, and that process starts with awareness. Once we are tuned in to ourselves during tasks, we can then use 'self-evaluation' to compare our progress to the goals and standards that we set for ourselves for that specific task or more widely. We then quickly engage in 'self-judgement' where we make decisions about whether our actions are helping or hindering us. This is a key stage in terms of both general self-efficacy and influencing efficacy as unwanted differences may dent confidence and we can't move to the next step unless we believe in our ability to enact change. The final element involves 'self-regulation' and is where the individual takes action to change their thoughts, feelings and actions so that they can correct any incongruence and get back on track towards their goal.

Techniques for developing self-reactiveness are varied and many of them like mindfulness, cognitive reframing, metacognition and self-talk have already been explored in the book. A strategy that hasn't been covered yet and has played such a big role in my life that I got a tattoo of it is controlling the space between stimulus and response. Viktor Frankl, an Austrian psychologist and holocaust survivor is a well know thinker in this area and once said that "Between stimulus and response there is a space. In that space is our power to choose our response. In our response lies our growth and our freedom" (Frankl, 1963). Frankl spent three years in Nazi concentration camps during World War II and noticed that amongst the unimaginable suffering and horrific experiences there were some prisoners who seemed to find meaning and purpose. He later suggested that regardless of the external stimulus, there is a mental space between it and the response we choose where we can decide our action. This idea of not being passively at the mercy of others or our own unconscious behaviours is an empowering thought, and it feels motivating to think that we can take back some of the agency and add a layer of intentionality. If you have ever taken a few breaths or counted to ten before responding to an angry customer or colleague, then you have been creating this stimulus-response gap, and I would imagine your response was probably more effective. Creating space between life's stimuli and our responses is not easy though and takes practice and conscious action to think a little longer, breathe a little deeper and put a bit more consideration into the most effective response. From personal experience, the investment is always worth it though, and not only will you feel a deeper sense of influencing efficacy it will do wonders for the relationships in your life and your personal and professional performance.

As we reach the end of this section, I want you to take a minute to think about the passive and proactive elements of your work as a leader. Which situations do you feel able to influence and which feel out of your control? How much of your performance do you have influence over, and is this due to external constraints or just the internal cognitive shackles you have put on yourself? How much intentionality would others say exists within your behaviours, and could you locate the purpose of your thoughts, feelings and actions? How much forethought do you engage in prior to action, and could scenario planning enhance that purpose? Which cognitive biases are you most prone to, and which ones did you only just become aware of during this chapter? The final thing I want you to think about is how much space you typically have between stimulus and response. Could increasing this be the key to gaining more control over yourself and becoming more confident about your influence on the world around you?

Learning Self-Efficacy

The second of the big three that we are going to look at is the level of confidence we have for learning. This is our belief in our ability to successfully acquire, store, retrieve and apply new knowledge, skills or understanding.

This fundamental belief plays a key role in anything that we want to develop and get better at as knowing more about something is typically the first step in improving it. Throughout time, philosophers and poets alike have espoused its importance. Confucius believed that learning was crucial for personal and social harmony, Aristotle agreed and saw it as essential for human flourishing and more recently, enlightenment thinkers like John Locke and Thomas Hobbes believed it was the key to liberation and progress. Over time, others have joined the fight with Maya Angelou, the famous American poet, once suggesting that we should do the best we can until we know better. Then when we know better, do better. Social activists like Mother Teresa, Mahatma Gandhi, Nelson Mandela and of course Malala Yousafzai have all strongly advocated for education and learning, seeing it as the bridge between societal divides, a force for empowerment and a key vehicle for change. Applying a scientific lens adds more weight to the argument and highlights not only the brain's ability to maintain neuroplasticity and learn throughout our lives but also suggests a direct link between our knowledge, our behaviours and our impact.

If this link is to be believed, then whenever we are dissatisfied with our own or other's impact, we should probably take a closer look at the knowledge that underpins it and go about improving that through learning. It really could be as simple as 'when we know better, we can do better' but the next question is how to build learning efficacy, and this is where we will go next. In the rest of the chapter, we will explore how we can build our learning efficacy by first developing the right mindset, then our metacognitive capacity and finally our ability to actively process information.

Mindset

In 2006 Standford University psychologist Carol Dweck shook up the world of self-awareness and development when she published her book *Mindset: The New Psychology of Success* (Dweck, 2006). In the book she drew an arguably crude line between an individual having either a fixed or growth mindset with the latter concept now becoming a popular focus in education, business and personal development. Having a growth mindset is pivotal to the development of learning efficacy, and so it is worth us unpacking it in more detail. Let's start with the characteristics of a fixed mindset and how damaging that can be to confidence creation. A fixed mindset believes that intelligence and abilities are innate and unchanging and so growth is not possible. It views obstacles as threats rather than opportunities and avoids them to prevent even the possibility of failure. People with a fixed mindset fail to see the benefits of practice or learning and lack resilience because of a belief that setbacks are permanent. Unhealthily, a fixed mindset also leads people to reject feedback from others and to see the success of peers as a threat.

On the flip side, a growth mindset views intelligence and ability as developable resources, and that effort and action can lead to improvement. People with a growth mindset willingly embrace challenges even if there is a risk of failure and believe in the power of practice. They see failure as a temporary setback, persist in the achievement of their goals and seek out the learning of any errors in order to develop even further. This type of mindset seeks out feedback from others because of its transformative power and actively encourages compassionate candour over ruinous empathy. The success of others is seen as a source of inspiration by those with a growth mindset rather than a threat or source of anxiety.

Before we move onto strategies for developing a growth mindset, it is worth recognising that Dweck positions the two mindsets on a dynamic continuum where individuals are rarely at the extremes and often move between the two states frequently. This movement occurs over time through experience, feedback and conscious effort, but can also move more responsively during a single task as parameters or performance changes. It is also worth noting that much like self-efficacy, our mindset can differ between tasks with the perception that some things are easier to change than others. Sadly, for us it is common for people to feel that skills and knowledge are more developable than personality characteristics like self-esteem and confidence. For this reason, it is important that we now explore some of the strategies that we can use and encourage others to use to grow our mindset.

The first step towards a growth mindset and unlocking the power of learning efficacy is to recognise, acknowledge and accept the idea that change is possible, and that biologically and psychologically we were designed with the capability to improve. The dichotomy of fixed and growth mindset can be off putting for many and lead to rejection of the concept, so the next step is to embrace the idea that our mindset sits somewhere on a dynamic continuum of which we have some control. A strategy that we have spoken about extensively in this book and can help with the shift towards growth is managing our self-talk. For many people, their inner voice is one of negativity and more aligned with a fixed mindset, producing declarations like "you are not good at this" or "you will never be able to do that". If we are subject to negative self-talk then we need to proactively counter the deterministic tone by adding a temporality to any immediate weaknesses and calls to action for any long-term prophecies. The examples above could then change to "you are not good at this yet" or "you will never be able to do that unless you study and work hard".

Our next strategy is linked to what we reward ourselves and others for and what is in our control. We saw in chapter 5 that self-efficacious people tend to have an internal locus of control and see themselves as the controller of their actions, and this has implications for our mindset as well. Dweck noted that shifting our rewards away from the outcomes of events and more towards the process and the attributes that support the outcome can be more beneficial for our mindset. Rewarding effort and resilience rather than scores or results sends the message that success sits within the individual and further promotes the idea that change is possible. Seeking out and embracing challenge is another strategy for not only developing a growth mindset but as we said in the previous chapter also great for developing confidence. Viewing challenges as opportunities and failure as part of the learning process increases motivation, sustains resilience and softens the perceptions and outcomes of any lack of success. The final strategy that we need to utilise is an interpersonal one and may be more difficult than the others depending on the flexibility of your work, family and social groupings. Fixed mindsets like low confidence can be infectious, and so if we want to develop a growth mindset, we need to surround ourselves with like-minded people and proactively limit our exposure to negativity or determinism.

Now that we have the right mindset and believe that we can learn anything, we need to explore the mechanics of learning and what we actually need to do to learn stuff. Coming to a consensus on how learning happens is an ongoing battle fought by neuroscientists, psychologists and educators and one that we sadly don't have time to explore in this book. We could focus on the different theories of learning, but again the complexity of the differences between behaviourism, cognitivism, constructivism, humanism and connectivism is too much for what little time we have left. Two areas that are in my opinion worth delving deeper into though are the fascinating topics of 'metacognition' and 'active processing'.

Metacognition

In the early 1970s, American developmental psychologist John Flavell was building on the work of William James and Jean Piaget and coined the phrase 'metamemory' to describe a person's knowledge and awareness of their own memory processes. Later in that same decade, Flavell broadened the scope of his thinking to include the entire spectrum of thought processes including learning, problem solving, reasoning and decision-making which he then called 'metacognition'. The term immediately became significant as it provided a unifying term for the various aspects of self-awareness and pulled together the disparate research that had been happening up to this point. Researchers have been exploring the concept in more detail ever since and uncovering its intricacies and importance. Metacognition's impact on confidence lies in its links to effective learning and the support it can offer the development of learning efficacy. If our growth mindset allows us to believe anything is learnable, then our metacognitive skills will then help us achieve it.

Figure 13.3 provides the structure for this next section and shows how we can divide metacognition initially into knowledge of our thinking and then the regulation of that thinking.

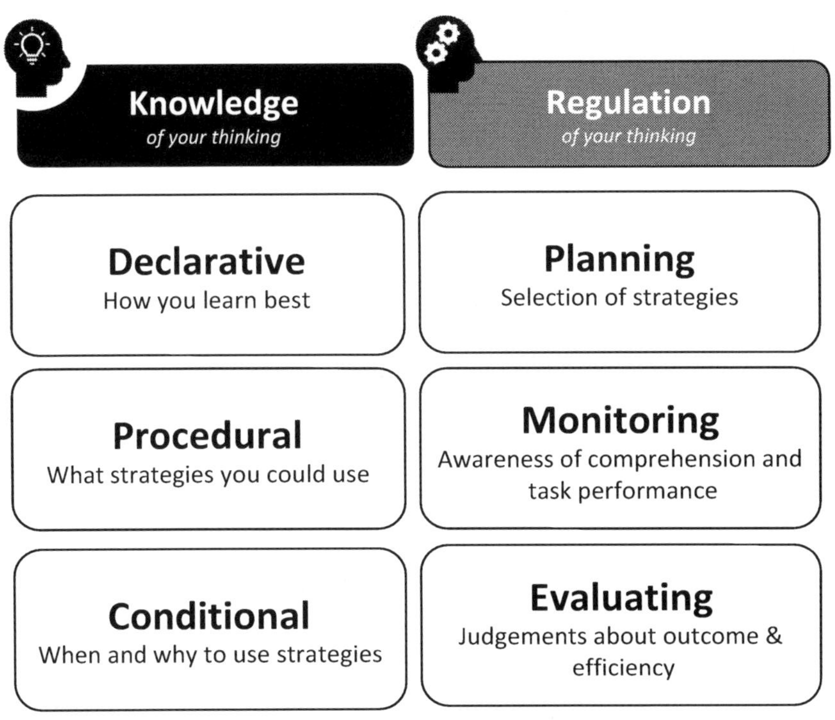

Figure 13.3 Elements of metacognition

The first step in becoming more metacognitive is to understand our thinking better and develop our knowledge of the way we think. We can break metacognitive knowledge down even further by looking first at the 'declarative' knowledge and factual information we have about ourselves as learners and our own cognitive abilities. It may be that we know we struggle with facts and figures more than concepts or that we particularly struggle transferring knowledge into action as with skill development. This knowledge is important if we are going to protect our confidence levels because if we are expecting resistance and difficulties then we can decide to allocate more resources to get through it. This knowledge of ourselves extends into what learning strategies exist and which of them typically work best for us. Understanding the nature or characteristics of a task is also part of our declarative knowledge and allows us to make decisions about the likelihood of success and what actions we need to take. It may be that we use that knowledge to put a rating on a task's complexity, unpick its different components, reflect on similar tasks from our past or identify possible barriers and challenges. Understanding task demands and having a toolbox of techniques at our fingertips can significantly improve our ability to learn and thus our learning efficacy.

As we have seen earlier in the book, knowing what something is and then knowing how to utilise it are often different challenges and this is the same for learning strategies. If declarative knowledge is what learning strategies exist, then our 'procedural' metacognitive knowledge is how to use them and use them successfully. We may know that summarising, paraphrasing, mnemonics and mind mapping are useful tools for learning, but do we know how to maximise their effectiveness. Mind maps are a great example of this and are a learning strategy that is used to varying degrees of complexity and success. Although similar visualisation techniques have existed for centuries, the modern use of a mind map is often attributed to the English psychologist and author Tony Buzan. For many people the mind map is a simple and quickly drawn web of different elements highlighting their connections but, in his book, *The Mind Map Book* (Buzan, 1993), he explains that they can be so much more. To get the most out of the strategy, we must ensure that we have a structure of branches and sub-branches that accurately describe the complexity of the topic and not seek oversimplification. We must ensure that we include links between sub-topics to highlight the rich interdependence of the different elements and help form the same connections in our brains. We also need to push ourselves to utilise the power of images and colour in our mind maps as these provide visual cues that aid retention and recall. The final step is to further strengthen our learning by adding key words or phrases which can also act as cognitive triggers when we come to use the knowledge later on.

Our final type of metacognitive knowledge is what we call 'conditional' and describes our knowledge about when and why to use specific learning strategies. We may know that mnemonics are a strategy, we may know what they involve but do we know when we should use them rather than other techniques like summarising or active listening? The knowledge about which strategy would be most appropriate comes from our knowledge of the strategy itself, the characteristics of the task and any experiences we may have had with the strategy in the past. Much like general self-efficacy, we are more likely to repeat behaviours or in this case, use strategies that have produced previous success.

Metacognitive regulation

So now that we have our metacognitive knowledge and our learning map, we can move onto using the map to regulate ourselves during the learning process. In the same way that we are able to break down the knowledge element, we can split the regulatory process down into three sequential steps. Mastery of these steps is another great way of improving our learning self-efficacy and building a strong foundation of all other confidences. The first step involves planning for the learning and starts with a clear definition of the goal and an examination of the more granular success criteria that will help us achieve it. We then need to activate our prior knowledge of the task or similar tasks to recall any important information that might enable us to select the right strategies and navigate any issues. The next part of the planning process involves selecting the most effective learning strategies, deciding on an appropriate sequence and prioritising the first step.

Once the learning task has begun, we can shift into metacognitive monitoring which involves the continual self-checking of our levels of understanding, application and strategy selection. Any issues or concerns associated with these areas should trigger an adaptive action which could involve re-reading information, repeating activities or selecting alternative strategies. Another key element of the monitoring phase is the moderation and maintenance of engagement and motivation. Regular progress checking and the recognition of success as it happens can help to maintain confidence, build resilience and keep our learning on track.

The third step in the metacognitive regulation process is called evaluation and closely aligns with the 'process' stage of our confidence code from the previous chapter. Evaluation is often used after the completion of the task to assess the effectiveness of the learning strategies and levels of engagement and motivation. It's during this stage that learners will ask themselves about how well the task went and explore the successful and unsuccessful elements. This final step is a key part of confidence creation because it focuses on what can be done to improve future performances. In this stage, individuals lock successful strategies into their mind for use in future tasks and explore the reasons for any failures so that they can be avoided in future performances.

When we pull of all of this together, we can see just how complex metacognition can be if purposefully developed and the almost infinite combinations of the three knowledges means that metacognitive knowledge is deeply personal and situationally specific. In his book *Smart Schools* (Perkins, 1992), David Perkins addresses the personalisation of metacognition by defining four levels of metacognitive learning and provides a useful framework for those wishing to develop it. At the most superficial level we have 'tacit' learners who are unaware of their metacognitive knowledge, merely accept if they know something or not and do not think about any particular strategies for learning. A level above that, we find our 'aware' learners who know something of the thinking that they do whilst learning but it is not necessarily deliberate or planned. As a learner improves their metacognitive learning, they reach the 'strategic' level where they organise their thinking by using a range of purposeful actions like problem-solving, grouping and classifying to help them learn. 'Reflective' learners are the highest classification and alongside the strategic application of thinking they also reflect upon their learning while it is happening, considering the success or failure of any strategies they are using and then revise them as appropriate.

If after reading that last section, you feel the need to boost your metacognitive knowledge and regulation then you are not alone and as far back as the original research by Flavell, it was found that people overestimated their abilities in these areas. A lack of understanding and the typically unconscious nature of metacognitive skills make it a difficult thing to develop, but there are some strategies that leaders can use themselves and encourage others to use in order to make progress. Improving our awareness of our thinking processes through self-reflection and journalling can make a real difference and the analysis of cause and effect, and patterns over time can push that learning even further. Metacognition itself is learnable and so we should seek out resources that explicitly improve knowledge, understanding and skill as well as learn from others through observation or discussion. Its skilful nature also makes it perfect for practice and experimentation, and for individuals to actively try out different strategies and reflect and refine along the way. To embed metacognitive strategies into our workplace performance, we need to systematically weave them into our working practices and find opportunities to create processes that force us into that level of planning, monitoring, evaluating and adaptation. We also need to not forget the power of recognition and praise in the learning process, which links back to our focus on operant conditioning in chapter 8. Rewarding ourselves and others when they engage in metacognition will help to build the levels of engagement, confidence and resilience required to ensure it becomes part of everyone's learning efficacy toolkit.

Active processing

In our pursuit of greater learning efficacy, we have so far developed a growth mindset that allows us to believe we can always get better, a metacognitive map of how we learn best and a set of regulatory strategies to help guide us through tasks but there is still one piece of the puzzle missing. At the very start of the book, we spoke about something called cultural passivity and how the apathetic norms of a group can mean that people expect things to just happen naturally and so take no proactive action. Learning is a good example of this and for some individuals, attendance at a training event or simply reading or transcribing something is in their minds, all they need to do for learning to happen. Sadly, this is rarely true but there is a strategy called active processing that we can use ourselves and encourage others to maximise learning and strengthen our learning efficacy. Active processing is often mistakenly associated with 'active learning' where learners are experientially involved in the learning processes and although there are similarities, there is also an important distinction.

Active processing describes a mental activity where learners use techniques to go beyond passively engaging with information. Like many of the things we have spoken about in this book, it has its roots in philosophy where dialogue and questioning were celebrated, and early learning theories advocated learning by doing. The rise of cognitive psychology in the 1950s gave us information processing theory which attempted to describe how information got from the environment into our minds. This complimented the work of people like Jean Piaget on constructivism, where the suggestion was that we actively constructed knowledge through our interaction with the environment and the people in it. More recently American psychologist David Ausubel developed the 'meaningful learning theory' which also emphasised the importance of actively connecting new information to existing structures for deeper understanding, retention and transfer. The research continues, and fields like neuroscience and social learning are continuing to shine more light on how we can actively engage in the learning process.

The purposeful and proactive nature of active processing requires the use of a range of different techniques which, you will be pleased to hear, are learnable and which the next part of the chapter will be devoted to explaining.

Selective attention

The first strategy we need to master is selective attention, which is described as the ability to focus on the learning stimulus while ignoring distractions and is like having a mental spotlight that we can shine on the most relevant elements of the environment. This deliberate blocking out of unimportant information is key to reducing something called cognitive overload, where our brains have too much information to process and so learning is hampered. Selective attention also means that only the most relevant information makes it into our working memory, which is important due to its small capacity and important links to our long-term memory. If we attend to the wrong stuff, then we think and remember the wrong stuff and of course, this has a negative impact on our learning.

Elaboration

Our next active processing strategy is called elaboration and involves us adding meaningful associations to incoming information to help us understand and remember it better. Many learning theorists and cognitive scientists see knowledge as a web, or a matrix of interconnected elements, and elaboration can help us to integrate new information into those structures. When we are elaborating, we are actively trying to link new knowledge to existing knowledge and to explore the new information in as much detail as possible. This may involve creating visual representations, breaking things down into their constituent parts, creating real-world examples and asking ourselves questions about how things work. Elaboration is a key step in the learning process as it means that knowledge is not left to just passively enter our minds and have nowhere to live or any clear path to it for future recall. Enriching and expanding the information we receive during learning means that we are much more likely to understand it, retain it and be able to use it to think critically and transfer it to new situations.

Clarification

Our next strategy, clarification, is one step further on from elaboration and is often a collaborative activity involving other people as the goal is to check whether our understanding is accurate. Many people believe that knowledge is constantly under construction and goes through an ongoing process of refinement as our experience grows. To this end, for us to fully engage in active processing and maximise our learning, we need to have the bravery to ask questions like "Am I right in thinking" or "Does this mean" to our peers, teachers and leaders. This process of clarification is vital if we are to avoid developing misconceptions that then go on to be barriers to new learning, stimuli for further misunderstanding or the root of errors which surface again much further down the line.

Organising

Organising is another active processing strategy and one that can help reduce forgetting and improve our ability to recall information from our memory when we need it. Grouping knowledge together in our mind because of shared characteristics or causal links is a great way to build an efficient matrix of information and creates cues that can be used during retrieval. Storing all of your knowledge about Excel spreadsheets or the performance management process together makes it easier to find something later because we know where to look for it. This is a tenuous analogy but if you are of an age that can remember the computer game Tetris, then you will be able to visualise new information as falling blocks which you need to manipulate on their way down before finding the best place for them to fit. Organisation of knowledge feels a bit like this in that we need to actively and purposefully find the right place in the matrix for new knowledge to go so that we can build a coherent and easily searchable web.

Thinking hard

So far, we have discussed active processing from a personal viewpoint and introduced strategies that individuals can employ but what about our impact on others and how can we facilitate active processing during the training and support we provide. The cognitive nature of learning means that the process is typically invisible in the moment and so we often need to use proxies to indicate that it is happening. Proxies as we spoke about in chapter 7 are things that we use in place of something else, and for learning we often use things like levels of engagement, the answering of questions and the completion of tasks to tell us that learning has happened. In 2015, Professor Robert Coe published what he called the 'poor proxies of learning' which include those above and also things like a calm, ordered environment and busyness. Professor Coe caused quite a storm by suggesting that these proxies were poor indicators of learning, but he was not suggesting that they are unimportant or do not correlate to learning, but just that the causal link is weak. One proxy that he said did have some weight was the degree to which the learner was 'thinking hard' in any moment, and this is what we will explore as our key lever for facilitating active processing in others.

Getting people to think hard is of course something we can do during learning through our use of questioning but there are also more systematic ways that we can achieve it through our task design. In his book *Why Don't Students Like School?* (Willingham, 2009), Daniel Willingham, an American cognitive scientist, talks about the need for 'desirable differences' during the learning process and how actively engaging with challenging material and tasks can lead to deeper understanding and stronger memory retention. The idea that we remember what we think hard about, creates an interesting task-design challenge for those of us wanting to facilitate active processing and improve learning efficacy. How can we create or adapt tasks to ensure that all learners are thinking hard and experiencing a desirable level of difficulty? Table 13.2 suggests a range of different activities that we

Table 13.2 Thinking hard tasks

Application Strategy	*Possible Activities*
Categorise	• Find common elements. • Create groups. • Describe characteristics for belonging to each group.
Compare	• Find similarities. • Find differences. • Describe the impact of it being the same or different.
Connect	• Identify key elements. • Draw links between elements. • Describe relationships between elements.
Criticise	• Give your opinion. • Have a debate. • Find conflicting evidence.
Deconstruct	• Split information into sections. • Create headings. • Highlight key terms, phrases, quotes, etc.
Derive	Explore the information by asking yourself: • What is the key message/hidden message? • Why did things happen? • What questions need to be asked?
Extend	• Finish a sentence, sequence, equation, image. • Add your own opinion. • Write the next paragraph.
Practise	• Repeat an activity. • Complete a partial example. • Explain a completed example.
Prioritise	• Rank things in order of importance. • Select the most important element. • Justify how you reached the decision.
Reduce	• Record the main bullet points. • Write a summary. • Write a heading which sums up the content.
Transform	Change the information into: • Images, diagrams, charts, tables. • Music, poetry, performance.

could design that require the learner to apply newly acquired knowledge and therefore force them to think hard about it.

And so, we reach the end of the second of our big three efficacies and lock in the idea that if we can improve our confidence to learn through having the right mindset, strong metacognitive abilities and actively process information then we provide ourselves with the tools to continually develop. If we do buy into the idea that all failure has its roots somewhere in a lack of understanding, then this perceived ability to learn anything also has the power to improve anything.

Coping Self-Efficacy

Our final foundational efficacy is the one that sets us up to deal with anything the world throws at us and describes our confidence to handle challenging situations effectively. If you are anything like most of the population, your life has already had and will continue to have ups and downs and hurdles to get over. For lots of people it's these pivot points that send their lives in unexpected directions and not always for the better. Imagine having the belief and the tools to navigate any difficult emotion, situation or event, and what a difference that would make to the choices you make and the things you accomplish. Well, that is what we are going to unpack in this part of the chapter, and as a first step we will explore where the term coping self-efficacy came from.

Albert Bandura's early work in the 1960s and '70s initially focused on general self-efficacy but quickly expanded to include specific types of confidence like collective self-efficacy which we looked at in chapter 7 and domain specific efficacies like health care, education and leadership. Self-efficacy's strong ties to the way we think and feel, and the increasing breadth of self-efficacy research eventually lead Bandura and others to examine its role in problem solving and our ability to cope. In 1989, a shift in the research on stress management away from a one size fits all model to a more personalised and contextual approach added weight to the role of the individual in stress reduction. In their book *Coping as a Transactional Process* (Lazarus & Folkman, 1984), psychologists Richard Lazarus and Susan Folkman suggested that the process of coping was more complex than first thought and that individuals needed to actively interpret and evaluate situations before selecting an appropriate coping strategy. This dynamic view of coping recognised the flexibility and adaptability that people need in order to cope with an ever-changing world and opened up the exploration of the appraisal process and the development of coping strategies. Another milestone in coping self-efficacy came in 1996 when Lazarus joined forces with two other psychologists, Susan Folkman and Marla Chesney, to create the Coping Self-Efficacy Scale, a standardized and reliable way to measure an individual's confidence in their ability to handle challenging situations. The creation of the scale allowed researchers to start assessing coping efficacy across diverse populations and explore its links to stress, depression and anxiety. The coping self-efficacy research continues to broaden all the time, and we now have a much clearer picture of it structure and impact on human functioning.

It is generally accepted that coping self-efficacy is a multi-dimensional concept that can be divided into problem-focused and emotion-focused coping. Problem-focused coping is used to target the issue or the problem itself and to gather information, seek solutions and take action. Being confident in this element means feeling that we have access to and are able to effectively use skills like strategic thinking, action planning and resource allocation to solve problems. Emotion-focused coping targets, as the names suggests the emotional impact of the situation and helps us regulate feelings of anxiety, sadness or frustration. Being confident in this element means knowing how to and actively taking advantage of mindfulness, relaxation, cognitive behaviour techniques and journalling.

In terms of impact, coping efficacy is definitely something worth developing as it has been linked positively to both mental and physical health. Individuals with strong coping efficacy typically feel less stress because of their perceived ability to manage challenge, regulate emotions and prevent neuroticism. They also tend to have enhanced sleep and immune functions because of this lowered stress and a reduction in conditions like anxiety and depression. In addition to the physical and emotional benefits, strong coping efficacy has also been linked to higher levels of motivation and perseverance because of the acceptance of challenge and the confidence to overcome it. A final and significant benefit of coping efficacy is the reduced levels of fear and risk avoidance that owners typically have. This willingness to take on things outside of their current efficacy circle as we saw in the last chapter is the key to sustained confidence growth.

Now that we know where it came from, what it is and how it affects us, I would imagine you are hooked and want to get started on building it, so let's have a look at some key strategies for its development. In this next section we will explore how the process of building coping-efficacy needs to be a combination of emotional regulation and problem solving.

Emotional regulation

Increasing our levels of self-awareness is often the first step in developing our coping ability to regulate our emotions and develop our coping self-efficacy because we can't change what we don't acknowledge and uncomfortably we ourselves are often the root of our own problems. These two abilities are often seen as key elements of a wider construct you may have heard of called 'emotional intelligence' (EI). As a concept EI was explored as far back as John Dewey's work on social intelligence in the early 1900s and again through the 1950s with Abraham Maslow's work on human needs before being introduced as a recognised term in the 1980s by Daniel Goleman. Goleman, an American psychologist and

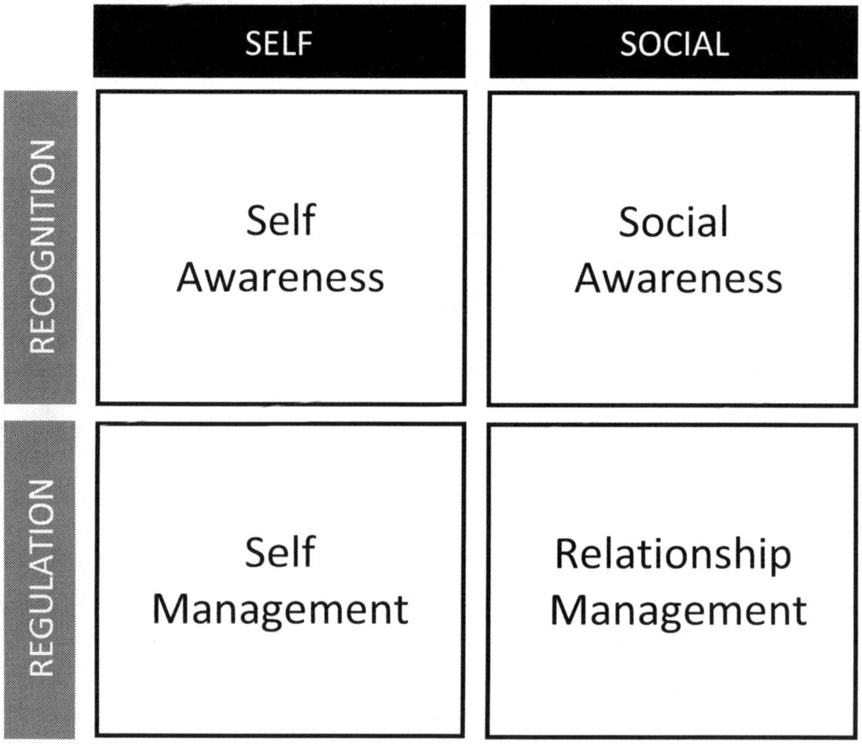

Figure 13.4 Emotional intelligence matrix

journalist, brought the topic into mainstream view and popularity with his 1995 book Emotional Intelligence: Why It Can Matter More Than IQ and it has been a source of fascination ever since. Figure 13.4 shows Goleman's revised model which splits the concept into four quadrants, each describing a component of EI and within that a set of associated competencies. The rows of the quadrants are separated into self and social, and the columns represent recognition and regulation. Self-awareness is therefore our ability to recognise ourselves, social awareness being the same but with others and the final two quadrants describe our ability to regulate ourselves and the interpersonal aspects of our lives.

Goleman's bold statement about the importance of EQ continues to prove itself just and I am sure you can think of people you work with or work for that have weaknesses that sit more in these quadrants than with their expertise or intelligence. It is worth noting that the four quadrants and their competencies are not mutually exclusive but interact and influence each dynamically. This complexity has led to a range of emotional intelligence models, but all point to its importance. For us its importance lies in our ability to understand our emotional triggers and be able to regulate them during challenge in order to effectively engage in emotion-coping as well as regulating actions to contribute to our problem-focused coping.

Reducing our levels of stress is vital if we want to gain better regulation of our emotions. The presence of stress has far-reaching influences and the influx of hormones like cortisol has been shown to impair cognitive functioning, limiting our problem-solving, decision-making and ultimately coping capacity. Stress has also been shown to reduce our emotional regulation, heighten our reactivity and cloud our judgement all which hampers our emotion-focused coping efficacy. Stress is also often the stimulus for some of the negative physical symptoms of poor coping efficacy and can interfere with our healthy habits of sleep, nutrition and exercise. A final negative consequence of stress is what it drives people in the pursuit of a solution, with many seeking quick relief from substance abuse, isolation or avoidance which typically worsens the situation in the long run. Much more sustainable solutions to stress management include regular exercise which releases endorphins and improves mood, and relaxation techniques such as progressive muscle relaxation, guided imagery, meditation and Tai Chi.

Another strategy for emotional regulation that is particularly helpful for busy professionals is time management, and there are a multitude of traditional and more high-tech ways of organising and prioritising. Strategies

Figure 13.5 Eisenhower Matrix

such as the Eisenhower Matrix, time blocking and the Pomodoro Technique are well known and widely used within organisations and can all significantly improving coping through enhanced time management. The Eisenhower Matrix is a popular productivity technique named after the 34th President of the United States and popularised by Stephen Covey in his book *The 7 Habits of Highly Effective People* (Covey, 2013). To use the Matrix, individuals place their to-do list items into one of four quadrants based on their level of urgency and importance. Items that are not urgent or important need to be 'deleted' from the to-do list. Items that are urgent but not important should be 'delegated' to other members of the team. Moving up into the top two quadrants, if we have items that are not urgent but are important then we need to 'decide' when they should be done, and the final quadrant is reserved for items that are both urgent and important and these are the one we need to 'do' as a priority.

Time blocking is another great productivity strategy and involves dividing your time into specific time slots with specific foci and goals. The tool works by creating tight boundaries which then focuses attention, minimises distraction and prevents any overloading. A similar technique popularised by Francesco Cirillo in the late 1980s is the 'Pomodoro Technique', named after the tomato shaped timer, that gave birth to the idea. The concept is that you should only ever work in 25-minute intervals (Pomodoros) with five-minute breaks if you want to maximise your effectiveness and reduce stress. Both techniques help with time management and coping self-efficacy by shrinking challenges into smaller chunks which then improves focus, reduces procrastination, increases motivation and decreases the chances of burnout.

Problem solving

The second key skill that we need to development if we want to improve our coping efficacy is problem solving, and as we saw earlier not only does it gives its name to one of the two major components, but it is also often what people say they are good at when they describe themselves as good at coping. People have been trying to solve problems and understand how to do it effectively since the dawn of time and so the theory behind it is vast and extremely complex. A good place to start is the broad classifications that are used to describe problems. Problems are often classified in terms of their scope as in broad versus specific or their time frame as in long-term versus short-term, and also in terms of their focus as in personal versus professional or internal versus external. The most fascinating distinction and one that causes a great deal of confusion and ineffective action is the distinction between complexity and complicatedness. Both complex and complicated problems have lots of different parts, but it is the nature of the relationship between them and the unpredictability that make the difference.

The parts of a complex problem are not linear or easily controllable, and small changes can therefore have large and unforeseen consequences making the problem even harder to solve. The solutions to complex problems often lie outside of our control and involve external components like other people, resources or the environment. Complicated problems are still hard to solve and can have many parts, but they can be tackled through systems and processes with logical steps. The solutions to complicated problems often rest on our ability to methodically work through the problem addressing them sequentially piece by piece. Some real-world distinctions might be that fixing a car is complicated but driving it through a busy city is complex, making a LEGO model is complicated but going rouge and making something new from a random collection of bricks is complex. In organisations we often encounter complex problems when we deal with Human Resource issues or supply chains and complicated problems when we design new processes or unjam the photocopier. This may seem like semantic pedantry, but the distinction becomes important when we start to look at problem solving strategies as the unpredictability of complex problems means that often there is no playbook and solutions need to be more creative.

As we mentioned before, the field of problem solving and its associated strategies is vast, so let's start by looking at some of the common characteristics of the different models, processes and techniques. Most problem solving should start with a robust understanding of the problem or problems involving the collection of valid and reliable information and an exploration of the root cause. Solution selection should be a narrowing activity which starts with the broadest set of possible evidence-based techniques and slowly and carefully weeds out the unsuitable ones. This process of evaluation should include consideration of each technique's effectiveness, feasibility, contextual alignment and potential consequences. Throughout each of these stages there should be a culture of collaboration and an embracing of different perspectives, as effective problem-solving is rarely done in isolation and if it is then the blind spots quickly show themselves.

Each organisation seems to either create their own problem-solving model and process or utilise some of the more popular ones like the U.S. Federal Emergency Management Agency's (FEMA) Analytical Problem-Solving Approach, the Plan-Do-Check-Act (PDCA) cycle or the Kepner-Tregoe Method. Sadly, we don't have space to explore these in detail but Table 13.3 shows common approaches that sit at the foundation of good problem solving.

The idea that collaboration is important to problem-solving and that it makes most things easier has been both a staple of ancient proverbs and regularly included in rousing speeches by politicians, activists and sportspeople. In Nigeria they say that "one tree cannot make a forest", Franklin D. Roosevelt said, "In unity there is strength and in division there is weakness" and the basketball hall of famer Micheal Jordan once said, "Talent wins games, but teamwork and intelligence win championships." Social support plays a key role in the development of coping efficacy because of the emotional, cognitive and practical support it offers. When we are talking about social support, we are referring to the network of relationships that we have amongst our family, friends and colleagues which is often face to face but increasingly online.

Table 13.3 Problem solving approaches

Strategy	*Description*
Analogy	Comparing the problem to another to find common characteristics and possible ways forward.
Evidence	Analysing the problem objectively through the use of qualitative and quantitative data to reach an unbiased evaluation.
Division	Breaking the problem down into its constituent parts or smaller chunks to lessen the challenge or distribute responsibility.
Hypothesis	Creatively assessing possible causes of the problem or solutions to add weight to or discount certain lines of thinking.
Means-End	Defining the problem, visualising the end goal, listing the differences between the two and then creating small sub-goals and actions.
Morphology	Viewing the problem as broadly as possible and how it fits into wider systems to make sense of the complexity.
Proving	Finding ways to prove that problems can't be solved or that solutions won't work can provide useful insights into ways forward.
Reduction	Progressively reducing problems into more and more simple problems or alternative problems where there is already a known solution.

Social support

An element of coping self-efficacy that spans across emotional regulation and problem solving is social support. Access the support of others can help us emotionally cope by reducing stress and anxiety through sharing problems with trusted others and the cathartic benefits of lightening the burden and making challenges seem less overwhelming. Our social connections can also offer a sense of empathy and validation for our feelings and experiences which provides reassurance that we are not alone or abnormal. This empathy often leads to collective problem-solving and the sharing of past solutions or the use of different perspectives and knowledge to create new ones. Another important emotional benefit of social support is the encouragement and increased motivation that can come from the bolstering of confidence and the reframing of negative thinking. The key for those wanting to build foundational and sustained coping efficacy is to proactively build and nurture a broad and supportive social circle so that there is a confidence that they will always be available and that their impact will make a difference.

Cognitively, social support can play an important role in our exposure to new perspectives and ideas which in turn can help us navigate the roadblocks that exist because of our limited and fixed thinking. Surrounding ourselves with diverse demographics, thinking and expertise can minimise blind spots and help generate new ideas. We have emphasised the importance of feedback on self-efficacy as various points in the book and the same is true for coping efficacy. Access to objective feedback from our social circle can also help us gain perspective and often hear the things that we are too afraid to admit or explore. A lack of clarity can often be overwhelming, and the resulting confusion can cause reduced coping efficacy. Having access to other people can improve our information processing and help us organise our thoughts, clarify situations, identify key information and refine our knowledge. Knowing that we have access to this in times of challenge is a comfort and a big contributor to our coping self-efficacy.

And so, we reach the end of our foundational three efficacies and lock in the idea that if we can improve our confidence to cope, then we provide ourselves with the tools to continual develop and create a foundation for all other confidences. If we buy into the idea that we can overcome any obstacle or setback then we can erode any boundaries to our abilities and supercharge our self-efficacy.

Nuggets

- The unpredictability of life makes self-efficacy development difficult.
- It would be unwise and unachievable to try to build self-efficacy is everything.
- It may be better to focus on developing three foundational forms of self-efficacy.
- Having high levels of INFLUENCING self-efficacy is the last of the big three.
- Being confident that our actions have impact galvanises our levels of motivation.
- Influencing self-efficacy requires strategies to successfully manage situations.

- Influencing self-efficacy also requires strategies to successfully manage people.
- Having high levels of LEARNING self-efficacy is one of the big three.
- Having the confidence to learn anything unlocks sustained development.
- Learning self-efficacy requires a growth mindset and all its characteristics.
- Learning self-efficacy requires strong metacognitive awareness and control.
- Having high levels of COPING self-efficacy is another of the big three.
- Having the confidence to cope with anything protects us against setbacks.
- Coping self-efficacy requires the development of strategies to manage problems.
- Coping self-efficacy also requires strategies to manage our emotions.

Next Steps

✓ Use the thinking hard activities in your next training session.
✓ Review your current levels of emotional intelligence.
✓ Use the Eisenhower Matrix and Pomodoro Technique for time management.

References

Bandura, A. (2006). Toward a psychology of human agency. *Perspectives on Psychological Science, 1*(2), 164–180. doi: 10.1111/j.1745–6916.2006.00011.x

Buzan, T., & Buzan, B. (1993). *The mind map book* (Full colour illustrated edition). Essex, England: Pearson Education Group.

Covey, S. R., & Collins, J. C. (2013). *The 7 habits of highly effective people: Powerful lessons in personal change* (25th anniversary edition). New York, NY: Simon & Schuster.

Dweck, C. S. (2006). *Mindset: The new psychology of success*. New York: Ballantine Books.

Frankl, V. E. (1963). *Man's search for meaning: An introduction to logotherapy* (5th ed.). Boston: Beacon Press.

Goleman, D. (1995). *Emotional intelligence: Why it can matter more than IQ*. London: Bantam Books.

Lazarus, R. S., & Folkman, S. (1984). *Stress, appraisal, and coping*. New York: Springer Publishing Company.

Perkins, D. (1992). *Smart schools: Better thinking and learning for every child*. New York: Free Press.

Willingham, D. T. (2009). *Why don't students like school? A cognitive scientist answers questions about how the mind works and what it means for the classroom*. San Francisco, CA: Jossey-Bass.

FINAL THOUGHTS

Wow, we made it!!

As we reach the end of the book, I am filled with hope – hope that you have enjoyed the experience, hope that you have found new insights into yourself and your own confidence journey, and finally hope that you have already started and are committed to continuing to create confidence by design through the four pillars of professional development (Intention, Acknowledgement, Learning, Deliberate Practice).

Intention

I hope that the early chapters of the book instilled in you a deep understanding of the power of confidence and the impact that it already has had and continues to have on all aspects of our lives. I hope that this new appreciation of its importance has fuelled an intention to make changes to the ways you live and work, to extend that action to support others and to ensure that in the future there will always be the optimal amount of confidence by design.

DOI: 10.4324/9781003558934-15

Acknowledgement

I hope that by engaging in the reflective activities throughout the book, you have reached a deeper level of awareness about your own confidence journey and the people, places and events that have shaped it. I hope that you have been brave enough to acknowledge the power that confidence has had and is having over your leadership and where the limiting forces are coming from. I hope that you have acknowledged the need for a proactive approach to confidence creation if change is required and the need to seek out support from others along the way.

Learning

I hope that your time with the book has been full of learning – learning about yourself, learning about your story and also learning a range of new strategies for improving confidence by design. I hope you learnt that confidence is not something we just inherit or that stays fixed but is a commodity that can be proactively grown if we do it by design.

Deliberate Practice

I hope that your experience with this book will not just be confined to your mind and the learning squandered. I hope that you have seen the importance of action and will go forward to engage in cycles of deliberate practice where you live out the four Ps of the confidence code. I hope that you will continue to **Pinpoint** specific and ambitious goals for yourself and others. I hope that you will **Prepare** for success by seeking out the knowledge, skills and experience that you need. I hope that you will have a go and **Perform**, not being afraid of mistakes but seeing them as just missteps towards your goal. I hope you protect time to **Process** your performances so that you can extract the learning, realign your resourcing, improve your preparation and then go on to be successful in future attempts.

And my final hope is that you have realised that if your confidence is not where you want to be or where it needs to be, then you don't have to passively sit by and be a victim. You now have the knowledge and tools to ensure that your approach to confidence creation will always be by design.

Next Step

- ✓ Complete your first 4P placemat.
- ✓ Get each member of your team to complete a 4P placemat.
- ✓ Integrate 4P placemats into the weekly/monthly/yearly routine of your team.

4P PLACEMAT

WHAT

The 4P placemat is a way for leaders to systematise their confidence creation and ensure that its development is not left to chance, but by design. The activity requires the leader to regularly utilise the confidence code to **pinpoint** confidence goals, **prepare** for success, pre-empt **performance** issues and **process** the outcomes of any attempts.

WHY

Knowing how to become more confidence is not enough, and the gap between knowing and doing is the source of most personal growth paralysis. Integrating the use of the 4P placemat into weekly, termly or yearly professional development cycles ensures that awareness levels stay high and action is planned for and taken.

HOW

Step 1 – **Pinpoint** the element of your role which you want more confident in.

Step 2 – **Prepare** by identifying the additional experience, observation, feedback and opportunities for rehearsal that would improve your chances of success.

Step 3 – Identify any blind spots you may have in terms of your **Performance** and what decisions you will need to make to maximise success.

Step 4 – After the performance, **Process** the experience by reflecting on its impact on your self-efficacy and what you need to be successful in the future.

INDEX

Made in the USA
Monee, IL
13 September 2026

62977458R00144